*Fourth Edition*

# Essentials *of* Criminological Theory

L. Thomas Winfree, Jr.
*New Mexico State University*

Howard Abadinsky
*St. John's University*

WAVELAND
PRESS, INC.
Long Grove, Illinois

For information about this book, contact:
Waveland Press, Inc.
4180 IL Route 83, Suite 101
Long Grove, IL  60047-9580
(847) 634-0081
info@waveland.com
www.waveland.com

# Contents

# Preface

## To the Student

Our goal for this text is to make criminological theory's implications for the study of crime and justice as clear, concise, current, and consumable as possible. We approached this task by providing the historical context for the theories, the basic assumptions they make about humankind and human behavior, their fundamental causal arguments, and a sense of what criminologists have learned from testing those theories since they were first proposed. Interestingly, the theory as originally proposed may not greatly resemble its most current incarnation. Change is part of the equation when it comes to discussing crime theory.

The imagining of crime theory—its discovery, testing, metamorphoses into something "new," and its rediscovery—is one of the most exciting aspects of contemporary criminological studies. Some aspects of crime theory seem never to change; most theories, however, are in a state of constant flux. After all, these are not laws of human behavior. They are theories about crime—sets of ideas that attempt to describe, explain, predict, and possibly control a specific phenomenon (e.g., property crime) or class of phenomena (e.g., all crime).

The study of crime theories, like the study of crime and justice, is all about interconnectivity. We cannot truly study one theory without an appreciation for the others. As importantly, our task as authors was to organize both our thoughts about crime theory's interconnectivity and our presentation of that material in a textbook format. What we—and others—have observed about crime theories is that they typically fit one of three main overarching themes or modalities. Yet, these divisions, and the others that follow, are somewhat arbitrary. There are many ways to organize the basic material necessary to gain an appreciation for the importance of crime theories. The tripartite classification scheme that follows is but one of many such teaching models.

First is *classical criminology*, an approach that dates from the mid- to late-eighteenth century and the cumulative work of such renowned philosophers as the Frenchmen Montesquieu, Voltaire, Jean-Jacques Rousseau, and René Descartes, the Britain Jeremy Bentham, the Italian Cesare Beccaria, and the American Thomas Jefferson. All of these individuals contributed in some way to the perspective that holds offenders accountable for their actions and views society's just and fair actions toward them as essential in the quest to control crime. The deterrence model, which flows from this perspective on crime and justice, has held the attention of criminologists and other students of crime since the 1760s. Deterrence-based models have proven both resilient and difficult to test, and they are among the most popular of all crime theories.

In the intellectual afterglow of Charles Darwin's pronouncements about evolution and survival of the fittest, as well as more sociological interpretations of his work, a second perspective on crime emerged, *positivist criminology*. Central to this classification model is the idea that the causes of crime, like the causes of many different phenomena in the physical world, can be measured by one or more of our senses. This perspective's explanations—theories—tend to be deterministic; that is, they view the causes of crime as beyond the ability of the individual to control—caused by some outside force. The causes can be biological, psychological, economic, or social in origin; from this perspective, it is wrong to hold the individual accountable for his or her actions, a position that stands in direct conflict with classical criminology.

Speaking of conflict, the third major paradigm or perspective in this tripartite classification scheme is based on the idea that individuals or groups seek to enhance their own societal positions, often at the expense of other individuals or groups. This diversity-based paradigm is called *conflict criminology*. It seeks to understand crime in terms of the exercise of power, which itself centers on those characteristics that set us apart, a kind of sociocultural heterogeneity, us *versus* them. Conflict criminologists focus on the exercise of power by those who have it and wish to keep it—especially the power to create and enforce laws.

We hope that you enjoy this journey to a greater understanding of the basics of crime theory. Open your mind. Cast out preconceptions about the ties between crime, criminals, and theory. If you are able to achieve that mental state, you will find that understanding crime theory is a far more enjoyable endeavor.

## To the Instructor

This book has undergone several major metamorphoses since publication of the first edition in 1996. Every book, if it is truly revised and not simply updated, undergoes changes over the course of its lifetime. This fourth edition is no exception. We responded to input from students and instructors who have used our book.

### Text Overview

We returned to a 10-chapter format for this edition of the text. The materials included in this edition reinforce three critical observations about contemporary criminological theory. First, these are the theories with either staying power—they have survived the many efforts to disprove them—or theoretical "newcomers," crime explanations that show considerable promise to join the first list. In some cases, both descriptors can be applied to the same grouping of theories (e.g., chapter 2's biological theories) or specific theory (chapter 6's social learning theory).

Second, these theories represent a cross-section of contemporary criminological theories. Collectively, they constitute an introduction to what we believe are the most exciting developments in criminological thinking. Crime theory is no longer simply the musing of "ivory-tower" scholars, if it ever was. Consider that one of the founding fathers of modern criminology, Beccaria, was not just a philosopher of law at 26, but he spent the rest of his life actively pushing a specific practical agenda: Make laws—

and the legal process—fair. Other criminologists, as will become clear, spent their entire careers trying to test their theories and, further, sought to find a place for them in the practical world of crime and justice. This latter focus, which was admittedly not found uniformly across criminology through the twentieth century, has assumed a high level of attention in the first two decades of the twenty-first century. In that regard, then, this book is true to the goal we set twenty-odd years ago: *Provide students with an overview of the essentials of criminological theory, its origins, assumptions, causal arguments, and applications, as well as insights into new directions being suggested by those currently testing, expanding, and using the theories.*

The material contained in this text is faithful to the original theories. Our intent is that the readers of this text master the terminology used by criminological theorists so that they can meaningfully discuss these theories with others. When discussing certain theories, complex terms and ideas cannot be avoided, as in neurotransmitters' role in the biology of crime, or cognitive learning's importance for behaviorism, or the significance of privilege and demystification for economic conflict and Marxism. To facilitate understanding, we provide a series of marginal notes and detailed definitions in the glossary.

## Chapter Summaries

Chapter 1: An Introduction to Crime Theory. This chapter addresses five important topics: defining what is a crime and who is a criminal, classifying crimes, defining and justifying an emphasis on theory, demonstrating the links between research and theory, and, providing an organizing framework for the text based on the tripartite division. This chapter provides readers with the tools to explore the broad landscape that is criminological theory.

Chapter 2: Deterrence Theories. This chapter reviews three topics. First, it lays out the classical eighteenth century philosophy and practice behind deterrence theory, including how it changed over the first 50 years of its existence. Second, it describes the ways that deterrence theory changed in the late-twentieth century, as models based on the work of both Beccaria (i.e., Classical Deterrence) and Bentham (i.e., Moral Calculus and Cost-Benefits Analysis) began to appear in the criminological theory literature. Finally, this chapter examines twenty-first century ideas about deterrence, many of which have direct implications for the criminal justice system.

Chapter 3: Biological Theories. Biological theories, which are highly deterministic and empirically based, introduce positivist criminology. After a brief summary of nineteenth century criminal anthropology, this chapter explores a biological topic that has generated a great deal of controversy: crime's genetic basis. We examine both the early tentative statements about the influence of genes and the more current research and theorizing on the topic. The final topic in this chapter examines in some technical detail the role of the brain on crime and related misbehavior, including the still-developing adolescent brain. As humans are essentially chemistry sets, influenced by both internal and external chemicals, this section of the chapter has important implications for the study of criminals, as well as the general discussion about crime and determinism.

Chapter 4: Psychological Abnormality Theories. Two theories open this chapter's dialogue about psychology's contributions to positivist criminology. First, psychoanalytic theory owes much to the work of Sigmund Freud. Others have taken his ideas about the unconscious mind, psychosexual development, and the evolution of the id, ego, and superego and applied them to crime and justice. The second topic in this chapter examines the abiding idea of a "crazy but sane" person who commits crimes: the psychopath. That is, such offenders may be clinically diagnosed as suffering from a psychological problem, but it is hard to discern this problem from their external persona; they seem normal, if a bit disconnected from the rest of us. This topic is also interconnected to biological influences on behavior.

Chapter 5: Intelligence, Learning, and Developmental Theories. The theories in this chapter employ an eclectic approach to the study of crime. A given theory may be psychological in name, but other academic disciplines have made contributions. For instance, consider the sections on intelligence and crime—sociology, psychology, and biology all play roles in determining a person's intelligence. The section on behaviorism provides insights into how humans learn to respond to various stimuli appropriately and inappropriately. The chapter reviews three specific theories that examine the role of learning on crime and analogous behavior. The concluding section reviews life-course and developmental criminology.

Chapter 6: Structural Theories. The two central topics in this chapter emphasize social structure. The first looks at social ecology and social disorganization theory. The idea that certain socio-geographic places in communities foster crime was discounted by the middle of the twentieth century, only to enjoy a resurgence at the end of the century and the beginning of the twenty-first century. The second macro-theoretical theme in this chapter derives from the work of French sociologist Emile Durkheim and his concept of anomie. As with social ecology and social disorganization theory, the anomie tradition saw a resurgence at the close of the twentieth century and remains important today.

Chapter 7: Social Process Theories. If any two theoretical paradigms have dominated criminological research for the past 50 years, they are social learning and control theories. The first paradigm emerged in the 1930s in Edwin Sutherland's differential association theory and was further expanded by Ronald Akers' social learning theory. Contrasted with this paradigm is the control perspective, which suggests that rather than being blank slates that must taught to be criminals, humans are born with a natural tendency to deviate, and it is up to society to control their behavior. The tension between these two social process theories has provided much grist to the criminological theory mill.

Chapter 8: Labeling Theory and Reintegrative Shaming Theory. There is a shift in this chapter from positivist criminology to a focus on power and its use and misuse by society. Labeling theory describes how formal agents of social control essentially stigmatize adult criminals and delinquents, as well as the impact of that process on their subsequent lives. Reintegrative shaming theory stands in opposition to labeling theory. Whereas disintegrative shaming, often the result of a negativistic labeling process, moves the offender to the fringes of society, reintegrative shaming seeks to place the offender back into the community.

Chapter 9: Conflict Theories. The conflict described in this chapter moves the discussion of the use of power to a different level. The chapter describes two main forms of conflict: economic (i.e., conflict resulting from a traditional Marxist view of capitalism, power, and conflict) and social (i.e., conflict between cultures and groups). The chapter closes with an examination of contemporary conflict-based crime theorizing, which essentially looks at the perceived "threats" posed by varying racial, economic, and social groups to the interests of those groups in society that hold power and wish to keep it.

Chapter 10: Crime Theory, Public Policy, and Criminal Justice Practices. The final chapter explores the ways the various theories influence, shape, or otherwise impact criminal justice policy and practices. It examines the various paradigms and specific theories across general crime control policies, focusing specifically on law enforcement. The common theme in this chapter is how theory influences or is reflected in current police policies and practices.

## Key Features

This text has a number of key features intended to enhance the student's learning experience.

1. Learning Objectives. Each chapter begins with a set of four or five learning objectives—statements that should help the student prepare for the content that follows. After reading the chapter and absorbing in-class material, the student can revisit the objectives to gauge their comprehension of key elements.

2. Marginal Notes. The sidebars are an excellent way for the reader/student to see immediately the significance of a particular term or idea in the context of the material discussed.

3. Boxes/Figures/Tables. Each chapter has at least two of these elements to help students gain additional insights into crime theory. For example, a box entitled "Consider This" is found in each chapter; each presents a key concern or question related to the material in the chapter to stimulate critical thinking. For example, in chapter 1 we ask readers to consider whether George Washington was a traitor to the British crown and his likely punishment had he been caught. In chapter 9, we review female genital mutilation as a form of culture conflict that has emerged in the U.S. and other nations that do not allow its practice.

4. Summary Material. We present the chapter summaries as bulleted items—comprehensive summations highlighting the specific contributions of the various theories and their concerns, characterizations, and conclusions.

5. Key Terms. At the end of each chapter is a list of the 30 or more key terms bolded in the text. The terms are also included in the index and defined in the glossary. However, it is important to consider each key term relative to the specific content discussed in the text. Definitions and marginal notes provide shorthand information only.

6. Critical Review Questions. These questions require students to assimilate, synthesize, and summarize the relevant material. The reader/student is asked to use his or her analytical and critical thinking skills to foster a better understanding of crime theory.

7. Glossary. Combined with the Marginal Notes, the glossary of almost 400 terms should provide a strong framework for understanding the basics of each theory. In many cases, the information in the glossary is more than simply a definition; it expands on the ideas found in the text. Where appropriate we cross-list or pair the terms with other related terms to make it easier to understand the context in which they are used.

## Acknowledgements

We would like to thank Neil Rowe of Waveland Press for having confidence in us, demonstrated by his willingness to publish the fourth edition of our criminological theory book. As this project evolved, he played an instrumental role in getting us to the finish line. The preparation of this edition was greatly facilitated by the fine editorial work of Carol Rowe of Waveland Press. Carol's work, which included helping the coauthors work as a team, was much appreciated. Thank you.

We would also like to thank the following individuals that helped in the production of this work: Deborah Underwood (manuscript preparation), Catherine Murphy (typesetting), and Gayle McSemek-Zawilla (indexing).

Several individuals read all of the chapters and made both editorial and substantive comments about them, including Eileen J. Winfree and J. Keith Akins (University of Houston-Victoria).

We also wish to acknowledge the debt we owe all of our students, past and, in the case of Howard Abadinsky, present and future. Had they not asked some difficult questions and otherwise challenged us to make this material more understandable and consumable, without sacrificing theoretical content, this book would never have been written. Thank you.

Tom Winfree, Los Lunas, New Mexico
Howard Abadinsky, Jamaica, New York

# About the Authors

*Tom Winfree* received a Bachelor of Arts degree in sociology from the University of Richmond in 1968. He served two years in the United States Army, which included a tour of duty as a member of the Berlin Brigade, Germany. In 1974, he earned a Master of Science in sociology from Virginia Commonwealth University. Tom received a doctorate in sociology with an emphasis in criminology and deviant behavior from the University of Montana in 1976. Winfree has co-authored seven textbooks and edited works that have been published in a total of 17 editions, including, most recently, *Introduction to Criminal Justice* (with G. Larry Mays and Leanne F. Alarid, Wolters-Kluwer) and *Essentials of Corrections* (with G. Larry Mays, Wiley-Blackwell). He has also authored or co-authored over 80 refereed journal articles and over 20 book chapters. Tom retired from New Mexico State University in 2012, after 25 years of service. He has also held faculty positions at the East Texas State University (now Texas A&M-Commerce) and Louisiana State University. He was a visiting faculty member at the following institutions: University of New Mexico, University of Canterbury (Christchurch, New Zealand), Catholic University of Leuven (Belgium), Tübingen University (Germany), Kiel Polytechnic University (Germany), and Arizona State University. Although formally retired, Winfree continues to contribute to criminal justice, criminology, and sociology through his active research and writing agenda.

*Howard Abadinsky* is professor of criminal justice at St. John's University. He was a New York State senior parole officer and an inspector for the Cook County (IL) Sheriff's Office. A graduate of Queens College, CUNY, he holds an MSW from Fordham University and a PhD from New York University. Dr. Abadinsky is the author of several books, including *Organized Crime* (Cengage), *Probation and Parole* (Pearson), and *Law, Courts, and Justice in America* (Waveland).

# 1

# An Introduction to Criminological Theory

## LEARNING OBJECTIVES

- The definition of crime and criminal is changeable over time and place
- We distinguish between the various types of laws, based on the seriousness of the offense and the punishments accorded those found guilty of violating them
- How to define theory and its connection to the study of crime and criminals
- The role of research in developing and testing crime theories
- The distinctions between classical, positivist, and conflict criminology

# Introduction

Jesus and George Washington are two of history's most illustrious criminals—their crime was sedition, which is inciting people to rebel against the ruling authority. In the process of further defining *crime*, we will add other names to this list. In this chapter we explore the meaning and importance of *theory* as it is applied to the study of both crimes and criminals. We will group the various theories on crime and criminals into three broad categories: classical, positivist, and conflict. Each perspective makes assumptions about humans and their conduct, as well as how the rest of us respond to those among us who break the law.

> Criminologists divide crime theories into three broad categories: classical, positivist, and conflict.

# What Is a Crime? Who Is a Criminal?

**Crime** is a violation of the criminal law, and a **criminal** is a person who committed the violation. These simple definitions ignore a great deal of real world complexity. For example, consider each of the following criminals and their crimes. As you read about each one, reflect on the purpose of the law in question at the time of its application and how it defined the criminal's status as a law violator.

- The Bible in *Exodus* tells us that when the Hebrew Moses, a member of an ethnic group identified as slaves, slew an Egyptian taskmaster who was beating a Hebrew slave, he had to flee pharaoh's wrath lest he be arrested and executed.

- In more contemporary times, Susan B. Anthony, who was over 21 years of age and born in the U.S., voted in the presidential election of 1872, an act for which a deputy U.S. marshal arrested her. At her 1873 federal trial, she was denied the right to speak, and the judge directed the jury to find her guilty, which they did. Anthony never enjoyed the right to vote—she died in 1906. The Nineteenth Amendment recognized the right of women to vote in 1920.

- On December 1, 1955, the Montgomery, Alabama, police arrested Rosa Parks, a black woman, for refusing to give up her seat on a Montgomery bus to a white man, as the law required. She was convicted of disorderly conduct and fined $10, plus $4 in court fees. Historians consider the actions of Rosa Parks and the bus boycott that ensued as the start of the civil rights movement.

- Martin Luther King Day honors a man who, by the time of his assassination in 1968, had been arrested dozens of times and incarcerated in a number of jails; his crimes stemmed from acts of civil disobedience that resulted from his leadership in the African American Civil Rights Movement.

• Nelson Mandela served 27 years in South African prisons for the crime of opposing apartheid. In 1994, four years after his release from prison, the electorate of South Africa elected the former criminal as their nation's president.

Apartheid was an official system of racial segregation enforced in South Africa from 1948 to 1994.

What is a crime? Who is a criminal? The best answer we can give at this point is it depends. Sometimes the label criminal is a status conferred on a class of persons. For example, in 1850, the U.S. Congress passed and President Millard Fillmore signed into law a statute requiring the apprehension and return of "fugitives from labor"—a euphemism for runaway slaves. Failure to obey the Fugitive Slave Law of 1850 subjected violators to a fine equivalent to $30,000 today and six months of imprisonment. In 1865, the Thirteenth Amendment abolished slavery. Being a runaway slave in the pre-Civil War United States meant being a criminal, in much the same way as did being a Jew in Nazi Germany (1933–1945). Once again: What is a crime? Who is a criminal?

Can behavior that is legal at one point in history later result in a person being defined as a criminal? Beginning in 1945, the victorious Allies prosecuted prominent members of Germany's Nazi government; ten individuals, whose actions had been lawful under German law from 1933 to the war's end, were hanged. On November 9, 1989, the citizens of East and West Berlin started tearing down the Berlin Wall, and residents of both Berlins freely crossed the infamous barrier. In the years before this event, East German border guards, obeying their government's orders, had killed 138 persons attempting to flee to the west. With Germany's reunification, the new German government prosecuted those guards for actions that, at the time, had been required by East German law.

Nazi officials and former East Berlin border guards found themselves prosecuted for behavior that was lawful when it was committed.

The criminalizing of one form of behavior often can have unforeseen consequences. Consider that for much of U.S. history, the nation could be characterized as a "drug fiend's paradise," as heroin and cocaine, among other drugs, were freely and widely available. In 1914, the **Harrison Narcotics Tax Act** (Ch. 1, 38 Stat. 785) and two 1919 Supreme Court decisions outlawed possessing and trafficking in opiates and coca products (*United States v. Doremus*, 249 U.S. 86), as well as prescribing addicts such drugs solely for addiction maintenance purposes (*Webb v. United States*, 249 U.S. 96, 99). What had been legal was now criminal, and that act of criminalization ultimately led to the creation of a vast black market in drugs. In 1920, the manufacture and possession of alcoholic beverages such as beer, wine, and whiskey, became a crime with the passage of the 21st Amendment and enactment of the **National Prohibition Act** (P.L. 66-66, 41 Stat. 305), also known as the Volstead Act. Prohibition presented opportunities for people like Al Capone and Lucky Luciano; their activities became known as "organized crime." Prohibition was repealed in 1933; alcoholic beverages once again became legal substances, and its manufacturers and purveyors ceased being criminals. The Harrison Nar-

Until 1914, drugs such as heroin and cocaine were freely available in the United States; sellers and users were not defined as criminals.

cotics Tax Act was not repealed, and illegal drugs became an alternate revenue source for the criminal organizations created by Prohibition.

The roots of many criminal laws can be found in religious beliefs. Jesus was ruled a criminal and executed alongside two common thieves. As Christianity spread, many of Jesus' followers met similar fates. Later generations of Christians defined heretics and non-Christians as criminals, and they treated them as badly as the Romans had treated Christianity's founder. For most of the medieval times, the Roman Catholic Church's canonical laws shaped how European nation-states responded to all sorts of behavior the Church viewed as threatening, including such crimes as heresy, **apostasy**, and witchcraft.

> Apostasy refers to the act of turning away from a formerly held religious belief system, and for many religions, past and present, this act is punishable by death.

Religious beliefs continue to influence contemporary legal systems throughout the world. In the 1950s, every U.S. state had laws against sodomy, laws that were largely based on religious beliefs and upheld by the Supreme Court in a 1986 decision (*Bowers v. Hardwick*, 478 U.S. 186). Chief Justice Warren Burger cited the "ancient roots" of prohibitions against homosexual behavior. In the early 1960s, states began to repeal these laws. In 2003, the Supreme Court, in *Lawrence v. Texas* (539 U.S. 558), ruled that private, non-commercial sexual conduct was a protected liberty. Yet, one has only to consider the current public debates over same-sex marriages or, for that matter, abortion to recognize that law and religion have an ongoing and dynamic relationship.

> Sharia law is based on an Arabic word meaning "way" or "path" and is the legal framework within which both public and private aspects of life are regulated for those living in an Islamic legal system.

Debates based on religious beliefs are not limited to the United States. Today, some followers of Mohammed deny the legitimacy of other Muslims and subject them and non-Muslims to corporal punishments and even execution for violating their particular version of Islamic **Sharia law**. Moreover, in many parts of the world, usually based on a theology, homosexual unions of any kind are a crime that can bring severe punishment.

Determining what is or is not a crime and who is or is not a criminal, ultimately depends on *time* and *place*, and on the views of those who wield authority to define or not define behavior as "crime." In other words, *power—* the ability to create and enforce laws—determines the definition of crime. This fact explains why the criminal justice system punishes the crimes committed by those with limited financial and political resources more severely than the misbehavior of corporations or even the government. Indeed, the legal codes may not even define the actions of corporations as criminal despite the harm caused. For example, consider the death and injury caused by faulty car ignition switches and the poisoning of water supplies and soil contamination linked to the indiscriminate discharge of industrial waste.

> What is or is not a crime and who is or is not a criminal, depends on *time* and *place* and the ability to control the process of writing laws to define what behavior is criminal.

## Classifying Crimes

Law defines crime. Not all crimes—nor the punishments accorded to those convicted by the legal system of committing them—are the same, at least in terms of how those who create the laws see them.

## *Mala in se* and *Mala Prohibita*

We can distinguish between classes of crime by considering the harm associated with a given act, allowing us to divide criminal behavior into two main forms: *mala in se* and *mala prohibita*. **Mala in se**, Latin for "evil in itself," refers to crimes that are intrinsically evil, such as murder. Although societies may differ on what constitutes murder, all prohibit the behavior. This term contrasts with **mala prohibita**, Latin for "wrong because it is prohibited," which refers to activities that have been outlawed not because they are obviously or inherently evil, but because they violate certain societal standards. For example, insider trading is a violation of accepted business practices—gaining an unfair advantage in business transactions and is not intrinsically evil; rather, some people profit, through knowledge that is not generally available to the public. When does an unfair business advantage become a crime? In 1909, the Supreme Court provided one answer to that question in the first case of insider trading, *Strong v. Repide* (213 U.S. 419). A corporate executive who knew that his company's stock was about to soar in value bought it from an outsider without revealing what he knew. The court viewed the executive's actions as fraudulent, although there was no obvious victim.

While behavior that is *mala in se* tends to be rather obvious—murder and robbery, for example—behavior that is *mala prohibita* tends to encounter the twin issues of *time* and *place*. For example, a civilian in Vermont can carry a firearm openly without a permit or license. In New York, a civilian carrying a firearm openly would be subject to arrest. In Massachusetts, open carry is allowed but requires a permit. The possession of marijuana for recreational purposes in legal in Colorado but is a crime in most other states.

We know that certain actions are defined as criminal. However, can a person be officially designated as a criminal for *failure* to act? Some examples include males who fail to register with the Selective Service at age eighteen, persons who fail to file a state or federal income tax return, and parents and other lawful caregivers that fail to provide sustenance and adequate care for their dependent children.

> Crime can be *mala in se* or *mala prohibita*.

## Formal Distinctions in Law

Law distinguishes noncriminal—or civil—offenses from criminal ones. The former centers on claims of *private* wrongs called **torts** brought by a plaintiff against a defendant, whereas criminal charges are public wrongs brought against a defendant by a prosecutor in the name of the people of a specific state or the United States. All criminal cases are referenced with the name of the involved governmental entity written first, for example, *New York v. Jones* or the *United States of America v. Smith*. While a criminal prosecution can result in the loss of liberty (or

> As opposed to criminal defendants, defendants in a civil case are not in jeopardy of losing their freedom.

*Misdemeanors* are usually punishable by no more than one year of imprisonment, while convictions for *felonies* carry a prison sentence of more than one year and, in some cases, the death penalty; *ordinances* are municipal or county laws whose violation entails fines, but not incarceration.

life, in extreme cases), private wrongs offer no such sanctions; a defendant can lose money or property, but not his or her freedom or life.

Law distinguishes crimes according to the *length of punishment* and the *place of confinement*. **Misdemeanors** are crimes for which the maximum punishment is usually no more than one year of incarceration in a city or county jail or federal correctional center, as well as the possibility of a fine up to an amount fixed by state or federal law. **Felonies** are punishable by more than one year in a state or federal prison and in some cases death; they represent far more serious crimes than misdemeanors, and their fines are much higher than those accorded misdemeanors. Even among felonies, not all are equal, either in contemporary criminal codes or in a historic one, such as that described in box 1.1. **Ordinances** are laws enacted by a municipal or county government whose violation generally does not result in incarceration—parking violations, for example.

**Box 1.1 Consider This: What Could Have Happened to Washington the Traitor?**

This chapter began with the premise that George Washington was a criminal. Indeed, he was a British citizen, as were nearly all members of the Continental Congress, not to mention the Continental Army. They were in open rebellion against King George III, an act of High Treason under British law. Had the British captured George Washington and sent him to London for trial, he could have faced, as a prominent leader in the rebellion, drawing and quartering, which was the standard punishment.

Drawing and quartering, which dated from the Treason Act of 1351 and was intended to deter offenders, consisted of being dragged or drawn to the place of execution by horses, hanged to the point of unconsciousness and revived, emasculated, eviscerated, beheaded, and then cut into four quarters, after which the body was often put on public display. Females found guilty of treason were subject to burning at the stake. Not actually carried out for decades, drawing and quartering was officially abolished by Great Britain in 1870.

*Sources*: Bellamy (2004); Block and Hostettler (1997); Wormald (2001).

## What Is Theory? Why Is It Important?

Now that we have examined the complex issue of defining crime, we will look at theory, which is sometimes dismissed as irrelevant or fanciful—"Oh, it's just a theory"—by those who do not understand its critical importance. Albert Einstein, an icon of intellect, is one example of the inappropriateness of such thinking. While he was *just* a theorist, his contributions to science and his impact on everyday life are legion. A **theory** is an attempt to make sense of a real-world occurrence, an explanation in the form of a highly organized statement based on systematic observations about the phenomenon or class of phenomena under study—in short, a highly informed and very logical guess.

Theory enables the prediction of when the phenomenon or phenomena of study will occur or why it or they occurred in the past. A theory provides an explanation for the relationship between two or more abstract ideas, which theorists call **concepts**. Consider, for example, the two concepts of intelligence and crime. We might assert that low intelligence causes crime (an issue we will examine in chapter 5). For example, in the 1920s, criminologists proposed that persons with "subnormal" intelligence were far more likely to abandon their children than were individuals with "normal" intelligence (Erickson 1929:604). To test this idea, we must first define each term. In this case, IQ is taken as a measure of intelligence, while the crime of child abandonment is defined as abandoning a dependent child. Next, we must create a measurable form of each concept, called a **variable**. A person's score on a specific standardized intelligence test could serve as a measure of IQ; the presence or absence of a criminal arrest or conviction for the criminal offense of abandoning one's dependent child could serve as a measure of child abandonment. Finally, we look at the extent to which this claim is true in the "real world." In other words, we must collect the data and analyze it to see the extent to which our claim (e.g., the testable idea that those with low IQ scores are more likely to commit child abandonment) is supported or not.

Sound complicated? At some levels, it is a complicated process. Generally, theory is a product of thinking, building, and testing, just like any other aspect in the advancement of human knowledge. In the physical sciences, such as chemistry and physics, researchers can subject theory to rigorous testing and replication. As we shall see, it is often a great deal more complicated in the behavioral and social sciences.

> The purpose of a theory is to describe something, enable the prediction of when it will occur, and explain why it occurred.

## Characteristics of Theories

Theories must be *comprehensive*, broad enough to apply to more than one specific set of circumstances, facts, or observations. They should also be *parsimonious*, meaning we should cast our theories in terms that are as simple and straightforward as possible without sacrificing explanatory power. We cannot determine the cause of a particular criminal behavior based on a satisfactory explanation for a single case; however, if enough individual cases fit the same explanation, we can develop a theory and test it against future cases of criminal behavior. The ability to predict is a measure of a theory's validity, and validity requires testing. Any "theory" that cannot be tested—and, therefore, disproved—is not, according to the guiding principles of all sciences, a theory. A purported cause of crime that does not permit testing has more in common with ideology and theology than criminology—it lacks scien-

> A valid theory is one that has been tested and found to perform as proposed, suggesting that it is well founded and corresponds to events in the real world.

tific merit. Hence, *testability* is a crucial characteristic of any criminological theory.

To determine the strength of a theory, the scientific method requires an assertion stated in the form of a **hypothesis** for testing. (Recall the "testable idea" that low IQ scores are associated with the crime of child abandonment.) For instance, what do we need to do to test a theory that maintains poverty causes crime? We might state the following hypothesis: "Poverty is a predictor of crime." We could test this assertion by comparing crime rates in areas with high poverty to the crime rates in areas with low poverty. Indeed, we are likely to find a link between poverty and crime. However, can we conclude that poverty *causes* crime? What if those who have committed a crime constitute only a small percentage of persons residing in areas of poverty—as is the case. What if we discover that police departments deploy larger numbers of officers in areas of high poverty than are deployed to middle-class areas? Assuming that the police are doing their job properly, more police officers will catch more criminals, driving up the *statistical* rate of crime. What if we discover that areas with high poverty also have a larger number of persons aged 15 to 25, the ages at which people are more likely to commit crime? Perhaps poverty predicts crime only indirectly. If the population in poor areas has more people in the crime prone years, there will be more crimes committed. Biological and sociological variables may explain *both* poverty and crime, so the poverty-crime connection may be *spurious*.

## Theories and Spuriousness

**Spuriousness** is a status accorded to a specific type of observed relationship between two events, occurrences, or variables. This observed relationship is alleged to be causal, but is, in fact, not causal, owing to the action of a third, unobserved event, occurrence, or variable (a confounding factor). For example, consider the often-observed relationship between storks and babies. That is, there must be a relationship, otherwise, why would so many ads and cards announcing a birth include a picture of a stork? Logic tells us that storks do not produce babies, or vice-versa—the connection is spurious—but both are related to a third variable. But what is that variable? One explanation for the stork-babies connection holds that medieval weddings in Germany took place in late June, around the time of the Summer Solstice, a popular pagan holiday for family and fertility. The storks, migratory birds, flew south for the winter, returning to nest in the roofs of the German towns and villages in March and April, about when the babies of the Summer Solstice were born. There is a correlation between storks and babies, but neither causes the other—the connection is spurious, owed to the coincidental overlap between the storks' migratory pattern and the sexual activities of a community's residents.

A spurious interpretation occurs when a relationship between two variables, described as causal, is really the result of a third variable causing the other two.

Does this idea hold for the study of crime? In this regard, consider the relationship between crime and broken windows. James Q. Wilson and George Kelling (1982) note that when a single window is broken in a building, say an abandoned factory, and no one bothers fixing it over a period of time, other windows will be broken, and eventually all the building's windows will be broken, giving rise to **"broken windows" theory**. Crime in the neighborhood surrounding the "broken windows" building increases at a rate that approximates that of the window-breaking in the building. The first diagram in figure 1.1 represents this correlation. The observed correlation seems to imply that the broken windows caused the crime, which is obviously incorrect. This statement represents a spurious interpretation of the facts. As James Q. Wilson and George Kelling (1982) maintain, both the broken windows and crime share a common cause: **community malaise**, which can be roughly defined as a general sense of

**Figure 1.1**  Correlation *versus* Causation: Crime and Broken Windows

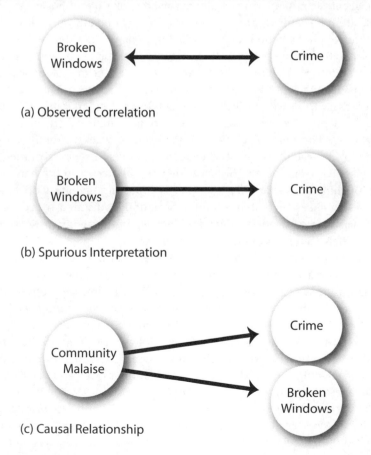

(a) Observed Correlation

(b) Spurious Interpretation

(c) Causal Relationship

disconnectedness that is present among a community's residents: the residents have no stake or emotional investment in their community—or each other. The same sense of uneasiness and disconnectedness within the neighborhood that failed to fix the windows—or demand that they be fixed—leads to increased crime. The appearance of disorder leads a would-be offender to conclude that committing a crime in this neighborhood entails little risk because residents "mind their own business" and are unlikely to call the police.

## Theories, Correlation, and Causation

As we explore theory, we must avoid confusing *causation* with *correlation*. A **correlation** ties two variables together, such as storks and babies or window-breaking and crime. When one variable changes, the second variable also changes, increasing or decreasing. The changes can be almost immediate or occur later. There is a strong correlation between low income and high birthrate, but low income is obviously not the cause of pregnancy. There is a strong correlation between poverty and crime: most *known* criminals are from an economically deprived background, but most poor people are not criminals and, of course, crime by persons of wealth is not an unknown phenomenon. Other variables, perhaps ones that are biological, psychological, or sociological in origin, may explain *both* poverty and crime, and those variables could also serve to explain crimes of the wealthy.

**Causation** refers to anything that produces an effect. Three criteria are necessary to prove causation (Eme 2009). *First*, the putative (alleged) cause must precede the effect in time, a requirement called time-order sequencing. The amount of time (e.g., seconds, weeks, months, years, millennia) is largely irrelevant, except for the person seeking to identify the cause. For example, the order sequencing of a burn to the hand of a child touching the surface of a hot stove is almost immediate. Conversely, the consequences of building homes on landfill poisoned by contaminated waste may not be evident for decades until medical researchers observe increased rates of birth defects or cancer.

> The term cause refers to anything that produces an effect; a cause makes something else happen.

*Second*, once researchers have established that indeed the cause precedes the effect in time, they must next demonstrate the presence of a correlation. If we can assign a number to the relationship between the correlated variables, we talk about the *strength of the relationship*. We describe relationships as strong, weak, or somewhere in between.

The *third* criterion is absence of a possible spurious interpretation of the observed relationship. Only when researchers show that the cause precedes the effect in time, and there is a correlation, as well as an absence of spuriousness, can they assert the existence of causation. While this is possible in the natural sciences, it is unlikely in the social or behavior sciences. In other words, we will never discover *the cause of crime* because so much depends on the issues of *time* and *place* that we have discussed earlier.

## Theories and Tautologies

When considering a theory, we need to avoid making a tautology, also referred to as circular reasoning. A **tautology** exists when someone defines the outcome variable, sometimes called the dependent variable, as its own cause. If we assert that flames cause fire, we are identifying the outcome by using a synonym for the cause. In the elementary grades, students are taught never to use the term being defined in its definition. Sigmund Freud's pleasure-pain principle provides an example of a tautology: "If one says that a man does what is pleasurable to him and that he does not do what is painful, then *everything* he does is pleasurable by *definition*" (Simon 1969: 211; emphasis in the original).

Years ago psychologists concluded that there is a strong correlation between psychopathy, a relatively rare mental condition (see extended discussion in chapter 4), and criminality. However, a common test to determine psychopathy includes questions about the person's inclination to break the law: The greater the inclination to commit crime, the more likely the person is a psychopath. Psychopaths by definition are persons who are likely to violate the law. In this criminological example, the researchers inappropriately used past behavior (i.e., prior rule-breaking conduct) to predict future behavior (i.e., subsequent illegal conduct), claiming the one as the independent cause of the other. In tautological terms, a psychopath is someone who acts psychopathic—circular reasoning.

At times, the issue of tautological relationships can be tricky. For example, one of the theories we will examine in chapter 7, *differential association*, argues that the strength of one's pattern of association—prosocial or antisocial—determines whether behavior is law-abiding or criminal. According to this explanation, criminal association leads to criminality, but criminal association is also the result of criminality—"birds of a feather flock together."

Does the use of these variables constitute a tautology? Perhaps, but if it can be shown that criminality did not exist prior to criminal associations, then a possible interpretation is that, due to increased criminality in a community, youths have fewer opportunities to associate with noncriminals. Thus, there is a feedback loop between criminality and criminal associations, a condition that is not, strictly speaking, a tautology. Crime can have multiple, complex causes.

## Theories and Research

While theory is the basic building block for the advancement of knowledge, the testing of crime theory is problematic. In the natural sciences, such as chemistry and biology, researchers subject theoretical claims to rigorous laboratory testing under controlled conditions and subsequently attempt to repeat the experiments. An example would be testing the effects of certain chemicals on genetically engineered laboratory rats. The social or behavioral sciences—including criminology—are concerned with behavior that is uniquely human—only humans can commit crime—and testing is limited accordingly. We could subject rats to extreme levels of physical stress, and then study their reaction when given morphine. Both law and morality do not permit researchers to subject human beings to similar levels of stress and then administer morphine to determine if they become drug addicts. Social scientists must study criminal behavior in a more circuitous manner.

The "gold standard" of research is the experimental design using random assignment, an approach difficult to apply in the study of criminal behavior. Conventional wisdom posits a connection between abuse in childhood and criminality in adulthood. However, we could not ethically or legally select a group of children at random and subject them to child abuse, comparing this group to another randomly selected group protected from such abuse. Criminologists could test the effectiveness of police preventive patrol by doubling the numbers of officers on patrol, while withdrawing all patrol units from similar beats, and comparing both to beats where the pattern of preventive patrol was not altered—as was done in the "Kansas City Study" (Kelling et al. 1974). This research, too, was not without ethical issues: If preventive police patrols do indeed protect citizens, withdrawing the police endangers the citizenry.

> Social science is interested in applying scientific principles of research to human behavior, an endeavor that is limited by law and morality.

In the search for causal relationships, theories that are too broad or too complex may prove hard to test, and attempts to test them may yield conflicting results. For this reason, it is interesting to note that even theories that have either not been subjected to empirical research or have garnered little support, may be endorsed by those who decide crime policy. Consider the following: "Increasing the number of police officers on patrol will reduce crime." While this is a popular policy argument (e.g., "Put 100,000 more police on the nation's streets"), existing research challenges this claim (Kelling et al. 1974). The policy of providing more police as a way of reducing crime may also defy logic. Many crimes, ranging from shoplifting to murder, occur in areas not routinely patrolled by the police, such as department stores and apartment buildings.

## The Significance of Nature and Nurture for Crime Theories

One way to categorize theories of crime is by how proponents view the fundamental force allegedly shaping the human behavior under study: Is it nature or nurture? Supporters of the **nature** position suggest that we can understand behavior primarily by genetic, biological, or other properties inherent in the individual. Proponents of the **nurture** position look to the social environment for causal factors; they believe human behavior is largely the product of social interaction.

> The issue of *nature v. nurture* can distinguish theories of crime.

If nature shapes criminal behavior, what can and should society do with law violators? If a person's nature determines that he or she will be a criminal, then, short of genetic engineering, the crime control policies directed at criminals are limited. If criminals are unchangeable, if unalterable nature caused their behavior, the choices for society are limited to executing them or, alternatively, incarcerating them until, because age or infirmity renders them harmless, they are no longer a threat to community safety and security. The "nature" view also conflicts with the legal system's need to prove **mens rea**—criminal intent—in order to hold offenders accountable. Alternatively, if the source of the problem lies largely within society's mechanisms of socialization, such as families and schools, what is society's obligation to ensure that the resources accorded these key nurturing forces are up to the task? Moreover, as we shall see later in this book, some crime theorists view the *nature versus nurture* position as outdated, proposing instead that the two interact—a *nature and nurture* perspective—to produce criminality.

> *Mens rea* is a legal term that describes the accused's mental state at the time of the crime's commission; specifically, the act was willful and the outcome was intended.

## On the Roots of Theory

Agreement about the cause of crime does not necessarily mean agreement about the "cure." For example, a greater police presence, increased punishments, enhanced employment-skills training, expanded drug and mental health treatments, widely available recreational opportunities, and neighborhood improvement collectively may (in theory) reduce "crime on the streets," but not "crime in the suites"—corporate crime. Economic inequality may precede crime, even cause it in terms of one's social conditions and opportunities. Nevertheless, whether you subscribe to this idea about the linkage between crime and economics may depend on how you answer the following question: Do you see crime as a natural condition of human beings, or do you believe that individuals chose the wrong path? We turn next to an understanding of what your answer to this question means.

### Classical Criminology

Before beginning our examination of specific theories of crime, we need to discuss a view that emerged out of the European Enlightenment period of the eighteenth century (sometimes referred to as the "Age of Reason") that provides the foundation for criminal justice in the United States. The classical view rejected spiritual and religious explanations for criminal behavior. During this era, philosophers such as Montesquieu (b.1689–d.1755) and Voltaire (b.1694–d.1778), spoke out against the French penal code and its accompanying punishments as both inhumane and inequitable. Jean Jacques Rousseau (b.1712–b.1778) and Cesare Beccaria (b.1738–d.1794) argued for a radical concept of justice based on equality. At a time when laws and law enforcement were unjust and dispa-rate, and punishment often brutal, the emergent classical philosophers demanded justice based on **equality** and **proportionality**—that all people are treated the same when it comes to the application of law (equality) and that the punishment fit the crime (proportionality). Today, the icon of such equality before the law is found on many court buildings—lady justice with a blindfold to avoid considering the person rather than the behavior.

Standing in opposition to the manner in which law was being—and had for centuries been—enforced, classical proponents argued that the law should respect neither rank nor station. As it is written in the Decla-ration of Independence (1776), drafted by advocates of the classical view, *all men are created equal*. This premise was formalized in the area of criminal justice by Beccaria who, in *An Essay on Crimes and Punishments* (1764; English edition, 1867), stated that laws should be drawn precisely and matched to punishment intended to be applied equally to all classes of men. The law, he argued, should stipulate a particular penalty for each specific crime, and judges should mete out identical sentences for each occurrence of the same offense (Beccaria 1963). According to the classical view, punishment is justified because the offender is a rational being, endowed with **free will**. That is, every person has the ability to distin-guish and choose between right or wrong, between being a law-abiding person and being a criminal. Law violating behavior is, therefore, a ratio-nal choice made by a reasoning person with free will. Criminal justice refers to this concept by the Latin term *mens rea*, or criminal intent, which is the willful and intentional elements that the prosecutor must prove in order for a defendant to be found guilty of a crime. Infancy (below a certain age) and mental deficiency, for example, are conditions that can mitigate the presence of *mens rea*.

The classical view argues that because human beings tend toward **hedonism**—that is, they seek pleasure and avoid pain—the fear of pun-ishment will restrain them from unlawful albeit pleasurable acts. Accord-ingly, the purpose of the criminal law is not simply retribution, but also **deterrence**. The law stands as a bulwark against the "natural" hedonistic tendencies of humans that society collectively views as threatening. In the classical view, equality and proportionality balance out hedonism because people will freely choose appropriate over inappropriate conduct when they understand the costs. If someone chooses inappropriately, punishing law transgressors will warn others not to follow that path and will deter offenders from future bad choices.

## Positivist Criminology

When we entertain even the possibility that biological, psychological, or sociological variables may influence criminal behavior, we move away from free will and in the direction of **determinism**—that forces beyond the person's control cause all or some human behavior. "Praise or blame only makes sense if there exists an agent who initiates an action that was not ultimately caused by environmental and genetic factors" (Slife, Yanchar, and Williams 1999: 80). Determinism in science, as opposed to theology, finds expression in positivism.

Positivist criminology searches for the underlying causes of crime. If successful, positivist theories allow for criminal behavior's prediction and, thereby, suggest ways of preventing or controlling its occurrence. While the basis of classical criminology is philosophy and law, positivist criminology finds its grounding in science and empiricism. Positivists search for universally applicable causes. As formulated by sociologist Auguste Comte (b.1798–d.1857), **positivism** refers to a method for examining and understanding social behavior. Comte argued that the methods and logical form of the natural sciences—the scientific method—are applicable to the study of humans as social beings. We must study and understand social phenomena, Comte stated, by observation, hypothesis, and experimentation.

> A scientific explanation of crime entails a denial of free will.

The positivist approach to the study of crime found early legitimacy in the efforts of Cesare Lombroso (b.1835–d.1909), a Venetian physician. In *L'uomo delinquente* ("The Criminal Man"), first published in 1876, Lombroso argued that the criminal is an atavist or "primitive throwback" to earlier developmental stages through which noncriminal "man" had already passed. Lombroso's research centered on physiological characteristics believed indicative of criminality. A later work, edited by his daughter, Gina Lombroso-Ferrero (b.1872–d.1944), and entitled *Criminal Man, According to the Classification of Cesare Lombroso* (1911), noted the importance of environmental factors in causing crime. In contrast to the classicalists' emphasis on criminal behavior as rational and freely chosen (*mens rea* and free will), the positivists saw it as a symptom of some form of biological, psychological, or social pathology.

## Conflict Criminology

Earlier in this chapter, we noted that Jesus, George Washington, Martin Luther King, Susan B. Anthony, and Nelson Mandela were criminals, persons who violated the criminal law. Their crimes? They sought to change the power relationships that controlled the definition of crime. People with the power to create and enforce the laws use the legal system to maintain and consolidate their power; moreover, those with power use the law to define as criminals anyone who threatens that power.

**Conflict criminology** emphasizes society's diversity. Diverse groups are often at odds with one another—farmers, industrialists, and union members; atheists and fundamentalists; liberals and conservatives—all competing for power and position within society. One important prize awaits the winners: they get to define crime. Thus, the definition of crime reflects power relationships in society and serves the interests of those in control. In capitalist societies, the owners of the means of production—wealthy capitalists—maintain the power to create the laws and oversee their enforcement.

Conflict theorists have little interest in the positivists' causes of crime—whether biological, psychological, or sociological. Instead, they offer a politicized perspective on crime causation; the political process determines law and defines crime and its enforcement. The common denominator is power; law serves the interests of the powerful who are able to criminalize the actions of those who would challenge them.

## An Organizing Framework

This text is organized around these three topical divisions: classical, positivist, and conflict criminology. Each adds unique insights into the study of crime and criminals. Moreover, each perspective gives us somewhat different answers to the following questions: What can we do about crime? What can we do with criminals?

Classical (chapter 2) and conflict criminology (chapter 9) generally discount deterministic answers to crime causation questions. Classical theories portray crime as emerging from a human decision-making process, while conflict theories frame their answers in the exercise of power by those who have it and want to keep it. Neither perspective views nature nor nurture as playing a major role in the creation of crime or criminals.

The positivist explanations, which tend to be deterministic, highlight the interaction between *nature* and *nurture*. Biological theories—*nature*—are the first such explanations explored in this text (chapter 3). Next we review the psychological theories (chapters 4 and 5), which in several cases include the influence of both nature and nurture. In subsequent chapters, this text also examines the influence of *nurture*, largely through the lens of sociological theories (chapters 6–8). Collectively, these deterministic theories raise the question of what society, and the criminal justice system in particular, can and should do to criminals whose propensity to offend is due in some measure, small or great, to factors beyond their control.

We should note that most of the theories included in this text derive from a positivist view of crime and are generally organized by academic discipline. But, as noted above, nature and nurture interact, so any division into separate chapters is for instructional purposes. For example, we begin our look at criminological theories in chapter 2 with an examination of deterrence theories—a set of ideas about crime and criminals that are generally non-deterministic, but which have become far more positivist in the past 30 years.

## SUMMARY

- Crime can be grouped into three categories: classical, positivist, and conflict.
- What is a crime and who is a criminal, depends *on time and place*.
- We can divide criminal behavior into *mala in se* and *mala prohibita*.
- Length of sentence determines if a crime is a misdemeanor or a felony.
- A theory attempts to make sense of an occurrence based on systematic observation.
- Theory must apply to more than one set of circumstances, facts, or observations.
- Testing a theory requires a hypothesis.
- A spurious relationship occurs when an apparent connection between two variables is actually caused by a third variable.
- A correlation ties two variables together; cause refers to anything that produces an effect.
- A tautology occurs when the variable being studied is stated as the cause or explanation.
- Theory is the basic building block for the advancement of human knowledge.
- Ethical and legal issues limit testing in social science.
- The issue of *nature v. nurture* influencing human behavior can distinguish theories of crime.
- The classical view of justice requires free will, equality, and proportionality.
- Free will is expressed as *mens rea* in the criminal justice system.
- Determinism denies free will.

## KEY TERMS

| | |
|---|---|
| apostasy | felonies |
| "broken windows" theory | free will |
| causation | Harrison Narcotics Tax Act |
| classical criminology | hedonism |
| community malaise | hypothesis |
| concepts | *mala in se* |
| conflict criminology | *mala prohibita* |
| correlation | *mens rea* |
| crime | misdemeanors |
| criminal | National Prohibition Act |
| determinism | nature |
| deterrence | nurture |
| equality | ordinances |

positivism                          tautology
positivist criminology              theory
proportionality                     torts
Sharia law                          variable
spuriousness

## CRITICAL REVIEW QUESTIONS

1. What are the three categories into which we can group theories of crime?

2. What was a "fugitive from labor"?

3. Why was the U.S. prior to 1914 as a "drug fiend's paradise"?

4. Give two examples of later prosecuting people for acts that were lawful when committed? How can such prosecutions be justified?

5. How do "time" and "place" affect what is or is not a crime?

6. How do *mala in se* and *mala prohibita* differ?

7. Is insider trading *mala in se* and *mala prohibita*? Why?

8. How is a misdemeanor distinguished from a felony?

9. What is the purpose of a theory?

10. Why is it necessary that a theory be comprehensive?

11. How can a relationship between two variables be spurious?

12. How does correlation differ from causation?

13. What is a tautology?

14. Why is theory important?

15. Why is theory testing in a social science more difficult than in a natural science?

16. Why can an improvement in economic conditions result in more crime?

17. What has research revealed about the economics-crime connection?

18. What two elements of the classical view that emerged in the Eighteenth century can we find in modern U.S. justice?

19. How does free will find expression in the U.S. criminal justice system?

20. What is the connection between the positivist view and determinism?

# Classical Criminology and Deterrence Theories

**LEARNING OBJECTIVES**

- The origins of ideas about deterring criminals
- The ties between classic deterrence theory and modern versions
- Crime as a reasoned and reasonable choice between alternative behaviors
- The routine nature of some offending, and the role opportunity plays in defining its routineness
- The twenty-first century merger of deterrence, choice, and opportunity as an explanation of how offenders think and act

# Introduction

Most organized religions describe the fate of those who fail to follow the rules laid down by a supreme being. Ancient laws were both prescriptive and proscriptive—telling people what they must and must not do. They also described, often in excruciating detail, the sanctions for those who stray from the righteous path. Historical and archeological evidence of such rules—and often-graphic accounts of the associated corporal and capital punishments—suggests a long-standing belief in their power to promote compliance.

Cesare Beccaria, the eighteenth century Italian social critic (called by some the father of criminology), provided an early treatise on the ties between formal sanctions—those flowing from governments and enforced by their social control agents—and compliant behavior. Criminological interest in the deterrent effects of formal sanctions diminished 100 years ago as positivists searched for the causes of crime in other venues.

Rediscovered in the 1960s, deterrence quickly became a mainstay of criminological research. Over the final two decades of the twentieth century, criminologists largely explored two deterrence-related processes. Rational choice suggests that some people have already decided what laws they will break, given a certain set of circumstances and rationalizations, whereas routine activities views crime as a response to life's opportunities. Beginning in the twenty-first century, criminologists took elements of prior theorizing about deterrence, combined them with parts of economic theory and additional elements from routine activities and rational choice theories to redefine deterrence theory.

The theories in this chapter explore the choices people make. All assume some level of volition or the exercise of *free will*, and all have deep roots in Western history and culture. These theories explore the mechanisms that shape and influence individual choices either to adhere to normative behavior or to violate rules, norms, and laws. We begin with Beccaria's version of deterrence theory, an idea that has proved to have great longevity.

# Classical Deterrence Theory

The origins of deterrence theory are found in classical theory, itself an outgrowth of the Enlightenment in the eighteenth century, when Europeans rejected traditional social, political, and religious explanations of crime. During this epoch, French philosophers spoke out against France's penal code and punishments as inhumane and inequitable. Jean-Jacques Rousseau (b.1712–d.1778) and Cesare Bonesana, marchese di Beccaria, usually referred to as Cesare Beccaria (b.1738–d.1794), argued for a radical new concept of justice. They demanded *justice* based on equality and *punishment* that was humane and proportionate to the offense. This doctrine of equality helped foment the American and French Revolutions. The roots of these ideas are found in the concepts of *natural law* and the *social contract.*

## Natural Law and the Social Contract

The term **natural law** refers to a philosophy that some elements of justice are universal and derived from nature rather than from the rules of society. Given this perspective, the search for absolute justice is possible (Levy 1988). At its core, natural law posits the belief that humans have an inborn notion of right and wrong; therefore, it does not rest upon the arbitrary will of a ruler or upon the decree of the masses (Rommen 1998). Natural law, while not requiring belief in a deity, refers to a higher law, primordial or natural—in other words, rules for living that are binding on all societies.

Thomas Aquinas (b.1225–d.1274) united natural law doctrines, derived from Aristotle and other ancient philosophers, into a Christian framework. In his *Summa Theologica*, Aquinas asserts that if **positive law** (i.e., law derived out of the political process) violates natural law, the former is not law but a corruption of law. According to Church doctrine, natural law is rooted in human nature; divine law is written on the human heart (Fuchs 1965), the principles of which are known or at least knowable by anyone (Boyle 1992).

Natural law places limits on political power. It transcends all formal human constructs, and any law contrary to natural law derives from the coercive force of the state, not the voluntary compliance of the governed. According to the *Commentaries* (1760) of William Blackstone (b.1723–d.1780), any human law contrary to natural law has no validity, a statement similar to the one made by Aquinas 500 years earlier.

Should positive law conflict with natural law, most legal and religious scholars side with natural law.

Expressions of European Enlightenment's natural law are to be found in the **social contract:** a mythical state of affairs wherein each person agrees to a pact, the basic stipulation of which is that all men are created equal. "The social contract establishes among the citizens an equality of such character that each binds himself on the same terms as all the others, and is thus entitled to enjoy the same rights as all the others" (Rousseau (1954:45[1762]).

## Classical School

The **Classical School**, opposed to the capricious nature of eighteenth century justice, argued that laws should recognize neither rank nor station. Beccaria formalized this premise in *An Essay on Crimes and Punishments* (1963[1764]: English edition, 1867), when he wrote that laws should be drawn precisely and matched to punishments applied equally to all classes of men. The law, he argued, should stipulate a particular penalty for each specific crime, and judges should mete out identical sentences for each occurrence of the same offense.

According to the position advanced by the Classicalist Beccaria and the Utilitarian Jeremy Bentham (b.1748–d.1832), a society can justify the punishment of any offender only if that person is rational and endowed with free will (see box 2.1). Moreover, they concluded that every person has the ability to choose between right and wrong, between being law-abiding and breaking the law. Law-violating behavior is, therefore, a rational choice made by a reasoning person with free will. Classical theory argues that human beings tend toward *hedonism*—that is, they seek pleasure and avoid pain. The fear of punishment restrains the populace from unlawful albeit pleasurable acts. Crime is "caused" by the failure of laws—and the punishments they endorse—to deter would-be criminals from committing their crimes. Accordingly, the purpose of law is not simply retribution but also deterrence.

Beccaria's theory requires three essential elements for lawful punishments to deter future criminality: certainty, celerity, and severity. **Certainty** refers to the probability that offending persons will receive a sanction for their miscreant deeds. If deterrence is to work as intended,

> Classicalists believe that the law must serve as more than simple retribution for bad deeds. Rather, it must be the embodiment of the pleasure-pain principle: guiding the delicate balance between attaining the highest possible levels of pleasure without incurring any pain.

---

| | **Beccaria and Bentham: On Criminology and Deterrence** |
|---|---|
| **B O X 2.1** | |

Although often discussed as co-founders of deterrence theory and, by some, as co-founders of criminology, Beccaria and Bentham made quite different and unique contributions to the study of crime and justice. Each one's views, in fact, gave rise to a singular perspective on how deterrence operates. They wrote their respective magnum opuses 25 years apart, Beccaria's work in 1764, and Bentham's *An Introduction to the Principles of Morals and Legislation* in 1789. Beccaria was an Enlightenment philosopher who saw the cruelty and barbarism of contemporary legal codes as unacceptable. Given the natural tendency of humankind toward hedonism, sanctions only deter crime, he maintained, when they meet certain conditions (i.e., certainty, celerity, and severity). A perfect system of education—on morality and self-restraint, plus knowledge about crimes and punishments—would encourage better choices without having to resort to punishments.

Beccaria's theorizing about crime, outside of stating that crime is a reflection of the self-interest found in everyone, was, according to Raymond Paternoster (2010), immature and incomplete. Bentham, on the other hand, saw all human behavior, including crime, as shaped by the twin concerns for pleasure (i.e., maximizing it) and pain (i.e., minimizing it). Behavior is guided by *utility*, which is a "weighted balance between these two considerations" (p. 770). Bentham also recognized many informal sanctions, imposed by self and others, that factor into the utilitarian equation that guides human choices. When it came to defining those pleasures and pains that shape choices, Bentham went a step further: The valuation is not an objective state; rather, it is a product of the human mind.

Beccaria and Bentham, whose contributions to criminology are often mentioned in the same breath, championed ideas that while similar were also quite different. The intellectual heirs of each philosopher emphasized elements that reflect those differences.

*Source*: Paternoster (2010).

the certainty of capture, trial, and, ultimately, punishment must be high. The elapsed time between when the illegal act occurs and when the sanction is applied should be minimal; **celerity** refers to the prompt application of the sanction. However, in formal operation, the gap in time between committing a serious (felony) crime and punishment is often quite wide. Beccaria's thinking about **severity** was complex. The pain of any sanction should only exceed the advantage derived from the crime. That is, the punishment should be proportional to the crime. Excessive punishment, as in sanctions motivated by retribution, can increase crime. People could commit additional crimes to avoid punishment for the first one if the sanction is excessive. Beccaria opposed the death penalty as excessive—an example of the state declaring war on the individual. While classical theory emphasizes the certainty of punishment over its severity, the reality of criminal justice is the reverse: Severity is more easily achieved than is certainty.

> In its ideal form, deterrence derives from the unfettered actions of certainty, celerity, and severity.

## Neoclassical Theory

Classicalism had one annoying shortcoming: Implementing a criminal code based on classicalism proved difficult. This problem became apparent to the drafters of the 1791 French Code. Since equality and proportionality proved more difficult in practice than in theory, the French added to the judges' discretionary powers, creating neoclassicalism (Roshier 1989).

In classical theory, the law assigned a penalty for a particular crime; the offender's characteristics or circumstances were not to be considered. **Neoclassicalism** maintains an emphasis on free will, while including mitigation or aggravation based on past criminal record, mental state, age, and gender. The neoclassicalists believed that a society ruled by law can justify punishment only if crime is reasoned behavior. Their revisions created a need for nonlegal experts, such as psychiatrists, psychologists, and social workers (Taylor, Walton, and Young 1973:8). Such experts determine the presence of mitigation, while maintaining the centrality of free will, creating wiggle room for neoclassicalists.

Classical and neoclassical philosophies underwrite the U.S. criminal justice system. Contemporary crime theories also reflect many of the ideas originally laid down by Beccaria and Bentham more than 200 years ago, including modern deterrence and opportunity theories. The idea that people are responsible for their own actions—and that society, through its social control mechanisms, can make clear that lesson—has proved quite resilient.

> Not only did French and Italian social critics provide a philosophical underpinning for the American Revolution but their ideas also can be seen in how justice is administered in the U.S. today.

Criminologists' interest in deterrence theory waned in the last quarter of the nineteenth century. Charles Darwin, Herbert Spencer, and Cesare Lombroso led a revolution in explanations of human behavior. Criminologists shifted from the study of laws and punishments to the study of criminals, both in society and in its prisons, a locus largely maintained until the 1960s. For 100 years, criminologists took one path, and policy makers followed an entirely different one.

## Deterrence Rediscovered

The 1960s brought changes to U.S. society, ranging from desegregation to near political anarchy. In those tumultuous times, two social scientists shifted criminologists' attention back to deterrence. In 1968, Jack Gibbs authored an article entitled "Crime, Punishment, and Deterrence," which owed much to Beccaria's views on deterrence. Gibbs offered a theory of criminal deterrence based on legal sanctions. One offshoot from this body of work is **perceptual deterrence**, which looks at the relationship between the perceptions of individuals about the risk of sanctions and their self-reported misconduct (Geerken and Gove 1975). By the 1980s, any inhibition in crime that could be linked either directly or indirectly to the threat of a sanction was part of the deterrence process (Williams and Hawkins 1986). The *perception* of severity, celerity, and certainty was what mattered—not the actual outcome (Paternoster and Bachman 2012).

Also in 1968, economist—and eventual 1992 Nobel Prize winner—Gary S. Becker published "Crime and Punishment: An Economic Approach," a work that employed **cost–benefit analysis**. The decision to commit a crime depends on the costs and benefits of both criminal and noncriminal conduct. Criminal penalties constituted only part of the costs associated with being caught, convicted, and sanctioned. In Becker's approach, the certainty of sanctioning was far more important than the severity of the sanctions themselves.

With the publication of these two works, deterrence theory was once more on the empirical-studies agenda of criminologists. One of the first consequences of the rediscovery of deterrence in the 1960s was to expand the forms of deterrence (see box 2.2 on the following page). The second was the creation of two separate but related approaches to deterrence research, one involving econometrics and the other largely driven by sociological concepts.

### Beccarian Models of Deterrence

Deterrence conceptualizing in the 1960s and 1970s benefited from the collective work of Jack Gibbs, Richard Hawkins, and Franklin Zimring, among others (Geerken and Gove 1975; Meier and Johnson 1977; Nagin 1978; Silberman 1976; Tittle and Rowe 1974). The sociological thinking about deterrence that emerged at this time little resembled Beccaria's ideas, but it owed him an intellectual debt nonetheless (Paternoster 2010). Raymond Paternoster and Ronet Bachman (2001:16) observed the following about what happens whenever sanctions are threatened or applied: "It is not difficult to see that the deterrence message may get mixed because often our personal and vicarious experiences are at odds." Sociology-based deterrence studies, then, tended to focus on punishments' certainty and severity effects (Blumstein, Cohen, and Nagin 1978; Gibbs 1975; Tittle 1969). Researchers evaluated the links between what people think about—their perceptions of—the certainty and severity of punishments, as well as their subsequent self-reported criminal behavior and deviance (Paternoster 1987). One development, then, was a shift from seeking insights into absolute deterrence to understanding perceptual deterrence.

Prisoner studies did provide insights into the experiential component of deterrence (i.e., specific deterrence). For example, Julie Horney and Ineke H. Marshall (1992), in a study of the experiential interpretation of sanctions by a sample of prison inmates, addressed the meaning of pun-

> Beccarian models on punishments and deterrence derive from Beccaria's notions of hedonism and the pleasure-pain principle, along with the roles played by severity, certainty, and celerity in making those punishments work.

---

**BOX 2.2**

### Expanded Forms of Deterrence

In Beccaria's day, **general deterrence** reflected the idea that those watching, hearing about, or otherwise becoming aware of a sanction would view the outcome as too costly and not engage in behavior that would be punished. The public display of punishments was believed to have a deterrent effect on potential offenders—those who had committed previous offenses without being caught and those contemplating crime. In fact, public executions often included the recitation of the sins that had led to the gallows. A minister, preacher, or priest often facilitated the confession. The targets of **specific** (or **individual**) **deterrence,** Beccaria's second major form of deterrence, were those who had been caught, convicted, and punished. Imprisonment or corporal punishment *encouraged* offenders to change their life paths to noncriminal ones. Otherwise, they would suffer increasingly harsh sanctioning.

Social scientists in the 1960s added two other forms of deterrence to the mix: absolute and restrictive deterrence. According to **absolute deterrence,** once individuals come to see either the error of their ways or the potential losses they face, they will refrain from all crime. Just as importantly, those who have never been caught in a criminal act, as well as those who have been caught and punished, may exhibit the effects of absolute deterrence. For example, suppose a young man spends 10 years, from age 18 to 28, in federal prison for dealing crack. At the time of his release, thanks to the federal prison industries program, he knows how to build furniture. He subsequently secures a good-paying job and leaves behind his life as a drug dealer. Meanwhile, a 16-year-old friend back in the neighborhood, who was also contemplating a career as a drug dealer, hears about the 10-year sentence and decides to return to high school, where he gets his degree, and then goes on to college. The same day his friend is released from federal prison, the reformed wannabe drug dealer assumes a position as a criminal justice professor at the local community college. In both cases absolute deterrence is at work.

The second concept is **restrictive deterrence,** whereby offenders may refrain from the act that previously landed them in trouble or that threatens trouble, but they only modify their criminal conduct rather than abandon it. For example, suppose our hypothetical drug dealer decides, upon release from prison, to stop selling crack because the police are targeting that particular drug and embarks on a new career in marijuana sales, knowing that the local police are less interested in retail marijuana sales. He has not entirely given up criminal ways, but he has modified them to reduce his risks to more manageable levels.

*Sources*: Gibbs (1968); Zimring and Hawkins (1973).

ishments for persons with a high propensity for crime. High involvement in crime should lead to perceptions of low certainty of punishment only in situations in which the offenders go unpunished for their criminal acts. The researchers found that, consistent with deterrence theory, active offenders, or those who reported any involvement in a given crime, formulated their perceptions of punishment probabilities based on their past experiences with legal sanctions.

In addition to those who end up paying for their crimes, and the impact of that payment upon future decisions, there is another side to this particular deterrence coin: What about those who escaped sanctioning? Mark C. Stafford and Mark Warr (1993) offered another modification to the deterrence model. They noted that previous definitions failed to take into account people who "got away" with crime. That is, each time someone escapes notice or punishment, what is the implication for the law's ability to deter? Stafford and Warr suggested several possible answers. First, people who commit crimes and escape apprehension (or conviction), having personal experience with attempts to deter them, may view this escape as license to commit more crimes. Second, individuals who know of others who escaped paying for their crimes—that is, vicarious experience—may be disposed to engage in crime as they see little risk. Third, individuals with personal or vicarious experience with a sanctioning process that was effective should be deterred. For example, a juvenile might be deterred from further offending as an adult by a stay in juvenile hall, or learning about a friend who was sent to "juvie" might serve as a deterrent. This theme—the impact of personal and vicarious experiences on risk perceptions—helped shape a new wave of deterrence theorizing and research in the twenty-first century.

Sociological research on sanctioning and deterrence from the late 1960s through the century's end was generally inconclusive. In his contemporary review of perceptual deterrence studies, Paternoster (1987) found that the theory generally did not fit the data, as available operationalizations of punishments' certainty or severity effects were not up to the task. Other critics of Beccarian-style deterrence theorizing saw several endemic shortcomings of the approach. First, they were not sure if it was a theory or a hypothesis. Deterrence is often called a hypothesis, meaning that it is a testable idea but lacks fully developed theoretical arguments—mainly propositions—about its putative operation and effects (Tittle and Rowe 1974). As Matthew Silberman (1976:442) noted, classical Beccarian deterrence employs strongly stated arguments steeped in untested assumptions about human nature and philosophical treatises on the use of punishments to secure normative conduct. This is hardly the level of conceptual thinking that leads to empirical verification.

Second, it was not clear that deterrence could stand on its own, or whether it must be tied to other theories. Modern tests of deterrence include variables never envisioned by Beccaria, including the opportunity and rational choice theories discussed later in this chapter. Deterrence theory is often integrated with other ideas about crime, such as chapter 3's genetic arguments, chapter 4's notions of psychopathic personality disorders, and chapter 5's IQ–crime links. For example, given various biological or psychological anomalies, certain people are undeterrable by penal sanctions. Theory integrations such as these reinforce the observation that deterrence is a hypothesis with limited utility to explain behavioral choices on its own merits.

Third, a major concern is whether deterrence works to control only minor crimes, such as nonserious delinquency, but is ineffective for more serious crimes, such as rapes and robberies (Paternoster 1989a, b). As interest in deterrence was growing in the mid-1970s, Isaac Ehrlich (1975) applied cost–benefit analysis to the death penalty. His conclusion: Executing one person saves seven to eight other lives; however, flaws in Ehrlich's data largely discredit this finding (Forst 1983; Klein, Forst, and Filatov 1978). Critics point to the Ehrlich study as an example of manipulating data to prove a specific point (Klein et al. 1978). The general absence of studies supporting the utility of severe sanctions, including the death penalty, to deter homicides suggests that the deterrent effect of criminal sanctions has limits (Pratt et al. 2006).

Finally, meta-analyses also report little support for deterrent effects of criminal sanctions (Pratt and Cullen 2005; Pratt et al. 2006; see, too, Paternoster 2010). Despite questions about whether deterrence works for both formal *and* informal sanctions, the absence of complete tests of the theory, and its utility for both major *and* minor crimes, Beccarian deterrence remains appealing. It makes sense to laypersons and practitioners alike. Its impact on persons likely to engage in crime remains less clear.

A meta-analysis is a statistical technique that allows researchers to pool the estimates of how well a theory's claims fare empirically.

## Benthamite Models of Deterrence

Economists, who view crime as they do any decision that has associated costs and benefits, provide a unique perspective on crimes and punishments. If someone analyzes the costs and benefits associated with purchasing a household item, goes the logic, then he or she will perform a similar **cost-benefit analysis** prior to committing crime (Becker 1968; Sullivan 1973). Gary S. Becker provided the groundwork for this perspective by suggesting that decisions to commit crimes involve the same decision-making processes as one uses to make the decision to buy a car. Even absent all needed information about possible outcomes (e.g., the roadworthiness of the car or its repair history), people make decisions based on an **expected utility principle.** This term describes the basis for deciding between uncertain outcomes or prospects while maximizing future returns on investments of time, talent, and other valuable or scarce resources—in the case of crime, this includes considering one's liberty or life. Simply put, a person utilizing this principle multiplies the value of the possible outcome by the probability that it will occur. Hence, decision-makers should glean as much information as possible about cars (or crimes), including bad things that can happen (buying a "lemon" or getting caught by the police), storing the data in their memory, and using it to analyze a specific decision (e.g., buy the car or commit an illegal act). The rationality they employ may be imperfect, but it is framed by the information they possess, recall, and act upon in a given situation at a given time. They may make imperfect decisions (e.g., buy a bad car or get caught committing a crime), but it is *the best decision at the time*. In other words, the cost–benefit analysis made by uninformed people will result in uninformed decisions. In computer lingo, garbage in, garbage out.

In addition, as box 2.3 suggests, it is also about timing. The decision to buy a car or commit a crime owes much to one's perceptions of when any possible debt—balloon payment or criminal sanction—comes due.

Criminology saw a resurgence in Benthamite deterrence theorizing and researching beginning in the late 1970s. This was largely due to Becker's (1968:170) simple and elegant suggestion that criminologists consider "the economist's usual analysis of choice" and Ehrlich's cost–benefit analysis, including his 1975 work on the death penalty. By the end of the twentieth century, these new-generation deterrence theories,

> Benthamite models on punishments and deterrence derive from Bentham's utilitarianism principle, meaning actions are taken based on the greatest return of pleasure.

## Box 2.3    Consider This: Time and Deterrence

The certainty of a sanction must not be in doubt for deterrence to work. However, when does certainty take hold? Deterrence generally assumes that all people look at time in the same way. That is, we all calculate events in the future in the same way: we worry about all future events equally, good or bad. Those persons not deterred, but arrested and punished, just made bad decisions. Time discounting, another idea from economics, has implications for how deterrence operates. The concept is also called delay discounting, and it refers to the idea that people tend to devalue a future reward in favor of one that is closer in time.

What if an offender sees a current event (think crime) as highly valued (think hedonism) and some future negative event (think prison or worse) as a long way off and not worth considering? The near event (pleasure from the crime) is more important than the far-off (and possibly avoidable) event (punishment). Consider an example from economics. A person offers you $20 in a week or $5 today; you take the $5, reflecting your time-discounting rate. However, experience may influence delay discounting. Consider a situation where your friend takes the $20 a week after you immediately take the $5. When your friend shows you the $20, you see the error of your ways. The next time you may value the future more highly. What if, however, you were offered either $100 today or $1,000 in a month? You might see that time horizon (a month) as short enough and delay receipt of payment until you received the $1,000. In this way, the amount of the reward (or sanction) is important as well. Time discounting plays a role in decisions of all sorts, including ones to commit crimes.

*Sources*: Klochko (2006, 2008); Nagin and Pogarsky (2004); Read and Read (2004).

called the **Neuve Classical School** (Paternoster and Bachman 2001:19), assumed two primary forms: rational choice theory and routine activities theory. There followed in the first two decades of the twenty-first century a new mixture of all three forms of deterrence theory, one with a decidedly more pragmatic focus. To get to that point, however, we must first understand the reasoning of those who commit criminal acts.

*Rational Choice Theory.*   In *The Reasoning Criminal*, Derek Cornish and Ronald Clarke (1986:1) observed that offenders seek to benefit personally from their criminal behavior. Their "reasoning" involves the making of decisions and choices, however rudimentary these processes might be. Finally, these processes exhibit a measure of *rationality*, which is constrained by the time available for the crime's commission and the offender's ability, as well as the availability of information about what could be gained by the crime and at what possible cost. Cornish and Clarke merged the idea of cost–benefit from economics with the idea of free will from the classical deterrence theorists, creating rational choice theory. Their theory frames the expected utility principle in terms of a crime-decision process that includes psychological forces. Indeed, rational choice theory includes a number of background factors in its explanatory schema—including intelligence, temperament, and cognitive style.

Given Cornish and Clarke's emphasis on criminal acts as possible sources of rewards or punishments, you might think that this theory applies only to property crimes; however, nothing could be further from the theory's intent. Proponents claim that violent crimes with no apparent motivation are explained by this theory. Even crime that appears purely impulsive has rational elements. For example, graffiti artists enjoy not only the act of creating their art but also the dangers associated with it (e.g., the possibility of contact with law enforcement, rival gang members and other graffiti artists, or just working over a highway overpass) and the notoriety that follows a successful act. Nonutilitarian violence appears to be rewarding to those who engage in such behavior, perhaps due to domination of victims and the senseless (and unpredictable) nature of such acts. In addition, the risks involved in criminal behavior can be exciting—in the jargon of behavioral psychologists, "reinforcing"—a topic to which we return in chapter 5.

Cornish and Clarke included several elements in the process of making choices, which in this case included the decision to commit a crime. First, Cornish and Clark saw **choice structuring** as taking place when individuals assess their own skills and needs in light of a specific crime's characteristics. They asserted that each crime has a unique choice-structuring process associated with it. Even the crime of burglary is not a single generic crime—in their words "it may be necessary to divide burglary simply into its residential and commercial forms" (Cornish and Clarke 1986:2). It may also be necessary to distinguish between burglary com-

Two theories, based on Benthamite notions about deterrence, formed the basis of the Neuve Classical School, including rational choice theory and routine activities theory.

According to rational choice theory, every crime has a unique choice-structuring decision associated with it.

mitted in middle-class suburbs, in public housing, and in wealthy residential enclaves. Having followed a choice-structuring process for one type of burglary does not lead automatically and inevitably to the choice to commit another type.

Second, the **involvement decision** is a multistage process that ends with the decision to get involved in crime. In this step, a person's demographic, social, familial, and psychological backgrounds constitute the interpretive context for crime involvement decisions. These background factors, along with various experiences (e.g., direct or vicarious criminal behavior, contact with police, and conscience and moral attitudes), provide the means to evaluate legitimate and illegitimate solutions for achieving generalized needs felt by everyone (e.g., money, sex, friendship, status, and excitement). The solutions include an appreciation for (1) the amount of work involved (i.e., too much or just the right amount), (2) the amount and immediacy of the reward (i.e., too little reward too far in the future versus the right amount immediately), (3) the likelihood and severity of punishment (an element easily recognized from classical deterrence theory), and (4) moral costs (i.e., values tied to one's upbringing, especially family factors). Once a particular illegitimate solution is seen as acceptable, a readiness to commit the crime is said to exist. Crimes occur when individuals with such readiness or a preexisting involvement decision react illegitimately to chance events, such as an easy opportunity, a need for cash, persuasive friends, drunkenness, or quarrelsome demeanor, among others.

Immediately before the commission of a crime but after the involvement decision, the criminal engages in the final element, an **event decision**, which is based on information about the possible criminal act. This step occurs quickly and without much thought on the offender's part. This decision becomes a rational response to chance events, a decision that is based on preexisting inclinations and a readiness to engage in illegitimate acts.

Cornish and Clarke did not see crime, even economic crime, as well planned and carefully executed. The rationality associated with crime goes into the decision to get involved in crime. Certain factors—including previous punishments and opportunity—constrain choices, moving the individual away from a decision to get involved in crime. After the initial decision has been made to commit a particular crime, however, the person moves quickly to its commission, given the right set of circumstances. Specifically, opportunity assumes an important role. Without the opportunity to engage in a crime, the involvement decision is, in sports parlance, all windup and no pitch.

Rational choice theory is itself the source of definitional problems. For example, it is not clear if rational choice theory overcame the definitional shortcomings of deterrence theory. Some critics see rational choice and deterrence as closely tied to both sociological and psychological variables (cf. Bachman, Paternoster, and Ward 1992; Paternoster 1989a,b). The tests that most support rational choice models are those that move away from strict measures of expected utility (Akers and Sellers 2013:26). Finally, students are often confused by the use of the word "rational" in rational choice theory. About the only thing the rational choice supporters and detractors agree on is that *rational* does not mean "careful thinking and sensible decisions by someone's standard" (Felson 1993:1497; see too Felson and Eckert 2016). Rational choice proponents argued that offenders may think about crime and its consequences—but not necessarily with great care, preferring to engage in "illegal decision analysis" (Felson 1993:1497). Offenders often engage in behavior that can only be described as "unrealistic," as in the case of repeat property offenders who demonstrated insufficient planning or understanding of the penalties for their crimes (Tunnell 1992). The issue may be a too-narrow definition of rationality, using only its instrumental meaning (i.e., what is the benefit gained from the act?), rather than its noninstrumental forms (i.e., what does engaging in the crime mean to the person doing it?) (Boudon 2003).

Recasting deterrence theory in econometric terms has silenced some critics, while others are less impressed, seeing new logical flaws in terms such as rational, restrictively narrow definitions related to its economic origins, or the conceptual commingling of rational choice with other theories. Moreover, finding empirical support for rational choice has proven difficult, a view reinforced by a meta-analysis of research on rational choice theory (Pratt and Cullen 2005).

***Routine Activities Theory.*** In the late 1970s, criminologists began to pull together several disparate theoretical ideas and empirical findings under an umbrella called routine activities or opportunity theory. Armed with the findings of victimization surveys and motivated by a general interest in better understanding the fate of crime victims, Lawrence E. Cohen and Marcus Felson (1979) articulated routine activities theory. They believed that both criminal motivation and the supply of potential offenders are constants: There is a never-ending supply of individuals who are ready, willing, and able to engage in **predatory crime**—violent crimes against persons and crimes of theft in which the victim is present. The statistical summaries of criminal victimizations, however, showed that crime was not evenly distributed throughout society.

Cohen and Felson saw predatory crime as dependent on the overlaying of a **motivated offender** (e.g., someone who feels the need for cash, items with immediate liquidity, or other items of value such as clothing or cars) with a **suitable target** (e.g., a well-heeled pedestrian in the wrong part of town, a rental car in search of the interstate, or a house with valuable goods), all occurring in the absence of a **capable guardian** (e.g., no homeowner present, no police, or a lone traveler). Cohen and associates

Routine activities theory maintains that the supply of perpetrators is virtually a constant; some potential victims can make themselves less attractive to offenders and, as a result, lower their individual probability of being victimized.

(1981) later stipulated that target suitability itself has four dimensions: (1) **exposure**—the visibility and physical accessibility of the target; (2) **guardianship**—the ability (and presence) of persons or objects to prevent crime from occurring; (3) **attractiveness**—the material or symbolic value of persons or property; and (4) **proximity**—the physical distance between potential targets and populations of potential offenders. Since the supply of motivated offenders is constant, a change in any of the four dimensions has the potential to reduce or to increase the likelihood of victimization.

According to routine activities theory, traditional law-and-order policies to reduce predatory crime may be doomed to failure. Certain features of modern life that improve the quality of life—such as better transportation, more electronic durable goods, and greater opportunities for recreational activities outside the home—may increase the opportunity for predatory crime, result in lower guardianship, and increase the pool of suitable targets. Cohen and Felson (1979) also disdained the idea that crime is related to the breakdown in the social structure of large cities. Crime is, alternatively, a by-product of "freedom and prosperity as they manifest themselves in the routine activities of everyday life" (p. 606).

Routine activities theory is a rich conceptual base from which to view crime and, as we shall see in chapter 10, crime-fighting efforts. However, critics are uncertain whether this a crime theory or a victimization theory. This distinction is not a trivial point. Some **victimologists**—researchers who study crime victims—have linked routine activities concepts to activity-specific risks of property and personal crime victimizations (Wilcox, Madensen, and Tillyer 2007), gender-specific risks for victimization (Mustaine 1997), college student lifestyles (Mustaine and Tewksbury 1998), and gang membership, gun carrying, and violent victimizations (Spano, Freilich, and Bolland 2008). Although nothing about the theory limits any tests solely to the explanation of criminal motivation and behavior, its use as a victimology theory is an important shift in emphasis.

Victimology may be considered a subbranch of criminology that addresses various aspects of becoming a victim.

Routine activities theory has proven to be resilient. Certain elements are underdeveloped, including the role of informal social control in both creating and eliminating specific geographical locations that have high crime intensity or "hot spots," and complete tests of the theory are unknown. Nonetheless, as we shall see in chapter 10, it is rich in its implications for both policies and practices.

## Deterrence Theorizing in the Twenty-First Century

Early in the twenty-first century, criminologists began to look critically at the application of deterrence principles to specific crime-fighting practices. This resurgence of interest in deterrence, at least the second in modern times, represented a combination of "lessons" from Benthamite and Beccarian models, which took several forms. One addressed the morphing of perceptual deterrence as an explanation of how offenders update and even modify their risk assessments, an idea reflected in restrictive deterrence. The second reflected the notion of differential deterrability, as not everyone responds in exactly the same manner to perceived threats. Finally, an idea born in the 1980s as "hot spot" criminology, reappeared in the twenty-first century as focused deterrence.

## Restrictive Deterrence

In the 1990s, criminologists studied the impact of offenders' experiences with the criminal justice apparatus on risk perceptions. Would such experiences, they asked, deter future criminality? The idea of restrictive deterrence comes from Gibbs (1975:33), "the curtailment of a certain type of criminal activity by an individual during some period because in whole or in part the curtailment is perceived by the individual as reducing the risk that someone will be punished as a response to the activity." Negative experiences with the justice system—apprehension, trial, conviction and imprisonment—are clearly important to the modification of offender behavior (see, e.g., Horney and Marshall 1992). Research on car thieves (Jacobs and Cherbonneau 2014) and computer hackers (Maimon et al. 2014) further suggests that the perceived threat of sanctions for their respective forms of misconduct can lead to behavioral modification (restrictive deterrence) but perhaps not crime abstinence (absolute deterrence).

A related idea suggests that risk perceptions are "updated" by prospective offenders (Nagin 1998). Shamena Anwar and Thomas A. Loughran (2011) took this idea a step further. Not only can the impact of such contact be calculated, but any risk updating also may be crime specific. They found that offenders who committed crime and were arrested perceive the probability of a subsequent arrest as increasing by 6% compared to not being arrested. This updating distinguished aggressive from income-generating crime, but only barely.

## Differential Deterrability

Twenty-first century studies of perceptual deterrence have also given rise to research on whether different types of offenders, given their experiences with crime and justice, may be differentially deterrable (Pogarsky 2002; Jacobs 2010). **Differential deterrability** derives from the idea that formal sanctions are more likely to work for some people and not for others. Assuming that all people are equally deterred by criminal sanctions is an idea that may have seemed logical in the eighteenth century, but not in the twenty-first century.

Who is less deterrable? Who is more deterrable? And under what circumstances are they differentially deterrable? Researchers have provided several answers to these questions. One approach captures the idea of ceilings and floors for the threats posed by sanctions. That is, there are deterrence boundaries that differentially impact offenders: some are more amenable to sanction threats when those sanction boundaries are breached, whereas others may be undeterred by those same threats. Thomas A. Loughran and associates (2012a:19) specified that the differences depend on the individual's offending pattern: "We identified a group of high-rate offenders who display lower perceived risks of detection and punishment for crime and also higher perceived rewards from crime. Alternatively, we identified a group of low-rate offenders who report higher perceived risk and lower perceived reward regarding offending" (see, too, Loughran, et al. 2012b). The researchers observed that low-rate offenders, medium-rate offenders, and high-rate offenders all exhibited sanction threat ceilings and floors, beyond which some individuals are more amenable to deterrence and others are undeterred by sanction threats.

It is also possible that peers have an impact on the rate of deterrability by formal sanctioning messages. Risk perceptions may vary by position in the social structure or types of peer groups (see chapter 6). The question becomes, then, how peers differentially influence perceptions of the certainty and severity of punishment. A study of street-youth found that the certainty of punishments is associated with increased violence; moreover, severity is also associated with greater levels of violence the longer the youth remains on the street (Baron 2011). How does this happen? The rewards of peer approval and the cost of peer sanctions hold greater cachet for street youth than do the potential costs of legal sanctions. If the peer group's moral code endorses the use of violence, if they see law enforcement as illegitimate, and if they report higher levels of anger, then the street youths are more likely to offend. In such cases sanction threats may encourage misconduct (see, too, Svensson 2015).

### Focused Deterrence

Finally, a virtual cottage industry has grown up around the use of deterrence-based police practices, called variously **focused deterrence** or "**pulling levers**," especially against street-level violence (Tillyer, Engel, and Lovins 2012). One such practice is related to "hot-spot" policing (Sherman, Gartin and Bueger 1989). By providing highly visible formal guardianship, including additional patrols and direct contacts by police with citizens, offenders may perceive a non-routine police presence. Police operations that target specific locations, including "corridors of crime," may also deter offenses, but the effects are often short-lived, and they may even be crime specific (i.e., business-based crimes) and place specific (i.e., high crime density locations) (Crank et al. 2010).

"Pulling levers" comes from the idea that when violence occurs, public officials, including the police, pull every available lever, call in every possible debt, and provide suspect populations with many examples of what could happen to them should they be caught; alternatives to their current crime path are also described to them (Braga and Weisburd 2012; Nagin, Solow, and Lum 2015). Police may, for example, target a separate but related activity as a lever. In the case of gang violence directed against non-crime-involved citizens, police may engage in full-enforcement by targeting all the gang's criminal activities, while they and other public service agencies make clear to gang members the consequences for continuing on this particular track as well as the available alternatives to gang involvement.

We will further explore focused-deterrence programming in chapter 10. Suffice it to say that the impact of focused policing tends to be short-term, lacking in sophisticated evaluative designs, and any outcomes appear based on flawed metrics, such as the clearance rate (Braga and Weisburd 2012; Nagin et al. 2015). Nonetheless, such programs are viewed as promising.

## SUMMARY

- The role of rules in shaping behavior by the threat of punishments is very old and reflected in most of the world's religions.
- Beccaria, the father of criminology, is also viewed as having created a perspective of deterrence based on the celerity, certainty and severity of criminal sanctions.
- Natural law has its roots in nature itself and, in the minds of many philosophers and religious persons, is superior to positive law, the latter coming out of a political process.
- The Classical School sees law and justice as recognizing neither rank nor station.
- The Classical School includes hedonism and free will as core ideas, the former referring to the natural tendency to seek pleasure and avoid pain, while the latter is an expression of the ability of human beings to make their own volitional life choices.
- Neoclassicalism added mitigating and aggravating conditions, based on an offender's criminal record, mental state, age, and gender.
- The emphasis on choosing between alternatives—one right and one wrong—is an enduring idea, based on equally powerful assumptions about human behavior.
- Academic interest in deterrence largely ceased with the growth of positivistic criminology in the nineteenth century.
- Cost-benefit analysis suggests that the decision to commit a crime depends on the costs and benefits that accrue to both criminal and noncriminal conduct.
- There are at least four forms of deterrence: general deterrence, specific deterrence, absolute deterrence, and restrictive deterrence.

- Contemporary Beccarian models emphasize perceptual deterrence of the certain and severity of criminal sanctions.
- Critics of Beccarian models question whether deterrence is a theory or a hypothesis, whether it must be linked to other theories to be tested, and whether it only works for minor crime.
- Even in the absence of definitive proof, deterrence theory remains a powerful idea.
- Contemporary Benthamite model's expected utility principle involves multiplying the value of a possible outcome times the probability that it will occur.
- Time discounting tells us that people tend to devalue a reward that is in the distant future for one that is closer in time.
- The Neuve Classical School is a term that refers to late twentieth and early twenty-first century ideas about deterrence, but especially rational choice theory and routine activities theory.
- Cornish and Clarke's rational choice theory consists of three elements: choice structuring, involvement decisions, and event decisions.
- Critics of rational choice theory question whether the theory addresses all of the costs a crime decision may accrue, whether this theory can be distinguished from embedded sociological and psychological variables used to test it, and the true meaning of the term "rational" in rational choice.
- Cohen and Felson's routine activities theory emphasizes that there is a near constant supply of individuals ready, willing, and able to engage in predatory crime and that such crimes occur when a suitable target lacks a capable guardian.
- Target suitability includes exposure, guardianship, attractiveness, and proximity, all of which are crucial to whether crime becomes a routine activity of everyday life.
- Critics of routine activities theory wonder whether this is a crime theory or a victimization theory.
- Deterrence theorizing and researching in the twenty-first century has emphasized three ideas: restrictive deterrence, differential deterrability, and focused deterrence

## KEY TERMS

| | |
|---|---|
| absolute deterrence | Classical School |
| attractiveness | cost-benefit analysis |
| capable guardian | differential deterrability |
| celerity | event decision |
| certainty | expected utility principle |
| choice structuring | exposure |

focused deterrence
general deterrence
guardianship
individual deterrence
involvement decision
motivated offender
natural law
neoclassicalism
Neuve Classical School
perceptual deterrence
positive law

predatory crime
proximity
"pulling levers"
restrictive deterrence
severity
social contract
specific deterrence
suitable target
time discounting
victimologists

## CRITICAL REVIEW QUESTIONS

1. Explain the links between natural law, the social contract, and deterrence theorizing.

2. How were Beccaria's and Bentham's ideas on deterrence the same, and how were they different?

3. Describe Beccaria's operational elements for deterrence.

4. Which of Beccaria's ideas might explain problems with mandatory sentencing?

5. Why do you think the classicalists profoundly influenced U.S. penal philosophy?

6. What is neoclassical theory, and why is it important to criminal justice processing?

7. List and define the four forms of deterrence.

8. Elaborate on the idea of contemporary Beccarian models of deterrence.

9. Elaborate on the idea of contemporary Benthamite models of deterrence.

10. What is the role of time discounting in influencing the deterrence process?

11. What do you see as the greatest flaw in deterrence research?

12. Do you believe people are calculating machines, constantly doing cost–benefit analysis?

13. "Choice structuring is like when a student considers what classes to take (e.g., X amount of work for Y credit and Z knowledge equals too much work for too little gain)." How accurate is this statement?

14. List and discuss the three elements associated with rational choice theory.

15. List and discuss the three elements associated with routine activities theory. What are the four dimensions of capable guardianship?

16. How might rational choice theory expand our understanding of the relationship between routine activities and predatory crime? What are the problems with both theories?

17. Deterrence theorizing in the twenty-first century has tended to emphasize three themes. What are they, and what have they added to our understanding of how deterrence operates?

# 3

# Biological Theories

## LEARNING OBJECTIVES

- The continued centrality of biocriminology, which has its origins in the late nineteenth century, to the study of crime and criminals in the twenty-first century
- Human behavior as the result of genetic forces that have connections to social and environmental factors
- Contemporary biocriminological explanations of crime nearly as contentious as those espoused by Lombroso in the nineteenth century
- Biochemistry, including the operation of the brain and other parts of the central nervous system, as a unique window into human conduct, including crime

# Introduction

The exploration of biology's links to crime, what some have called **bio-criminology**, has generated a great deal of controversy over the past 150 years. As Francis McAndrew (2009: 331) observes: "There is little question that a predisposition to behave in a physically violent way is linked to biology." Molecular and behavioral genetics have demonstrated that many behaviors have in part a genetic basis. According to Adrian Raine (2013: 8): "Genes shape physiological functioning, which in turn affects our thinking, personality and behavior—including the propensity to break laws of the land, whatever those laws may be." At the same time, Raine, author of *The Anatomy of Violence: The Biological Roots of Crime*, makes no claim that genes are destiny, as other factors in a person's physical, social, and psychological environs also play significant roles in shaping human conduct.

Biocriminology is a criminological sub-discipline that examines the biological and hereditary origins of criminal behavior.

This chapter explores biological links to crime. Before turning to that topic, however, we must first note the specific ways in which biological explanations have proven controversial, ways that have had a significant impact on how criminologists look at biology as a viable explanatory factor (Berryessa, Martinez-Martin, and Allyse 2013). Specifically, the controversy centers on three issues (Ferguson and Beaver 2009):

1. A biological explanation for criminal behavior negates personal responsibility/free will—*mens rea*;

2. A biological explanation is decidedly deterministic—criminal behavior as incurable—and misuse can label people unfairly, for example, as "dangerous"; and

3. In the past, biological explanations have provided a foundation for racism, sexism, eugenics, and the belief in racial differences in intelligence.

Biological explanations for criminal behavior have been (mis-)used to promote racism and negative social policies and practices.

Each of these points are examined in this chapter and subsequent chapters, particularly with regards to how they have shaped criminologists' views of biological explanations. Moreover, these ideas are also important to the discussions in chapter 10 of the implications of such explanations for criminal justice policies, procedures, and practices.

# Criminal Anthropology

Humans have long blamed evil forces for troubling events. Early attempts to rid the community of a perceived demon or evil spirit involved the use of severe physical abuse inflicted to drive the demon from the host's body. In medieval times and well into the seventeenth century, people believed that witches made a pact with the devil. Communal attempts to rid European and colonial American society of this evil gave rise to the term "witch hunt." During the eighteenth and nineteenth centuries, the search for evil gave rise to the pseudo-science of **phrenology**: the view that the shape of a person's skull and facial imperfections could reveal a proclivity for criminal behavior, a view advanced by German physician, Franz Josef Gall (b.1758–d.1828). Cesare Lombroso (b.1835–d.1909), an Italian physician whose name figured prominently in chapter 1's discussion of positivism, advanced the view that external physical traits revealed the true "inner person."

## Cesare Lombroso, Prison Doctor/Positivist Criminologist

Lombroso was a military doctor early in his professional life, treating and studying soldiers. Lombroso was also a prison doctor and psychiatrist at an asylum for the criminally insane. He studied thousands of convicts using anthropometry, a part of anthropology that uses body measurements to identify differences in races and individuals. In 1876, pulling together his diverse studies on diseases of the nervous system, the brains of criminals, and their anthropological measurements, Lombroso published *L'uomo delinquente*, or *Criminal Man*. Perhaps influenced by the work of Charles Darwin (discussed below) and other evolutionists, Lombroso concluded that criminal behavior is the result of immature evolution, a state he called **atavism**, from the Latin word for ancestor.

Atavistic man is an evolutionary throwback with peculiar physical characteristics that Lombroso called **stigmata**. Stigmata included facial asymmetry; an enormous jaw; prominent cheekbones; large ears; fleshy, swollen, and protruding lips; abnormal teeth; a receding or excessively long chin or a short and flat chin, such as found in apes; excessive arm length; more than the normal number of fingers, toes, or nipples; and a series of behavioral characteristics. He stressed that stigmata in themselves were not the cause of crime, simply the external signs of atavism. Moreover, stigmata were offense specific; that is, different types of offenders also have unique external stigmata. A born criminal, he claimed, was one with five or more stigmata.

> Lombroso believed that many criminals were products of an immature evolution; external physical characteristics he called stigmata revealed such individuals.

Facing mounting criticism toward the end of his life, Lombroso modified his position, adding environmental factors to later editions of *L'uomo delinquent*. Further, he stated that only about 30 percent of all law violators were *born* criminals. He noted that a milieu with access to money and the ability to steal tempts even the non-atavist. Non-atavists avoid discovery or prosecution, he observed, by exercising influence. Gina Lombroso-Ferrero included many of these modifications in an English-language version called *Criminal Man* (1911), which she edited after the death of her father. While no longer linking all criminality to atavism in this volume, she argued that atavists pose the most serious threat to society.

## Challenging Criminal Anthropology

The shortcomings of Lombroso's research became obvious even in his own time. In a 12-year effort, Charles Goring (b.1870–d.1919), a British prison system physician and statistician, examined 3,000 convicted offenders and a comparison group of Englishmen without criminal convictions. In *The English Convict: A Statistical Study*, Goring (1913) reported that he was unable to find statistical correlations between the objective measures of physical and mental anomalies and known criminals. Not only was Goring unable to distinguish offenders from non-offenders using these anomalies, he also failed to find significant differences between types of offenders. Goring concluded that there was no such thing as a physical criminal type and certainly no such thing as a born criminal.

In 1939, as a response to Goring's critique, Harvard physical anthropologist Earnest Albert Hooton (b.1887–d.1954) published *The American Criminal: An Anthropological Study*. For years, he and colleagues at other universities collected body measurements from 17,000 individuals, including roughly 14,000 prison inmates. His comparison/control group was a cross-section of college students, police officers, and firefighters, persons whose measurements were easily obtainable. Hooton performed meticulous comparisons between the inmates and the control group. He found that there were significant differences between the criminals and the civilians on more than half of the anthropometric measurements. He further concluded that criminals are an organically inferior class of human beings. The physical inferiority of the criminals, Hooton argued, is an important link to mental and moral inferiority.

> Hooton failed to provide a truly comparable control group in his study of prison inmates.

While Hooton used a control group, he failed to appreciate that police officers and firefighters, especially during the Depression when such positions were prized, would be physically superior—e.g., had to meet weight, height, and strength requirements—to prison inmates who were typically from economically deprived circumstances with poor diets. As for college students, especially those from Harvard, they represented an advantaged population with good nutrition and opportunities for healthy physical recreation.

> Natural selection is the process whereby beneficial characteristics that aid survival become part of that organism's inherited traits, while less helpful traits and characteristics die out.

As suggested in box 3.1, the history of eugenics clouds any efforts to link criminal behavior to biology.

## Genetics and Crime

Genetics is the study of **heritability**, the idea that certain traits, characteristics, or even behavior can be transmitted biologically from one generation to the next. The science emerged in 1900 when scientists rediscovered Gregor Johann Mendel's (b.1822–d.1884) work on the inherited characteristics or traits of certain plant species. Mendel, an Augustinian friar living in Moravia, a part of the modern-day Czech Republic, viewed every trait as potentially transmittable within a species. He believed that both parents, as hereditary units, contributed some of

**BOX 3.1**

### Eugenics: An Ugly History

Charles Darwin's (b.1809–d.1882) first book (*Origin of Species* 1859) was concerned exclusively with nonhuman organisms—he was a botanist; however, his second book (*Descent of Man* 1871) included the idea that natural selection shaped humanity. Influenced by Darwin, English social philosopher Herbert Spencer (b.1820–d.1903) maintained that survival of the fittest was an idea that could and should be applied to society. Spencer and his supporters disapproved of humanitarian efforts at expending public funds to improve the lives of the less fortunate members of society. This position, later labeled social Darwinism, argued that government should not expend public funds on behalf of those who are labeled as "inferior." Is contemporary opposition to social welfare and subsidized housing a modern form of social Darwinism?

The work of Darwin also influenced his cousin, the eminent British scientist and statistician Francis Galton (b.1822–d.1911). In 1883, Galton coined the term **eugenics**, which morphed into policies encouraging high rates of reproduction by those with desirable human traits and discouraging any reproduction by those with undesirable traits (see, too, Galton 1906). Many states outlawed intermarriage between races; in others, government controlled the reproduction of "inferior stock" through sterilization, with Indiana enacting the first law authorizing the practice in 1907. By 1915, thirteen states had such laws; by 1930, thirty states permitted the sterilization of certain criminal offenders and people deemed mentally defective in public institutions (Lombardo n.d.).

The U.S. Supreme Court upheld these practices in a 1927 decision. Associate Justice Oliver Wendell Holmes, Jr., declared his support for Virginia's sterilization law in *Buck v. Bell* (274 U.S. 200), Carrie Buck was described as the daughter of a "mental defective" and the mother of a female daughter adjudged feebleminded at age seven months. Referring to Carrie, Justice Holmes remarked: "We have seen more than once that the public welfare may call upon the best citizens for their lives. It would be strange if it could not call upon those who already sap the strength of the state for these lesser sacrifices. . . . *Three generations of imbeciles is enough*" (emphasis added).

*Sources:* Degler (1991); Locurto (1991); Lombardo (n.d.); Spencer (1961/1864); Sumner (1906).

their respective traits to their offspring through reproductive cells called gametes. In the field of genetics, two key technical terms are *chromosomes* and *genes.*

**Chromosomes** are high-density genetic storage devices, the carriers of human hereditary characteristics that reside in all of the body's cell nuclei. Males have an X and a Y chromosome in each cell; females have two X chromosomes. An ordinary body cell contains 23 pairs of chromosomes each with thousands of genes. **Genes** are chromosome segments by which living organisms transmit inherited characteristics to the next generation. Genes consist of **deoxyribonucleic acid** (**DNA**) and array themselves along the length of each human chromosome.

One way to visualize gene segments is to think of a spiral staircase with two intertwining rails, described by geneticists as the double helix (Watson 1990). One rail contains subunits called **nucleotides**, which are subunit building blocks of the nucleic acids found in DNA; the other rail

The human genome is essentially a set of unique instructions written at the molecular level in the form of DNA for the construction of each human being.

has a mirror image of subunits, arrayed in chemically bonded groups that form traits or alleles. The human organism has more than 3 billion nucleotides. Scientists believe humans have around 25,000 protein coding genes. Hence, every human cell, except red blood cells, contains an exact copy of an individual's DNA. The sum of these genes is the **human genome**—instructions written at the molecular level for each human being.

The science of genetics is at the core of much contemporary biocriminology. Indeed, today DNA is nearly synonymous with genetics. Before the discovery of DNA in 1953, however, researchers employed a straightforward approach to the genetic transmission of criminal tendencies. They looked for answers to the central question, "Is crime caused by nature or nurture?" The researchers looked for their answers in the criminal conduct found among adopted children and twins. Do biological parents pass along their crime-prone tendencies to their children as a kind of genetic inheritance or, conversely, does a child's environment shape their behavior? These were the types of questions posed by criminologists employing both adoption and twin studies.

## Adoption Studies

Beginning in the 1930s, research into criminal inheritability centered on **adoption studies,** which involved comparing the crime and delinquency rates of adopted children with those of both their biological *and* their adoptive parents. When the adopted children's behavior more closely resembles that of their biological parents, supporters point to this as evidence of a genetic predisposition (nature). Studying the criminality of adopted children separated from their biological parents at an early age accomplishes what would be an unethical, if not illegal, alternative to employing the classical experimental approach with random assignment and control groups.

Adopted children whose natural parents have criminal records are much more likely to be convicted of a crime than when the natural parents have no criminal records (Hollin 1989). Barry Hutchings and Sarnoff Mednick (1977) compared adopted children who had a criminal biological father and a noncriminal adoptive father with those who had a noncriminal biological father and a criminal adoptive father. The researchers concluded that those with a criminal biological father were twice as likely to become criminals as those with a noncriminal biological father.

But adoptions are not all equal and do not provide the same unbiased sample as would random assignment. Selective placement is a biasing factor: Children whose biological parents have a history of criminal behavior are more likely to be placed later and in an inferior environment, such as one with greater poverty. They are also more likely to experience negative prenatal influences, including a lack of obstetrical care and parental substance abuse (Burt and Simons 2014). Lee Ellis and Anthony Walsh (2000) state that adoption studies provide evidence of the interaction between genetic and environmental factors, a *nature plus nurture* view.

## Twin Studies

Twins exist in two genetic versions: (1) identical or **monozygotic (MZ) twins,** which evolve from a single fertilized ovum or egg and share identical genetic material; and (2) fraternal or **dizygotic (DZ) twins**, which evolve from two separate eggs, fertilized by different spermatocytes with less shared genetic material. We know that there are many more behavioral similarities among reunited MZ twins than among reunited DZ twins (Rowe 2002). But MZ twins might be treated more similarly given their similar appearances, a tendency for parents to dress them alike, for example, than DZ twins—thus an environmental explanation. And there is a presumption of similar socializing environments.

**Concordance** is the key measurement in twin studies; it refers to the degree to which twins share a particular behavior or condition. What about criminal behavior? Again, as with adoption studies, the ideal, but ethically unacceptable, research design would be to separate MZ twins at birth and have them randomly assigned to adoptive parents (Rowe 2002). Instead, **twin studies** must settle for twins separated by circumstances and look for concordant sets of MZ and DZ twins, where both siblings subsequently engaged in criminality. Germany's Johannes Lange published the first such criminological twin study in his 1930 book *Crime and Destiny*. Among MZ twins, 75 percent were concordant pairs for subsequent criminality, but only 12 percent of the DZ twins exhibited the same propensity for crime concordance.

Nearly 70 years later, Patricia Brennan and associates (1995) reported on eight twin studies, three from Germany, and one each from Holland, the United States, Finland, England, and Japan. These eight studies, published between 1929 and 1979, examined 138 pairs of MZ twins and 145 DZ twins. Brennan and associates identified crime concordance levels for MZ twins ranging from 50 to 100 percent, with most between 60 and 70 percent. Crime concordance levels for DZ twins were much lower, ranging from zero to 60 percent, with most between 10 and 15 percent. Indeed, the overall average was 52 percent for MZ twins and 21 percent for DZ twins (see Raine 1993:79).

The twin studies have important shortcomings. First, the high concordance for MZ twins involved as few as two to four sets of twins. There are relatively few separated MZ twins available for study. The three studies with the largest numbers of MZ twin pairs, between 28 and 37 sets, exhibited concordance levels between 61 and 68 percent. Few medical researchers would accept so few cases as definitive. Moreover, the chief outcome variables—crime, delinquency, or some other indicator of misconduct—rely on the timely intercession of the criminal justice system or a judgment by a researcher. These facts make the conclusions of the twin studies highly suspect.

Given null findings, twin researchers may turn to rather interesting explanations for the absence of concordance. For example, when a major Norwegian study failed to show a significant difference between the criminality of MZ and DZ twins, Karl Christiansen, who also studied Danish twins, was troubled. Christiansen (1977:82) suggested that perhaps "some special conditions exist in Norway that would dampen the expression of genetic factors." Given the high level of cultural and racial homogeneity found in most Scandinavian countries, this is a rather remarkable statement. The same qualification is true for nearly all such genetic studies because the largest and most sophisticated ones have taken place in Scandinavia. These conclusions beg an important question: What are the researchers measuring? Is it, perhaps, the impact of nationality or geographic boundaries on genetics? And if so, how is that possible?

The first wave of twin and adoption studies into the biological origins of criminality continued from the 1930s into the early 1970s. Another gene-linked approach, **karyotype studies**, a rudimentary form of chromosome study, represents an unfruitful but instructive biocriminological offshoot that briefly held the attention of the public and scholars alike. The karyotype studies represent a return to Lombroso's basic question: How can we identify the criminal? As the information contained in box 3.2 suggests, the answer provided by the karyotype studies was highly problematic and, in the end, inaccurate. The twin and adoption studies, on the other hand, proved far more resistant to the critics, and, indeed, as we make clear in the next section, have enjoyed a resurgence since the start of the twenty-first century.

## Contemporary Biocriminology

Early in the twenty-first century, John Wright and associates (2008a) began testing the genetics–crime link with large, longitudinal data sets, particularly the National Longitudinal Study of Adolescent Health (Add Health). The Add Health study included a sample of twins. The researchers explored the extent to which being a twin accounted for variations in the youths' identification with delinquent peers and their own self-reported delinquency. Wright and associates reported that both genetic influences and non-shared environmental influences accounted for the variability in the outcomes they encountered. While they found many similarities among the MZ and DZ twins included in the Add Health sample, there were also differences. Their research supported a convergence of biogenetic and social/physical environmental factors on the study of crime and delinquency (Barnes, Beaver, and Boutwell 2011; Wright et al. 2008a).

Biocriminologists have criticized contemporary graduate education in criminal justice and criminology, suggesting that the unfortunate leg-

Despite their shortcomings, twin and adoption studies tend to support a nature view of criminal behavior but also have shortcomings.

The idea of a man with an XYY chromosomal structure being a supermale and, as a result, prone to violence and aggression is a myth.

A longitudinal study is one that repeatedly looks at a general societal pattern (i.e., a trend study), an identified and specific group (i.e., a cohort study), or a group of individuals (i.e., a panel study); the Add Health is a panel study.

**Box 3.2    Consider This: The Supermale/Superviolent Criminal—Genetic Fact or Journalistic Fiction?**

During the night of July 13–14, 1966, eight Chicago nurses were systematically tortured, raped, and murdered. Within days the police had a prime suspect: Richard Speck, a drifter and social outcast. Speck was found guilty at his April 1967 trial and sentenced to die in the electric chair. A year later, the *New York Times* carried a story about Speck being a **supermale**, an XYY chromosomal male for whom violent crime was part of his genetic programming.

In 1965, Patricia Jacobs and associates pointed to a genetic abnormality as a possible key to some criminal behavior in *Nature*, a preeminent British scientific journal. The researchers based this claim on the fact that sex chromosomes determine gender: An XX pairing is a female, and an XY is a male. A karyotyped chromosomal abnormality occurs when the fertilized ovum receives an extra Y chromosome. Jacobs and associates speculated that the extra Y chromosome created an extremely rare XYY pattern—an aggressive, hyper-violent supermale. The XYY pattern was found to be overrepresented in the prison population. The traits associated with the extra-Y chromosome included: being taller than six feet, exhibiting low mental functioning, acute acne, and clumsiness. Such men were no more likely to commit crime than other people, but their physical and mental characteristics made it more likely that they would be caught and convicted. By the late 1970s, the scientific consensus was that the hyper-violent XYY male was a myth. Indeed, such individuals, when compared to genetically normal males, tend to exhibit higher levels of passivity.

Was Speck an XYY male? He was tested using a standard karyotype study, but found to have a normal chromosomal structure. This story did not get as much play in the press as the one stating that he was XYY and that his attorney refused to use this fact at trial as a mitigating factor. Speck's death sentence—but not the guilty verdict—was overturned by the U.S. Supreme Court; he was remanded to the trial court for resentencing. He was sentenced to life in the Illinois prison system, dying of a heart attack in 1991 at age 50.

*Sources*: Clark, et al. (1970); Hoffman (1977); Jacobs, et al. (1965); Lyons (1968); Sarbin and Miller (1970); Telfer (1968).

acy of Lombroso resulted in an absence of any biocriminological arguments in the career training of the next generation of criminologists. They accuse sociologically trained criminologists of misstating the theorizing of biocriminologists and ignoring the findings of biocriminologists—all in an attempt to enforce disciplinary boundaries (Wright et al. 2008a).

Criticism of biocriminology has led to a debate about the utility of twin studies and an alternative but related genetic approach, epigenetic studies. **Epigenetic studies** examine the influence of environmental forces that essentially turn off genetic switches, causing cells to misread one's DNA; moreover, most of these changes are viewed as heritable, that is, capable of being passed from one generation to the next (Bird 2007). The twin studies represent an empirical and theoretical dead-end, claims one side (e.g., Burt and Simons 2014, 2015; Massey 2015; see, too, Fraga et al. 2005), owing to far too many methodological shortcomings in how the data are collected and how the key genetic variables are measured (see, too, Gill 1978).

Biology may be important, but as epigenetic researchers demonstrate, environmental factors can turn on and off genetic switches so that DNA essentially responds differently in different environments. In this regard, cancer, mental illness, and possibly violence or other criminal actions are essentially "caused" by alterations to DNA in response to changes in one's physical and social environments. Because of the variable influence of epigenetic forces on humans, it may not be possible to separate out the uniquely biological forces at work creating criminals (Burt and Simons 2014, 2015).

This debate amplifies two important points about biological studies generally and genetic studies in particular. First, even after 150 years of research on genetics and more than a decade after mapping the human genome, we simply do not know to what extent genetic forces influence certain kinds of human behavior, crime among them. Second, biogenic explanations are controversial. Anyone who questions the validity or reliability of the arguments on either side—relying on a purely nature or nurture argument—is likely to be seen as an **oppositional ideologue**. Those challenging the *validity* of current biocriminological studies ask a basic question: Are we truly measuring the actual biological and heritable aspects of crime or are the measures we employ too indirect and, therefore, invalid? Those challenging the *reliability* of such results are asking a different question: Are the reported results likely to stand up over time and be repeated from study to study? Biocriminologists and their critics continue to seek answers to these questions.

What is not in dispute is that many physical characteristics are inherited. Most humans have two eyes, two hands, and ten fingers; tall parents tend to have tall children, just as the reverse is true. But, in the final analysis, are *behavioral* traits passed on from parents to offspring? And most important, is criminal behavior inherited? Some fascinating anecdotes indicate otherwise. Arnold Rothstein, considered the "godfather" of organized crime in America, was the wayward son of a pious Jewish businessman. The murderous labor racketeer Louis "Lepke" Buchalter had three brothers: one earned a PhD, later becoming both a rabbi and college professor; the second became a pharmacist; the third was a dentist. Lepke died in Sing Sing's electric chair in 1944.

Adrian Raine (2013: 52), echoing the epigenetic studies perspective, claims that "genetic and biological factors *interact* with social factors in predisposing someone to later antisocial and violent behavior." He further notes: "Studies over many decades from a variety of Western nations and ages converge on a simple truth; that genes give us half the answer to the question of why some of us are criminal, and others are not" (p. 47). Moreover, there is a great deal of sophisticated research indicating that environment can influence genes (Dobbs 2013). Raine believes that social influences can modify DNA, impacting the future of crime. Clearly, after

In this context, an oppositional ideologue is a person who unequivocally supports one side in a binary argument (either A or B is right) and selects or fabricates the evidence to support his or her position.

150 years, our understanding of the biogenic forces at work on criminals remains rudimentary. And, as discussed in chapter 1, there remains the issue of defining behavior as criminal, a legal not a scientific construct influenced by issues of "time and place."

## Crime and the Central Nervous System

The body consists of cells organized into tissues, and specialized cells along the surface of the body receive information about the environment that is translated into electrochemical signals we experience as sight, sound, smell, and touch. Information from the internal and external environment—collectively known as stimuli—is received by the **central nervous system (CNS)**, consisting of the brain and the spinal cord, whose specialized cells send information to specific processing centers in the brain.

A **neuron**, the basic working unit of the central nervous system, is a specialized cell designed to transmit information from the brain to other nerve cells or to muscle or gland cells. Neurons come in many sizes and shapes and form chains of cells. They differ from other body cells in that they can conduct information in the form of electrical impulses over long distances. There are over 100 billion neurons in the body and electrical signals move across them, from neuron to neuron (Twardosz and Lutzker 2010).

A neuron consists of a cell body **(soma)** containing three parts: (1) a nucleus and electricity-conducting fiber called an **axon**, which also gives rise to many smaller axon branches before ending at nerve terminals; (2) **synapses**, which are contact points where one neuron communicates with another; and (3) **dendrites**, which appear as branches of a tree and extend from the neuron cell body and receive messages from the synapses of other neurons. Each neuron has multiple dendrites that form structural networks for receiving information from another neuron or from the environment in the form of light, sound, smell, and so on; it subsequently converts this information into electrical activity that flows to the axon.

Axons may be long or short. For example, neurons in the brain stem have axons that extend down into the spinal cord, where they divide into thousands of branches, making contact with different receiving neurons. The microscopic complexity of this system explains why a spinal injury usually cannot be repaired. The axon conducts (i.e., "fires") electrical impulses to nerve terminals, which react by releasing **neurotransmitters**, the latter being highly sensitive electrochemicals stored in **synaptic vesicles**, which are button-like sacs that exit at the ends of axons. These neurotransmitters move across the synaptic gap to receptor sites on the dendrites of a neuron existing on the other side of the gap, triggering activity in that neuron. Through this mechanism an impulse is directed neuron by neuron to the spinal cord and into the proper circuit for transmission to the brain. The process is similar to that found in a car battery,

The central nervous system produces electricity in a fashion similar to a car battery.

producing electricity through the action of chemicals; indeed, human bodies are low-wattage batteries.

The brain, a dense mass weighing about 3 pounds and consisting of 10–50 billion anatomically independent but functionally interrelated neurons, is connected to the spinal cord by fibers and cells (the peripheral nervous system) that carry sensory information and muscle commands to the rest of the body. "This single organ controls all body activities, ranging from heart rate and sexual function to emotion, learning and memory" (Blank 2013:2). Poor nutrition, maternal stress, and toxins such as alcohol can affect the prenatal brain as can postnatal abuse and neglect (Twardosz and Lutzker 2010). Research indicates that individuals with impulsive aggression may have abnormalities in brain regions involved in the control of emotion (Seo, Patrick, and Kennealy 2008).

> Impulsively aggressive persons may have abnormalities in the region of the brain that controls emotion.

## Neurotransmitters and Behavior

Neurons do not interlock or even touch each other; rather, they are separated by synapses, fluid-filled microscopic gaps (0.0002 mm) that provide a chemical bridge for signals in the form of charged particles (ions) from one neuron to another. A single neuron may have over 10,000 synapses. When activated by electrical charges, neurotransmitters cross over the synaptic gap where they bind to receptors on the surface of an adjoining neuron—a lock-and-key effect. Each type of neurotransmitter has a specific receptor site designed to receive it. Depending on the type of neurotransmitter, electrical charges from the adjoining neuron are either *inhibitory* (i.e., slow electrical impulses across the synaptic gap) or *excitatory* (i.e., speed up electrical impulses across the synaptic gap). The body uses the first type of neurotransmitters to depress pain impulses, while the second type prepares the body for "fight or flight."

Once neurotransmitters have performed their assigned task—conveying messages to nearby neurons—they are recycled by the sending neuron in a process called **reuptake**. This process conserves the neurotransmitters by bringing them back into the presynaptic terminal for storage in the synaptic vesicle for future use. Proteins called **transporters**, located on the surface of the sending neurons, latch onto the neurotransmitters and move them back inside. Psychoactive substances, such as heroin, not only cause the release of neurotransmitters but they also inhibit the transporters from performing reuptake, causing the neurotransmitters to continue stimulating the receiving neuron until it is exhausted—that is, used up. When this happens, the person requires a continuing intake of heroin or a heroin-like chemical just to feel normal.

Receptor sites, where neurotransmitters attach (i.e., the lock-and-key effect) causing chemical substances to interact and produce pharmacological actions, can generally distinguish between substances. Only upon receiving the correct substance, by creating a chemical fit that turns the key in the lock, will they transmit signals that bring about pharmacological action. However, some psychoactive drugs called **agonists**, such as morphine and heroin, can mimic the action of neurotransmitters and "fool" the receptor into accepting its key into the lock. Competing drugs, called **antagonists** or substances that *inhibit* the action of a receptor site, can counteract the effect of an agonist by their ability to occupy or block receptor sites without triggering activity, providing a basis for using chemicals to deal with drug abuse.

*Dopamine and Crime.*    One of about 100 neurotransmitters found in the central nervous system, **dopamine** has received special attention because of its role in the regulation of mood and affect and because of its role in motivation and reward processes. Studies have revealed that the reinforcing effects of psychoactive drugs in humans are associated with increases in brain dopamine (Volkow et al. 1999). Dopamine is necessary to sustain life. The release of dopamine also generates feelings of euphoria for behaviors such as eating and sexual activity. Dopamine is constantly being released in small amounts, which allows the brain cells receiving its electrochemical signals to function properly. A dopamine malfunction is linked to various types of problem behaviors, such as violence, alcoholism, gambling, and drug abuse—activities that can substitute for a dopamine insufficiency (Seo, Patrick, and Kennealy 2008). It can also explain risky, albeit legal, behaviors such as mountain climbing, skydiving, and competitive martial arts.

Dopamine malfunctioning in the brain can account for a number of illegal behaviors (i.e., violence and drug abuse), socially problematic action (i.e., alcoholism and gambling), and even risky but legal behaviors (i.e., mountain climbing and skydiving).

*Serotonin and Crime.*    Human patterns of sleep, mood, depression, and anxiety are influenced by **serotonin**, which also moderates primitive drives such as aggression, sex, and food seeking. In addition, it influences the ability to interact socially. A deficiency in serotonin is associated with aggressive behaviors in animals *and* humans, particularly the impulsive type of aggression—that is, without regard for its consequences (Chichinadze, Chichinadze, and Lazarashvili 2011). Persons with low serotonin levels are more inclined toward aggression and violence than those with normal amounts. We do not know the exact causal processes at work whereby serotonin influences behavior or whether it has a direct impact or lessens impulse control. However, serotonin levels are a rough predictor of criminal behavior.

While the statistical correlation between serotonin and crime is clear (i.e., under conditions where a human being has too little serotonin, aggressive behavior is likely to follow), it is unclear whether one's environment influences serotonin levels. It is possible that serotonin and dopamine dysfunction have roots in social conditions, such as extreme poverty and accompanying malnutrition. Genetic influences may be at work, as genetic variations in both dopamine receptor genes and serotonin transporter genes can, given various social conditions, predict violent episodes

(Kreek, et al. 2005). One study of African-American youth living in Georgia and Iowa found that when environmental conditions were adverse, persons with a "suspect genotype" (i.e., combination of a unique dopamine receptor gene and an equally unique serotonin transporter gene) exhibited higher levels of violence than those with other genotypes; when the social environment was favorable, those with this suspect genotype were less violent than those with other genotypes (Simons et al. 2011). While not definitive in nature, such studies suggest we still have a lot to learn about the genetic origins of human conduct, especially as it relates to biochemistry and crime.

> Serotonin levels in humans are correlated with crime, especially violent crime.

*MAO and Crime.*   Human neurotransmitter levels are controlled by chemicals in the presynaptic terminal known as monoamine oxidase (MAO) that deactivate neurotransmitters in order to maintain equilibrium—keep the body in balance, a state referred to as **homeostasis**. In some individuals an excess of MAO lowers the amount of dopamine, norepinephrine, and serotonin, which results in depression. Serotonin selective reuptake inhibitors (SSRI), such as Prozac (fluoxetine) increase the availability of serotonin in the brain and are commonly used to treat depression; they are also effective for the treatment of aggression (Umukoro, Aladeokin, and Eduviere 2013).

Low MAO persons exhibit a tendency toward aggressive outbursts, often in response to anger, fear, or frustration. Several studies report relationships between MAO deficiency and abnormal aggressive behavior in males (Brunner, et al. 1994). Cocaine and methamphetamine can compensate for the tendency of low MAO persons to be depressed. Easily bored persons may suffer from MAO-overload. This condition could induce risk-taking activities, such as contact sports, mountain climbing, or skydiving, or criminal behavior. The possession of illegal drugs, or the use of legal drugs without medical authorization, is by definition criminal. The behavior, however, could be a form of **self-medication**, using a drug to offset an existing chemical deficiency or dysfunction.

> The use of illegal drugs may reflect a case of self-medication, allowing the user to "escape" the unpleasant life experiences associated with certain biochemical deficiencies.

## The Adolescent Brain, Delinquency and Crime

Research indicates that anti-social behavior is a common characteristic of adolescence. The human brain, particularly the prefrontal cortex (PFC), is not fully mature until the mid-twenties (Wilson, Hansen, and Li 2011). This executive or higher-thinking part of the brain is involved in the regulation of many social functions, especially what is commonly called ethics and morality; it also controls aggression and violence (Fallon 2006). The immaturity of this part of the brain accounts for the mood swings and impulsive behavior of adolescents.

When adolescents make decisions involving risk, they are incapable of fully engaging the still immature higher-thinking area of the brain, and this deficit can result in overstating the reward without fully evaluating the long-term consequences or risks involved. Furthermore, emotional or physical trauma associated with childhood abuse affects brain maturation and results in poorer executive functioning, contributing to the serious misbehavior of adolescents (National Juvenile Justice Network 2008). Abuse is also associated with lower levels of scholastic achievement and IQ scores, which are risk factors for anti-social behavior (Wilson, et al. 2011).

Biologically oriented studies of crime and criminals, whether in their incarnation as criminal anthropology or as positive eugenics or as biocriminology, have attracted many followers as well as detractors. That crime and biology are linked in some significant way seems beyond dispute. The role assigned to biology in contrast to other forces impinging on human behavior continues to be disputed. In the next chapter we continue our exploration of deterministic perspectives on crime, this time examining psychology and theories of crime derived from that discipline.

## SUMMARY

- Biological explanations for criminal behavior are controversial.
- According to Lombroso, serious criminal behavior is the result of immature evolution or atavism.
- Goring failed to find characteristics of atavism peculiar to the prison population.
- Hooton compared prison inmates to college students, firefighters, and police officers and found significant differences. He failed to recognize that the control groups were not representative of the general population.
- Eugenics argues for selective breeding and prevention of reproduction by persons of inferior characteristics.
- Social Darwinism argues against assistance to the "unfit."
- Genetic and biological factors interact with social factors in predisposing someone to antisocial and violent behavior.
- The use of the classic experimental design to seek a definitive answer to the "nature versus nurture" question would be both immoral and illegal.
- The genetically derived idea that the XYY-supermale is prone to violence and aggression is a media-driven myth.
- Twin and adoption studies support a nature explanation of crime but have serious shortcomings.
- Biocriminology is a controversial yet intriguing perspective on crime and criminals, one whose contemporary claims are met with skepticism by some and applause by others.

- Information from internal and external environments is received by the central nervous system, consisting of the brain and the spinal cord, whose neurons send information to a specific processing center of the brain.

- The complexity of the central nervous system essentially prevents repairs if any part of the system is damaged.

- A neuron is a specialized cell designed to transmit information from the brain to other nerve cells or crucial body parts.

- The axon of a neuron conducts electrical impulses to terminals, which react by releasing neurotransmitters, chemicals stored in synaptic buttons at the ends of axons, similar to the actions of a battery that converts chemicals into electricity.

- Neurons are separated by gaps across which neurotransmitters transmit information.

- Some neurotransmitters inhibit information transmission to the brain, while others speed transmission.

- Neurotransmitter dysfunction may explain drug abuse.

- An immature brain is implicated in risk-taking and anti-social behavior in adolescents.

## KEY TERMS

| | |
|---|---|
| adoption studies | human genome |
| agonists | karyotype studies |
| antagonists | monozygotic (MZ) twins |
| atavism | neurons |
| axon | neurotransmitters |
| biocriminology | nucleotides |
| central nervous system (CNS) | oppositional ideologues |
| chromosomes | phrenology |
| concordance | reuptake |
| dendrites | self-medication |
| deoxyribonucleic acid (DNA) | serotonin |
| dizygotic (DZ) twins | soma |
| dopamine | stigmata |
| epigenetic studies | supermales |
| eugenics | synapses |
| genes | synaptic vesicles |
| heritability | transporters |
| homeostasis | twin studies |

## CRITICAL REVIEW QUESTIONS

1. Why are biological explanations for criminal behavior controversial?
2. What did Cesare Lombroso mean by atavism?
3. What was Charles Goring's criticism of Lombroso?
4. What was the mistake Earnest Hooton committed in his study of prison inmates?
5. What is eugenics?
6. What policy flows from social Darwinism?
7. What is the connection between genes and criminal behavior?
8. With respect to criminal behavior, why is it impossible for a classical research design to determine a definitive answer to the "nature versus nature" question?
9. What have twin and adoption studies revealed with respect to criminal behavior?
10. What are the lessons we can derive from the discredited view of the XYY male as a supermale—an aggressive and violent criminal?
11. What comprises the central nervous system?
12. What is a neuron, and what purpose does it serve?
13. What is the purpose of a neurotransmitter?
14. How can the nervous system process be compared to a battery?
15. How can drug abuse be explained by a neurotransmitter deficiency?
16. How does brain development explain risk-taking and anti-social behavior by adolescents?

# Theories of
# Psychological Abnormality

## LEARNING OBJECTIVES

- The distinctions between psychology and psychiatry, as well as who practices each discipline

- The origins and evolution of psychoanalytic theory, including the work of the theory's most significant proponents

- The implications of psychoanalytic theory for understanding and treating criminals

- The definitional journey taken by psychopathy from moral insanity to psychopathic personalities

- The application of psychopathy to the study of crime and criminals

- The methods currently employed to determine who among us is a psychopath

# Introduction

Psychological theories explore criminal behavior at the level of the individual offender. This chapter explores two such theories: (1) psychoanalytic theory, which owes much to the clinical work of Austrian neurologist and psychiatrist Sigmund Freud, and (2) the psychopathy perspective, the modern form of which owes its foundation to the research of Canadian psychologist Robert D. Hare. Before turning to these topics, however, it is instructive to look at the origins of topic-specific key terms used in this chapter and the subsequent one.

The Greek word **psyche** means the soul. Two distinct forms of scientific inquiry and practice have addressed questions of the human mind or, as defined by the ancient Greeks and Romans, the human soul. **Psychology** examines individual human and animal behavior; it is concerned chiefly with the mind and mental processes—feelings, desires, motivations, and the like. Psychology is both an area of scientific study and an academic behavioral science. **Clinical psychologists** engage in the treatment of mental disorders, while **forensic psychologists** (generally practitioners of a subcategory of clinical psychology) bring criminological and psychological principles to bear on legal questions, either in the investigation of crimes (e.g., criminal profilers) or in court as expert witnesses (e.g., sanity and competency hearings). The most common degrees for people working in these fields are doctor of philosophy (PhD) in psychology or doctor of psychology (PsyD); both types of practitioners have considerable practical experience dealing with mentally troubled or disoriented patients. Some states, however, license psychologists with lower levels of education, and many license other practitioners, such as psychiatric social workers, who have a Masters of Social Work degree. The literal meaning of **psychiatry** is "healing the soul"; it is a branch of medicine concerned primarily with the study and treatment of mental disorders, including **psychoses** (very serious personality disorders) and **neuroses** (milder personality disorders). Psychiatrists are physicians, possessing a medical degree (MD), and the diagnosing of mental illness is usually exclusive to them. In sum, psychology is dedicated to both normal and abnormal behavior, while psychiatry, as a branch of medicine, employs the disease model and deals principally with abnormal behavior.

Few psychogenic theories, ones that look for the origins of criminal behavior in the mind or in a mental condition or process, evolved as purely criminological theories. Crime is a *legal* term and not a medical one. Accordingly, psychologists and psychiatrists seek explanations for human behavior, not *criminal* behavior. Like biological explanations of criminal behavior, psychological theories are *deterministic*; that is, such theories contend that criminals lack free will. As Gresham Sykes and Francis Cullen (1992: 324) noted about the development of early twenti-

Psychiatrists are medical doctors who specialized in mental health issues, while most psychologists usually earn either a doctor of philosophy or a doctor of psychology in clinical or counseling psychology.

eth century psychological theories: "Crime, it was said, was a bursting forth of instinctive impulses, and the criminal was acting out what most civilized men and women had learned to restrain. *The criminal was regarded as abnormal, but the abnormality was now centered in the mind*" (emphasis added).

Two ideas dominated much psychological thinking about abnormal behavior through the first 50 years of the twentieth century: psychoanalytic theory and psychopathy or psychopathic personality theory.

Psychological theories of criminal behavior are deterministic.

## Psychoanalytic Theory

Psychoanalytic theory and its therapeutic derivation, psychoanalysis, are based on the work of Sigmund Freud (b.1856–d.1939). Over the years both theory and method have undergone change, although Freud's (1933, 1938) basic contribution, his exposition of unconscious phenomena in human behavior, remains unchanged. He viewed the unconscious as being malleable and capable of altering one's conscious values and emotions without individuals being completely or even marginally aware of what was happening to them (Healy, Bronner, and Bowers 1930). In short, people are not aware of what determines their behavior—it is unconscious. Standing in stark contrast to Classical Criminology (chapters 1 and 2) and more in line with Biogenic Criminology (chapter 3), psychoanalysts believe that neither reason nor free will rule or even guide human behavior (Cloninger 1993).

Freud postulated three sets of mental processes that, although not directly observable, he inferred from his patient case studies:

1. **Conscious**: This group consists of those phenomena about which the individual is currently aware, or the here and now of our existence.

2. **Preconscious:** These thoughts and memories are just below the surface and can easily be called into conscious awareness, standing as a "buffer" or "waiting room" between conscious and unconscious.

3. **Unconscious:** The final group consists of repressed memories and attendant emotions; we can pull them into the conscious level, if at all, only by exerting much effort; they are, in the view of Freud, the primary source of human behavior.

The unconscious drives conscious behavior.

Clearly the unconscious plays a central role in psychoanalytic theorizing. Before we can appreciate how these mental processes connect to crime and criminals, two more key pieces in the psychoanalytic puzzle must be examined. First, one's psychosexual development, a highly criticized but nonetheless important part of Freudian thinking, owes much to what occurs at the unconscious level. Problems that may occur during these stages of development can profoundly influence a person's ability to integrate into society. Second, three psychic phenomena evolve as one moves through the five stages of psychosexual development: the id, ego, and superego. These phenomena, but especially the superego, are essential to understanding the ties between psychoanalytic theory and criminal conduct, including the use of psychoanalytic theory to change the offender.

## The Unconscious and Psychosexual Development

The unconscious serves as a repository for, among other things, unpleasant memories and highly charged emotions stored with these memories. Humans accumulate these repressed memories and emotions as they pass through life on their way to adulthood or **psychosexual maturity**. The stages of psychosexual development are *repressed* and, therefore, unconscious. Yet they serve as a guiding force of conscious behavior. Moreover, they are a source of anxiety and guilt, the basis for neuroses and psychoses. As we shall see, some individuals are waylaid in their journey to psychosexual maturity.

Freud described **psychosexual development** as consisting of five stages. In the first, the **oral stage** (birth to eighteen months), the mouth, lips, and tongue are the predominant organs of pleasure for the infant. In the normal infant, the source of pleasure becomes associated with the touch and warmth of the parent who gratifies oral needs. Infants enter the world as asocial beings, not greatly dissimilar from criminals: unsocialized and without self-control.

In the **anal stage** (one to three years), the anus becomes the primary source of sexual interest and gratification. Children closely connect pleasure to the retention and expulsion of feces the bodily process involved, and the feces themselves. During this stage, the partially socialized child acts out destructive urges, breaking toys or even injuring living organisms, such as insects or small animals. Disruptions in this stage may yield a great deal of adult pathology, including psychopathy, a topic covered later in this chapter.

Third, the **genital stage** (three to five years) signals a shift from anus to genitals as the main sexual interest; in "normal" persons this shift is permanent. During this stage, boys develop an **Oedipus complex,** while girls manifest an **Electra complex**, both characterized by erotic fantasies or wishes about the opposite-sex parent. The path to normal psychosexual maturity lies through relinquishing this paternal or maternal attachment and the unhappiness that ensues.

The fourth stage is the **latent stage** (five years to adolescence). The child begins to lose interest in sexual organs. Nonsexual, expanded relationships with same-sex and age playmates become paramount in their lives. The choice of play for both genders is influenced by the culture; thus, boys playing with dolls may be labeled "sissies," while girls who enjoy activities generally associated with the male gender may be labeled "tomboys."

Finally, in the **adolescence/adulthood stage** (thirteen years to death) genital interest and awareness reawakens. The incestuous fantasy is relinquished, replaced by mature sexuality—attraction to appropriate sexual partners.

The stages overlap, and transition from one to the other is gradual—the time spans are approximate. Each stage is left behind but never completely abandoned. Some amount of psychic energy, also called **cathexis**, remains attached to earlier objects of psychosexual development. When the strength of the cathexis is particularly strong, it is expressed as a **fixation**. For example, rather than transferring affection to an appropriate adult, the adolescent/adult may unconsciously stay fixated on the opposite-sex parent. **Regression** is said to occur when a person reverts to a previous mode of gratification—for example, moving backward from the adolescence/adulthood stage to the latent stage.

> There are five stages of psychosexual development: oral, anal, genital, latent, adult.

## Id, Ego, and Superego

While a person is passing through the first three stages of psychosexual development, three psychic phenomena evolve. The first to evolve is the **id**, a mass of powerful drives that consist of instincts and impulses seeking immediate discharge or gratification and lacking any restraint. The **ego** emerges second and is associated with the anal stage; it acts as a mediator through which infants modify their id drives by contact with the physical world around them. The goal is to obtain maximum gratification with a minimum of difficulty from restrictions that the environment places on the child. For example, the ego controls an id drive (desire) to harm sibling rivals. The ego provides an awareness of the consequences of one's action—the punishment that may result.

Without the ego to act as a restraining influence, the id would destroy the person through its blind striving to gratify instincts in complete disregard for reality. The id impels a person to activity that is likely to reduce the tension or excitement caused by the drive; the person seeks discharge or gratification. For example, the hunger drive will cause activity through which the person hopes to satisfy (gratify) the hunger experience; if unchecked, the id could drive a person to obesity. A person may remain at the ego level of development if he or she experiences disturbance in psychosexual development: "The child remains asocial or behaves as if he had become social without having made actual adjustments to the demands of society" (Aichhorn 1973:4). Feelings of rage and aggression associated with the anal stage lurk in the background awaiting an opportunity to break through to satisfaction.

The third phenomenon is the **superego**, which is sometimes referred to as a conscience-like mechanism, a counter force to the id. The superego also exercises a criticizing power, a sense of morality over the ego. Psychoanalytic theory connects the superego to the genital stages' incestuous feelings. The development of self-control becomes an internal matter and no longer exclusively dependent upon external forces such as parents. A healthy superego, then, is the result of identification with society's values and norms, normally occurring at the genital stage of psychosexual development. A healthy superego can also support criminality when the child internalizes the actions of antisocial parents (Smart 1970). Lastly, some individuals may simply not have the neurobiological capacity for attachment to society's values and norms, despite adequate parenting efforts (Yakeley and Meloy 2012).

The unconscious maintains a delicate balance, as the individual experiences the various sociocultural and biological aspects of life. This balance is easily upset. According to psychoanalytic theory, there is a thin line between normal and neurotic or between neurotic and psychotic. When repressed material begins to overwhelm the psyche, threatening to enter one's consciousness, external defense mechanisms come into play as neuroses and, in severe cases, psychoses. These responses take the form of phobia, or unreasonable fears involving, for example, heights, insects, or closed spaces. In a paranoid reaction, the person projects his or her thoughts onto imagined enemies. Employing reaction formation, for example, a person may channel the destructive urges of the anal stage into pro-social activities, becoming a surgeon or veterinarian, for example. Failing in this, the threat posed by the repressed wishes and desires may take on extreme antisocial dimensions, such as those found in serial killers or violent rapists.

> Not every person who fails to move smoothly from one psychosexual stage to the next becomes a deviant or criminal, as many are able to find pro-social alternatives for their abnormal urges.

Dysfunction during psychosexual development can express itself in the adult as socially inappropriate or, in more extreme cases, criminal behavior. For example, a failure to satisfactorily relinquish the normal erotic attachment of a child toward his mother can result in an adult inability to fulfill a mature sexual role. Sexual attraction to an appropriate partner is unconsciously experienced as incestuous, and the adult male may seek an unlawful alternative—a child. Even a passive pedophile may violate the law by indulging in child pornography.

## Crime and the Superego

Psychoanalytic theory divides id drives into a primary process that tends toward immediate and direct gratification and a secondary process that shifts the focus away from the original object or method of discharge when something blocks a drive. A classic example is when gratification is inaccessible by legitimate, acceptable means. According to Freud, at that juncture the secondary process accesses a series of defense mechanisms, including:

1. **Displacement:** In this case, an individual expresses unacceptable id impulses through an acceptable outlet. For example, a child may unconsciously transfer—displace—a desire to play with feces to playing with mud or clay.

2. **Reaction formation:** This mechanism allows an individual to replace socially unacceptable behavior with behavior that is socially acceptable. As distinct from displacement, reaction formation involves behavior that is the opposite of that expressed by the original desire or drive. For example, a child who wants to kill a sibling will become very loving and devoted. In adulthood, a sadistic impulse can result in a person becoming involved in the care and treatment of highly dependent persons or animals.

3. **Repression:** As a defense mechanism, repression prevents unwanted id impulses, memories, desires, or wish-fulfilling fantasies from entering the conscious-thought level. Psychoanalysts believe that the repression of highly charged material, such as incestuous fantasies, requires much psychic energy and the result is often a permanent conflict between the id and the ego. The delicate balance between the charged material and the opposing expenditure of energy is called **equilibrium**. When the means of repression are inadequate to deal with charged material, psychoneurotic or psychotic symptoms develop.

4. **Sublimation:** An individual who cannot satisfy a continuous drive in its primary form may employ sublimation. Specifically, the socially unacceptable impulses are unconsciously transformed into socially acceptable actions or behavior. Thus, a sadist might overcome the urge to cut people by substituting acceptable alternatives, such as becoming a surgeon or a butcher.

> Faced with a blockage of the primary methods of achieving fulfillment of an id drive, the secondary process provides at least four mechanisms that shift the focus away from the original object or method of discharge.

From a psychoanalytic perspective, antisocial behavior is a neurotic manifestation whose origin can be traced back to early stages of psychosexual development. For example, a craving for excitement can be fulfilled by lawful behavior ranging from skydiving and mountain climbing to action movies and amusement park thrill rides, or by risky criminal behavior. The superego's role in this process is central. The superego restrains people from acting on primitive id impulses. For persons with a poorly developed superego, the ego alone cannot exercise adequate control over id impulses. Such individuals—psychopaths—suffer almost no guilt from engaging in socially harmful behavior (discussed later in this chapter). At the other extreme is the person with a destructive superego. This person's superego cannot distinguish *thinking bad* from *doing bad*.

In some individuals, unresolved conflicts combined with id impulses normally repressed or dealt with through reaction formation or sublimation create severe unconscious guilt. Such people experience a compulsive need for punishment that is equally unconscious. To alleviate this guilt, the confused mind impels the person toward committing acts for which punishment is virtually certain. Criminals of this type are the victims of their own morality (Aichhorn 1973). For example, an offense is so poorly planned and executed it appears the perpetrator wants to be caught. Consider the case of a bank robber who, while he wore a black ninja mask, stood over seven feet tall; the easily identified 26-year-old suspect was arrested two days later. Or, there is the case of the bank robber who wrote his "give me your money" directions to the teller on his own check deposit slip, complete with current address. Relatedly, consider the rigid superego of the "true believer," a person whose religious or political belief provides entitlement to take his or her own life and the lives of others to advance a particular religious or political belief system. Such people do not fit the definition of the psychopath as developed later in this chapter, but their violence derives from an unyielding superego that propels the person forward as "an agent of a spiritual or religious authority" (Yakeley and Meloy 2012: 235). As suggested in box 4.1, the treatment of such individuals, especially in a correctional or prison setting, is a difficult proposition.

---

**BOX 4.1**

### Psychoanalysis: Treating Offenders

Psychoanalysts treat mental disorders using **psychoanalysis**. According to Freud, the intent of psychoanalysis is to induce the patient to reveal his or her early life repressions and replace them with feelings and perspectives that are more conducive to a healthy mind. This is achieved by asking patients to dredge up repressed experiences and forgotten memories. Psychoanalysts tie present symptoms to these repressed elements of early life—linked to the primary stages of psychosexual development. The symptoms will disappear when patients reveal the repressed material and learn to understand it through psychoanalytic treatment.

Psychoanalysis, in order to expose repressed material, uses three main devices. First, **free association** is a practice in which the patient verbally expresses ideas—often while they are relaxing on a couch—as they come to mind. Analysts then work with patients to understand why they uttered the words or phrases, their true meaning. Second, **dream interpretation** encourages patients to recall dreams. Freud believed that dreams hold the key to the individual's makeup. He saw a difference between the recollected content of a dream and its actual meaning. The former was what the patient was doing or having done to him or her in the dream; the latter was the significance of the dream, which the unconscious mind concealed. The analyst helps the patient to understand the actual, repressed meaning. Finally, the analyst may take therapeutic advantage of **transference**, whereby the patient develops a negative or positive emotional attitude toward the therapist. This attitude is a reflection or imitation of emotional attitudes that the patient experienced in earlier relationships that occurred during his or her psychosexual development. Thus, the patient may unconsciously come to view the therapist as a parental figure. By using transference, the therapist recreates the emotions tied to early psychic development, unlocking repressed material and freeing the patient of his or her burden.

Generally, psychoanalysis is not used to treat delinquents or criminals. Psychoanalysts are highly trained and often expensive; treatment takes many years and, as a "talking therapy," needs verbal ability beyond that of most criminals. Therapists may underestimate how hard it is to verbalize experience, even for otherwise verbal patients.

*Sources*: Freud (1938); Omer and London (1988); Reiff (1963).

In recent years, Freud has been at the center of questions about psychoanalysis. He based the theory on a very limited number of case studies involving mostly middle-class Jewish women. The context of Freud's medical practice also must be considered: He practiced in late nineteenth and early twentieth century Vienna, a time of repressed human sexuality. His theory takes on all of the limitations of a narrow clientele during a particular historical period. Nevertheless, psychoanalytic theory provides insight into a host of human maladies, and its explanation for problematic behavior such as substance abuse, has strong intuitive qualities (Abadinsky 2014a). Psychoanalysis is also the basis for therapeutic efforts in many treatment disciplines. Behavior theory (chapter 5) is a psychological alternative to the far more psychiatrically oriented psychoanalytic theory.

In summary, psychoanalytic theory connects criminal behavior to superego function, which is the result of an actor's relationship to parents or parental figures during early childhood. Parental deprivation through absence, lack of affection, or inconsistent discipline stifles the proper development of the superego. In adulthood, the actor is unable to control aggressive, hostile, or antisocial id impulses. At the other extreme, the presence of rigid or punitive parents/parental figures can result in the creation of a superego that is likewise rigid and punitive, leading one to seek punishment as a means of alleviating unconscious guilt.

> Psychoanalytic theory is not a theory of criminal behavior *per se;* rather, it is a way of viewing the processes at work when inappropriate behavior (some of which may be classified as criminal) manifests itself due to issues with superego development.

## Psychopathic Personality Theories

The terms **psychopath** and **sociopath** have the power to elicit an almost visceral response from laypersons and criminal justice professionals alike. Both terms are labels applied to the diagnosis of antisocial personality disorder. As a preliminary method of distinguishing between the two, psychopath is generally favored by psychologists; sociopath by those with a sociological background. In this context, then, sociopathy refers to antisocial behavior whose cause is social and environmental—more nurture than nature; the source of psychopathy is found in biology and genetics, as well as the environment.

More is involved in the distinctions between these two "diagnoses" than just the academic training of the person doing the diagnosing. Sociopaths may violate social norms, seemingly unconcerned about the consequences of their actions (Pemment 2013). Psychopaths act in much the same fashion but are oblivious as to the inappropriateness of their conduct and act simply to feed their own egocentric desires (Roberts 2013: Internet). Pamela R. Perez (2012), looking at the neuropsychological causes of psychopathy, extended the distinctions:

> While the psychopath does not experience feelings of remorse for his or her deeds, no matter how cold and heinous, the sociopath may be capable of feeling guilt and regret for his or her deeds, at least in the context of group (such as in gang affiliation) or familial relationships.

The sociopath, however, cares nothing for social norms, and will violate them without hesitation if doing so satisfies his or her own
desires or purposes. (p. 520)

Moreover, the term psychopath, more than sociopath, is used loosely and
with little definitional rigor by a variety of participants in the criminal justice system—police, prosecutors, judges, probation and parole officers,
and prison officials—as a synonym for an incorrigible offender. In order
to understand what various professions see and why that is important, we
must first look at the historical development of the notion of a hyper-dan-
gerous personality type.

## The History of Psychopathy: Describing a Personality Type

The study of individuals who are psychologically disturbed but
appear to be normal has a long and convoluted history, taking shape and
form in a little more than 100 years (Arrigo and Shipley 2001). At the start
of the nineteenth century, French physician Phillipe Pinel (b.1745–
d.1826) observed that some of his patients committed impulsive acts,
engaged in episodic violence, and harmed themselves; he called this specific mental disorder *manie san délire,* or "insanity without delirium"
(Millon, Simonsen, Birket-Smith, and Davis 1998). Thirty years later a
British physician, J. C. Prichard (b.1786–d.1848) used the expression
**moral insanity** to describe people with "a morbid perversion of the natural feelings, affections, inclinations, temper, habits, moral dispositions,
and natural impulses, without any remarkable disorder or defect of the
intellect or knowing and reasoning faculties, and particularly without any
insane illusions or hallucinations" (Pritchard 1837/1973:16).

At the turn of the twentieth century, German psychiatrist J. L. A.
Koch (b.1841–d.1908) was the first to describe this condition using the
term psychopathic; he viewed people who had emotional and moral aberrations derived from congenital factors as suffering from psychopathic
inferiority. Koch's goal in using this term was to rid the condition of the
moral condemnation associated with Pritchard's moral insanity. The German psychiatrist Emile Kraepelin (b.1856–d.1926) expanded upon Koch's
basic diagnosis so that it could contain categories for especially vicious
and wicked offenders; moreover, his categories of psychopathic personalities closely resemble those currently in use. Kraepelin also reinstituted a
moral component, calling psychopaths "the enemies of society" (quoted
in Millon et al. 1998:10).

While the search for an understanding of psychopathy clearly has
deep roots, even dating to Greek mythology, the modern construct
derives from Hervey M. Cleckley (b.1903–d.1984). In his classic book
*Mask of Sanity* (1941), he set forth the notion that the psychopath publicly exhibits psychiatrically normal behavior, while engaging in destructive behavior in private. In Cleckley's view, the psychopath, despite the

substantial number who are incarcerated, is typically nonviolent; more over he included as likely occupations businessmen, doctors, and lawyers His view contrasts with more contemporary conclusions that often connect psychopaths to violence.

Contemporary descriptions of psychopaths, ones linked closely to Cleckley, provide an instructive, if somewhat unsystematic, shopping list of characteristics:

- As a personality construct, "psychopathy is defined by lack of empathy, impulsivity, grandiosity, callous and manipulative interpersonal interactions, and the tendency to engage in socially deviant behavior. Psychopathy has been associated with aggression, recidivism, and other behaviors harmful to others" (Berkout, Gross, and Kellum 2013: 620).

- Superficially charming, psychopaths tend to make a good first impression and appear remarkably normal. Yet, they are largely devoid of any feelings of guilt and the capacity for empathy (Eme 2009).

- The psychopath has a well-developed capacity for empathy that "he employs to understand the minds of those he seeks to manipulate for his own ends" (Carveth 2010:112).

- Knowing is not caring and the psychopath exhibits a "callous and remorseless disregard for the rights and feelings of others, and a pattern of chronic antisocial behavior" (Meloy 1997: 630).

The nonfiction characters portrayed by Joe Pesci in the motion pictures *Goodfellas* and *Casino* exemplify the psychopathic personality.

As suggested earlier in this chapter, psychopathy also can be expressed in psychoanalytic terms. From this perspective, the psychopath does not experience the normal tripartite structure of id, ego, and superego (Meloy and Shiva 2007). There is a failure to internalize *values*. "The psychopathic adult is a valueless person" (p. 341). There is also an absence of mature defenses such as *repression* and *sublimation* (discussed above). Psychopaths exhibit a lack conscience, superficial charm, high verbal skills, and a lack of long-term interpersonal bonds. They are characterized by low-arousal, a low resting heart rate, and fearlessness. There is speculation that psychopaths have been victims of child abuse who turn off their emotions to reduce the abuse impact. This muting strategy contributes to the development of a psychopath who as an adult appears as a "hardened" person with strong/tough demeanor (Porter 1996).

## Psychopathy Versus Sociopathy: Final Observations

A central assumption of personality theory is that the ways in which people express their habitual patterns and behavioral qualities hold the key to understanding their behavior. These habitual patterns and qualities are physical or mental, behavioral or attitudinal. In 1952, the American Psychiatric Association (APA) substituted the term sociopathic personality disturbance (shortened to sociopathy) for psychopathy, which helps explain the conceptual confusion previously described about the distinctions between the two diagnoses. The occasion was the publication of the first DSM, or *Diagnostic and Statistical Manual of Mental Disorders*. The DSM criteria for sociopathy varied little from Cleckley's personality inventory for psychopathy. The terms psychopathy, sociopathy, and antisocial personality disorder (ASPD) are frequently used to describe the same constellation of traits, even in the DSM's fifth and most recent (APA, 2013) incarnation. The shared traits of both psychopaths and sociopaths include the following:

- A disregard for laws and social mores
- A disregard for the rights of others
- A failure to feel remorse or guilt
- A tendency to display violent behavior

Beyond those traits, sociopaths are described as nervous and easily agitated, prone to outbursts and fits of rage; psychopaths, on the other hand, are more controlled, but unable, as Cleckley observed nearly seventy years before, to form meaningful or long-term relationships. While both can be violent offenders, there are important differences. For example, sociopaths tend to engage in spontaneous and unplanned criminal activities, ones which nearly always result in their apprehension; psychopaths are cool, calm, and level-headed offenders, who generally offer few clues to the authorities as to their identities. They are the prototypes for serial offenders, whether their targets are property or sexual in nature, and organized criminals. Thus, definitions of each condition tend to emphasize the traits and behaviors associated with persons having, first, ASPD and then, second, being either a sociopath or a psychopath. Indeed, as suggested at the beginning of this section, it is the psychopath who most concerns those criminologists who employ the personality theory perspective.

---

While there are many similarities between psychopaths and sociopaths, the differences are important, especially to criminologists and criminal justice practitioners.

---

## The PCL and "Diagnosing" Psychopathy

After World War II, public and private sector employers, deeply immersed in scientific management practices, turned increasingly to psychometric screening devices. The idea was to restrict employment decisions only to those candidates who had the right personality traits for the job (Houston 1995). American correctional philosophy and practices were also undergoing a revolution of sorts and scientific management practices extended to correctional facilities as well. The "clients" of that system required review to determine entry into rehabilitative programs and for general institutional management (Mays and Winfree 2014). Policy makers and practitioners in criminal justice came to recognize that personality theory developed for other purposes, such as employee screening, offered diagnostic instruments that gave uniform and relatively quick answers concerning desirable and undesirable personality traits. Enter the **Hare Psychopathy Checklist** (PCL).

The PCL-R ("R" refers to revised), developed in the 1970s by Canadian psychologist Robert D. Hare (b.1934–), is a 20-item rating scale that takes several hours to administer. Hare based the checklist on his work with male offenders and inmates in Vancouver, British Columbia, as well as the work of Cleckley (Hare 1996a, 1996b, 1998). Summated scores range from 0 to 40, with 30 generally being the threshold for a diagnosis of psychopathy. Each item (see box 4.2) is scored as 0, 1, or 2, depending on how well the PCL-R administrator believes that a specific item applies to the person being tested. Noncriminals normally score around 5, while many non-psychopathic criminal offenders score around 22. There is also a PCL-YV for youths and PCL:SV for screening. Administrators of the PCL-R should possess an appropriate terminal degree and relevant training.

The interview portion of the evaluation, two sessions of two to six hours, covers the subject's background, including items such as work history; education; marital and family status; and criminal background. As psychopaths frequently lie, the information they provide is confirmed by a review of documents in the subject's case history.

> The characteristics or traits associated with psychopaths would make for good businessmen, doctors and lawyers, as well as vicious criminals.

## Psychopathology: Biogenic and Sociogenic Origins

There is much evidence indicating that the brains of psychopaths are abnormal (Kiehl 2014). For whatever reasons, their brains seem to work differently from non-psychopaths and other psychologically disordered persons. In the late 1990s and early 2000s, clinical comparative studies of brain activity revealed differences in the brains of persons diagnosed as psychopaths (Raine et al. 1990, 2000). The "application of the principles

---

**BOX 4.2**

### PCL-R Traits, Facets, and Factors: An Overview

The PCL-R groups 20 traits into four clusters or facets: (1) a *manipulative interpersonal style*, which measures affective or emotional involvement with others such as pathological lying and manipulativeness (4 items); (2) *deficits in affective resonance*, which measures responses to people and to situations such as callousness and a lack of remorse or guilt (4 items), (3) a *socially deviant lifestyle*, which measures evidence of socially unacceptable behavior such as a "parasitic" lifestyle and impulsivity (5 items), and (4) *antisocial behavior*, which measures instances of misconduct such as juvenile delinquency and criminal versatility (5 items). Two additional items measuring martial and sexual relationships are used by some but not by all researchers/practitioners employing the PCL-R.

Early research using the PCL-R suggested that there were only two factors: Factor 1 (consisting of facets 1 and 2) expressed the interpersonal and affective deficits of the psychopath; Factor 2 (consisting of facets 3 and 4) addressed antisocial behavior. The basic traits are assessed as either a full match with the subject (2 points), a reasonably good subject match (1 point), or does not apply to the subject (0 points); a summated score of 30 generally defines a psychopath, although there are divergences from this standard.

*Sources*: Hare (1998, 2007); Skeem, Polaschek, Patrick, and Lilienfeld (2011).

and techniques of neuroscience to understand the origins of antisocial behavior" gave rise to *neurocriminology* (Raine 2013: 8). Researchers contend that some 40 percent of the variability in psychopathy measures can be attributed to genetic factors (Beaver et al. 2011a).

Advances in brain imaging has led to the identification of specific areas of the brain responsible for behavior control and, hence, psychopathy (da Silva, Rijo, and Salekin 2012). A horseshoe-shaped band of tissue nestled in the limbic area may be the source of malfunctions in psychopaths. Neuro-criminologists key in on the areas that register feelings and other sensations, as well as their related emotional value. Researchers have noted that these regions also control decision-making, reasoning, and even impulse control (Kiehl and Buckholtz 2010: 27). Of particular interest is damage to the limbic region's amygdala, located in the prefrontal cortex positioned directly over the eye sockets that is involved in the generation of emotion. This part of the brain is involved in the regulation of many social functions, in particular what is commonly called ethics and morality, and also controls aggression and violence (Fallon 2006). While the amygdala and areas of the prefrontal cortex have well-understood relationships with emotional learning and the estimation of rewards and consequences, several other brain regions with subtler supportive roles in these processes have also been shown to be abnormal in psychopaths (Anderson and Kiehl 2014).

> Areas of the brain responsible for psychopathy have been identified, including the limbic region, also called the paleomammalian brain, the oldest regions of the human brain.

Environmental issues may also influence the neurology of psychopathology. Raine (2013), for example, reports that "social factors are critical both in interacting with biological forces in causing crime, and in directly producing the biological changes that predispose a person to violence" (p. 9). Raine offers a number of factors, such as smoking, drinking, and poor nutrition during pregnancy. Nutrition is linked to IQ; poor nutrition is a predictor for low IQ that results in poor school performance and the likelihood of anti-social behavior. Moreover, exposure to the relatively high rates of murder in many African-American communities can negatively impact the brains of young residents that affect school performance and, by extension, their ability to secure employment, a predictor for crime. We return to the IQ question in the next chapter. Suffice it to say at this point that the ties between psychogenic and biogenic causes of crime are complex and merit more study.

In addition, it also appears that culture plays a role in psychopathy. Rates of psychopathy are far from uniform when one nation or region of the world is contrasted with another. For example, North America is estimated to have a prevalence rate for the general population of 1.2 percent, while for the United Kingdom the estimated general rate stands at 0.6 percent (Coid et al. 2009; Neumann and Hare 2008). For prisoner populations, the North American prevalence rate is 25 percent, but only 8 percent for Germany (Beaver et al. 2011b; Hart, Hare, and Forth 1994; Ullrich et al. 2003).

Differences also exist in how the instruments themselves perform internationally. For example, a global study by Neumann and associates (2012) studied over 33,000 subjects living in a total of 58 nations in 11 major world regions. Rather than using the PCL-R, which was viewed as too cumbersome owing to requirements for training and administration, the researcher employed the Self-Report Psychopathy (SRP) scale, which included interpersonal, affective, lifestyle, and antisocial factors. The four-factor psychopathy model worked differently in the various regions studied, although the interpersonal and antisocial factor worked best, leading the researchers to conclude that culture affects "the expression of SRP-based psychopathy" (p. 571).

One might suspect that language, an important cultural element, also may be at work. A meta-analysis by Andreas Mokros and associates (2013) explored the use of the PCL-R and PCL:SV in German-speaking nations (i.e., Austria, Germany and Switzerland); the researchers found that the score necessary to define a psychopath in those nations was lower than in North America (25 points versus 30 points). They also found that antisocial facets played a far larger role in defining psychopathy in German-speaking nations than in North America. Other research ers report threshold scores for psychopathy diagnoses in various nations ranging from 18 to around 29. These studies and others that focus on lan guage and culture suggest that forces beyond simply either psychological or biological ones are at work to shape the diagnosis of psychopathy around the globe. It is worth noting that although Europe generally and German-speaking nations in particular employ a lower PCL-R summated score threshold, the overall prevalence rates and prisoner rates in these regions are lower than those reported in North America. Moreover, as suggested in box 4.3 (on the following page), even the PCL-R can lead to confusing results.

Several concerns about the utility of psychopathy for criminologists remain largely unresolved. First, researchers overwhelmingly conclude that treating the psychopath remains an elusive goal, as treatment modal ities intended to prevent, alter, or even ameliorate the condition of psy chopathy have yet to be confirmed as effective (cf., da Silva et al. 2012; Polaschek and Daly 2013). There may be hope for the treatment of juve nile psychopathy, however (Kiehl and Hoffman 2011). It would appear that with respect to reversing the condition of psychopathy, the jury is still out.

Second, gender has proven to be a problematic variable in the study of the links between psychopathy and crime. Researchers tell us that there are few female psychopaths and, further, that the female psychopathic criminal is even rarer (Beaver et al. 2011b). The psychometric methods used to diagnose psychopathy perform differently for males and females, although generally they yield the same ultimate diagnosis. The differences

> ### Box 4.3    Consider This: Corporate Executives versus Mafiosi
>
> The obvious implication in the search for psychopathy is a belief in the danger posed to society. But what about the "corporate psychopath," the successful businessman or professional who fulfills most criteria for psychopathy but has not committed crimes or has avoided detection? Perhaps psychopathic traits are an advantage in certain business environments; "a mix of psychopathic features might be compatible with good performance in some executive positions in some corporate milieus" (Babiak, Neumann, and Hare. 2010:176). In one study of corporate executives, researchers made use of personnel records and observations of social and work-related interactions to complete a PCL-R that omitted two items dealing with criminality. They found that the results in their sample of corporate executives were similar to those found in studies of criminals.
>
> What about members of the Sicilian Mafia? Herein lies an irony: Mafiosi are not ordinary criminals, but men whose murders are often sadistic—to convey a "message "—albeit rational and well planned to advance the business interests of their organization. According to recent research carried out by psychologists in Sicily using the PCL-R, Mafiosi are not psychopaths. Among other traits indicative of psychopathy, Mafiosi reportedly lack *impulsivity*—the "tendency to act on the spur of the moment, with little planning or consideration of the consequences" (Schimmenti et al. 2014:124)—often cited as a key characteristic of psychopaths by experts such as Hare. This view is challenged by N. G. Poythress and Jason R. Hall (2011) who point to psychopaths who coolly and deliberately plan their actions as seen in the case of professional criminals, such as Mafiosi. They argue that psychopathy is not a unitary concept; rather, it consists of various subtypes. They question if *impulsivity* should even be considered a marker for psychopathy.
>
> *Sources:* Babiak, Neumann, and Hare (2010); Poythress and Hall (2011); Schimmenti et al. (2014).

---

A psychometric test is a standard and scientific method employed to measure an individual's mental capabilities, behavioral style, personality characteristics, or aptitude (including cognitive abilities); it can be self-administered or administered by another person.

---

are found in the specific traits, facets, and factors used to create the scores (Neumann et al. 2012). Currently, even identification of the female psychopath remains a difficult task (McCuish et al. 2014).

Third, simply agreeing on a method for defining who is and is not a psychopath is far from settled. Researchers and clinicians employ at least three psychometric techniques, including ASPD (DSM-V), various versions of the Hare PCL-R, and the CPS or Childhood Psychopathy Scale. The ASPD is self-reported by the subject; the PCL-R is generally administered by a highly trained professional; and the CPS is completed by another person, usually a parent. The comparability of the diagnoses yielded by these various methods is open to question. In some cases, the best that can be said is that they generally yield similar results, but not exactly the same.

Previously, sociologists tended to discount the diagnosis of psychopathy as a catch-all category for mental disorders that did not fit other categorizations (Sutherland and Cressey 1974). Researchers found that a sample of adults defined as psychopaths in their youth were no more crime-prone than other delinquents (McCord and Sanchez 1983).

Recently, several criminologists have argued for the use of psychopathy (and one assumes the various methods currently employed to diagnosis it) as a general theory of crime. For example, Matthew DeLisi (2009), noting the strong links between the condition of psychopathy and general crime as well as violent crime, suggests that it may serve as a unified theory of crime. Problematically, we currently know little about the causes of psychopathy, and it may be premature to talk about psychopathy as a general theory of crime (cf., Beaver et al. 2011b; Perez 2012; da Silva et al 2012). Relatedly, we must not lose sight of the fact that even among the incarcerated offender population, psychopathy remains a rare condition. As Devon L. L. Polaschek and Tadhg E. Daly (2013) state, "it seems increasingly unlikely that what we call 'psychopathy' can be conceptualized as a single coherent disorder" (p. 594). Indeed, the preponderance of evidence suggests that psychopathy is not a distinct category that exists in nature but rather a configuration of traits. Cynics might argue that a psychopath is someone who acts psychopathic —a prime example of a tautology.

## SUMMARY

- Psychological theories explore criminal behavior at the individual level.
- Psychiatrists are medical doctors who treat mental illness.
- Few psychological theories have been developed exclusively to explain criminal behavior.
- Psychological theories of criminal behavior are deterministic.
- Psychoanalytic theory is based on the work of Sigmund Freud.
- The unconscious is central to understanding psychoanalytic theory.
- Psychosexual development consists of five stages.
- The id, ego, and superego explain how the psyche functions.
- The superego is crucial to understanding criminal behavior.
- Psychoanalysis is seldom ever used to treat criminals.
- The process of defining and diagnosing psychopaths has been fraught with controversy and disagreement.
- While they are similar, sociopaths differ from psychopaths.
- Sociopaths may violate social norms, seemingly unconcerned about the consequences of their actions, but are not necessarily criminals.
- Psychopaths have a tendency to engage in anti-social behavior that is often criminal; they do not experience feelings of remorse.
- The *Psychopathy Checklist-Revised* (PCL-R) can be used to diagnose psychopathy.

- Besides the PCL-R, there are several other psychometric techniques that can be used to determine who the psychopath is.
- Brain imaging has identified areas of the brain responsible for psychopathy.
- The expanded use of psychopathy by criminologists may be limited by several key factors.

## KEY TERMS

| | |
|---|---|
| adolescence/adulthood stage | oral stage |
| anal stage | preconscious |
| cathexis | psyche |
| clinical psychologists | psychiatry |
| conscious | psychoanalysis |
| displacement | psychology |
| dream interpretation | psychopath |
| ego | psychoses |
| Electra complex | psychosexual development |
| equilibrium | psychosexual maturity |
| fixation | reaction formation |
| forensic psychologists | regression |
| free association | repression |
| genital stage | sociopath |
| id | sublimation |
| latent stage | superego |
| moral insanity | transference |
| neuroses | unconscious |
| Oedipus complex | |

## CRITICAL REVIEW QUESTIONS

1. How do psychological theories differ from sociological theories?
2. How do psychiatrists differ from psychologists?
3. What does it mean that psychological theories of criminal behavior are deterministic?
4. In psychoanalytic theory, what is the role of the unconscious?
5. What are the five stages of psychosexual development?
6. What are the three psychic "phenomena" that emerge during psychosexual development and exercise, to a greater or lesser extent, control over human behavior?
7. What is the relationship between the superego and criminal behavior?
8. Why is psychoanalysis seldom ever used to treat criminals?
9. Describe the evolution of the ideas associated with the modern term psychopathy.

10. How is the sociopath different from the psychopath?

11. List and describe five or more characteristics of a psychopath?

12. One could argue that the study of the psychopath is a classic case of nature-and-nurture. What do you think about this argument, explaining your rationale?

13. What is the *Psychopathy Checklist-Revised* (PCL-R)?

14. What has brain imaging revealed about psychopathy?

15. What is the evidence of sociogenic influences on psychopathy?

16. What are the four critical issues surrounding the contributions made by psychopathy to the study of crime?

# Intelligence, Learning, and Developmental Theories

*LEARNING OBJECTIVES*

- How humans can be taught to respond in certain ways through the employment of behaviorist learning models
- The ties between behaviorism and crime
- How mental processing came to be linked to crime and measured as intelligence.
- Contemporary views on the intelligence-crime link in criminology
- The conflict created in criminology by longitudinal studies of offenders, including "career criminals"
- How life-course criminology and developmental criminology evolved as integrated theories that drew from psychology, sociology, and biology

# Introduction

This chapter examines three psychogenic clusters of theories about crime and criminals. The first, which held sway for decades, was the idea that criminals are somehow lower in intelligence than noncriminals. The connection between intelligence and crime was first proposed in the late nineteenth century, and it was based on what is by today's standards very questionable information. Moreover, in spite of considerable evidence concerning high-functioning offenders, this perspective had, as the saying goes, "legs." Specifically, prison inmates are subject to intelligence testing as part of the "classification process," which helps to determine their suitability for various types of institutional programming and treatment.

The second cluster derives from behaviorism and bridges both clinical psychology and experimental psychology. As we learned in chapter 4, clinical psychology focuses on diagnosing and treating mental, emotional, and behavioral disorders; **experimental psychology** emerged from the practices of those researchers who employed experimental methods to study behavior and associated processes. For its part, behaviorism is a type of psychological learning theory that emphasizes the objective, measurable investigation of individual actions and reactions. For nearly 100 years, psychologists have applied elements of behaviorism both experimentally and clinically to the study of human behavior, including criminal activities.

The final cluster of psychogenic-related theories is unique in that it draws from several academic disciplines. This theoretically integrated perspective emerged in response to what is described as the robust empirical relationship between crime and age. As social scientists tried to make sense of this relationship, they moved in several directions simultaneously. Taken collectively, the emergent integrated theory is known as developmental and life-course criminology. It consists of crime concepts taken from biogenic theories (chapter 3), structural theories (chapter 6), control theories (chapter 7), labeling theory (chapter 8), and developmental psychology. **Developmental psychology** is a branch of psychology that explores how and why humans grow, develop, and adapt over the course of their lifetime. It plays a central role in developmental and life-course criminology by explaining how some delinquents develop and emerge to become adult criminals, while for others delinquent involvement plays out well before adulthood.

The theories reviewed in this chapter, unlike those in chapter 4, make no assumptions about an offender's mental health itself as a precursor for crime. Rather, they provide insights into how psychology can help us understand the ways apparently normal people become delinquents and criminals. They represent a range of psychological explanations for crim-

Integrated theory is the idea that we can take ideas from two or more theories, combine them, and achieve a greater understanding and insight than was possible for either of the emergent theory's constituent parts alone.

inality—from the simplistic (as in feeblemindedness), to the very complex (as in behaviorism), to integrated multidisciplinary ideas (as in developmental and life-course theories). In all three sets of theories, biology also plays a role, including the linkage between intelligence and crime.

Before we turn to our examination of intelligence and crime, it is important to note that psychologists do not agree completely about the definition of "intelligence." Some argue that there are many different "intelligences," only a few of which can be captured by standard IQ tests (Neisser et al. 1996). For example, there is "practical intelligence," or being able to give an extemporaneous talk, or possessing a "sense of direction," or having interpersonal skills. At the same time, IQ tests do not assess mechanical or athletic ability, those of a football quarterback, for example.

While IQ tests correlate well with school success, other variables also assert influence in this regard, including a willingness to study, the encouragement of peers and family, and the quality of the educational experience. Culture also asserts an influence as evidenced by the success of Asian Americans, especially those of Chinese and Japanese heritage, who exhibit extraordinary ability in math and science, although their IQ scores do not exceed those of non-Asian Americans (Neisser et al. 1996). In short, intelligence and available measures of it are the source of much disagreement, and it should, therefore, surprise no one that it is equally divisive in crime theory.

## Intelligence and Crime

At about the same time as Lombroso was writing about born criminals (chapter 3), journalists, psychologists, and others in the United States began investigating what was believed to be an inherited mental condition, "feeblemindedness." They saw a person's mental capacity as providing behavioral insights, criminal and otherwise, an idea that helped generate popular support for intelligence testing (Davenport 1915). As late as 1913, for example, England and Wales had a two-pronged definitional test for mental deficiency: the person suffers from a mental defect other than insanity and the level of mental defectiveness is such that the person cannot manage his or her own life (Burt 1935). Early advocates rarely looked for any explanatory factors positioned between intelligence and crime; rather, they concentrated on an often-reported correlation: the lower the mental functioning, the higher the crime activity. What was missing in this argument was a standardized means to measure intelligence. As suggested in box 5.1 on the next page, this missing element was corrected in the early twentieth century by psychologists studying human intelligence. The next step was to show the links between feeblemindedness, IQ and crime.

B
O
X
5.1

**Measuring Intelligence: The IQ Test**

Exploring the connection between mental functioning and crime requires an "objective" measure of intelligence. In 1905, the French psychologist Alfred Binet (b.1857–d.1911), working in collaboration with Theodore Simon (b.1872–d.1961), provided this measure as a series of tasks laid out in terms of increasing complexity from those intended for children through adulthood. Three years later, Simon assigned a mental age to groups of tasks. He divided mental age by chronological age and multiple the results by 100, creating in 1912 the first intelligence quotient or **IQ score**: smarter people had IQ scores above 100 and duller ones below that figure.

Today the Stanford-Binet Intelligence Scale is often used for testing children and adolescents, while intelligence testing for adults often uses the Wechsler Adult Intelligence Scale (WAIS). The WAIS compares scores of the test-taker to those of others in his or her general age group. The average score is fixed at 100, with approximately two-thirds of all scores falling somewhere between 85 and 115. Scores that fall between these two numbers are considered average, normal intelligence. The modern version of the Stanford-Binet test uses a similar scoring scheme with 140 classified as "genius."

## Feeblemindedness, IQ, and Crime

Henry Goddard (b.1866–d.1957), an American psychologist, translated Binet's work into English and, using a modified Binet-Simon test, studied IQ-score distribution in U.S. society. He concluded that as few as 28 percent and as much as 89 percent of the nation's prison population had IQ scores of 75 or less (Goddard 1914). The link between weak morals and weak minds gained in popularity during the first two decades of the twentieth century (Degler 1991). A proponent of eugenics—he advocated colonizing and sterilizing "mentally defectives"—Goddard provided two types of support for his view. First, in 1912, he published *The Kallikak Family: A Study in the Heredity of Feeble-Mindedness* in which he detailed the crimes and other aberrations of the 976 descendants of Martin Kallikak and two women. During the Revolutionary War, Kallikak had an affair with a "feebleminded" girl with whom he had a son; 480 descendants were linked to this branch of Kallikak's family tree. After the war he married a Quaker girl raised in a "good family." Goddard found records for the 496 descendants of this union. In the first branch he found 143 feebleminded descendants and dozens of criminal or "immoral persons." In the second, only one mental defective and no criminals were found. He later repudiated the study as deeply flawed.

In 1914, Goddard published *Feeblemindedness: Its Causes and Consequences*, in which he reported on intelligence tests given to all inmates of the New Jersey Training School for the Feeble-Minded. No inmate had a mental age greater than 13. Goddard (1914) deduced the upper limit for **feeblemindedness** at a mental age of 12 or an IQ of 75, establishing an operational definition for feeblemindedness. In *Feeblemindedness*, Goddard also reported on many studies linking feeblemindedness and crime. These studies of prison inmates typically found high levels of feeblemindedness and Goddard believed they firmly established the IQ-crime connection.

Goddard (1921) reckoned that the feebleminded accounted for only 1 percent of the population; however, based on his experiences with youthful offenders, where the rate of feeblemindedness was far greater, Goddard maintained that at least half of all criminals are mentally defective. Carl Murchison (1926) challenged this claim, maintaining that intelligence was a negligible factor in crime causation. The matter was "settled" in the late 1920s by a massive study by M. H. Erickson (1929), who found that there was a definite correlation between IQ and crime, which was decidedly stronger for those in the lowest IQ group, whom he labeled low-grade feebleminded. He also reported that some crimes required greater IQ than others (e.g., financial crimes). Further, he speculated that the causal links between IQ and crime were indirect, as intelligence did not appear to be a causal factor in producing all criminals. Between the 1920s and the 1960s, criminologists, like the U.S. penologist Vernon Fox (1946) acknowledged the tie between IQ and crime but speculated little about what it meant. For years the correlation was relegated to that of an invalid and spurious connection (Bartol 1999). That characterization was to change dramatically in the 1960s.

## Contemporary Explorations of the IQ-Crime Connection

The IQ-crime connection became a subject of controversy when in 1967 Nobel laureate and physicist William Shockley (b.1910–d.1989) stated that the difference between African-American and European-American IQ scores was one of genetics. Moreover, Shockley (1967) claimed, genetics might also explain the variable poverty and crime rates observed between the two groups. He urged others to study this problem. He did not have to wait long, as psychologist Arthur Jensen (b.1923–d.2012) had already spent several years looking at the race-IQ link.

Jensen (1969) published an essay on genetic heritage. He divided intelligence into **associative learning**—the simple retention of input or rote memorization of simple facts and skills (level I)—and **conceptual learning**—the ability to manipulate and transform information input or problem solving (level II). Jensen believed that IQ tests measured level II intelligence. Jensen was interested in how culture, development, and genetics influenced IQ and began extensive testing of minority-group children in the 1960s. His research led to two conclusions. First, 80 percent of intelligence is genetic (nature); the remaining 20 percent comes from the environment (nurture). Second, Jenson contended that while all races were equal in terms of associative learning, conceptual learning occurred with significantly higher frequency in whites compared with blacks and with Asians somewhat more frequently compared with whites.

He concluded that whites were inherently more able to engage in conceptual learning than blacks, a conclusion viewed by many as racist (Lederberg 1969).

Robert Gordon (1976), citing Jensen's belief in the dominant role of genetics in IQ, saw striking parallels between IQ scores and delinquency rates revealed in juvenile court records and commitment data. Gordon, largely without supporting data, went on to argue for a connection between IQ and delinquency that was common to both African Americans and Caucasians. Gordon (1987) later completed this argument in an attack on the sociological argument that what IQ tests measure is socioeconomic status (SES). He conducted a series of analyses of lifetime delinquency prevalence rates (official designation as a delinquent at least once by age 18). He reported that IQ was a better predictor of delinquency than SES. As for the race-IQ-crime connection, Gordon concluded: "It is time to consider the black-white IQ difference seriously when confronting the problem of crime in American society" (p. 92).

In fact, sociologists have long observed the ties between intelligence tests and crime. Four decades ago, Travis Hirschi and Michael Hindelang (1977) concluded:

- Low IQ was at least as important as low social class or race in predicting official delinquency, but more important in predicting self-reported offending.

- Within social classes and racial groups, persons with low IQ are more likely to be delinquent that higher IQ individuals.

- The relationship between IQ and crime is mediated by negative school experiences; low IQ results in poor school performance, which is a marker for criminal propensity.

In *The Bell Curve*, psychologist Richard Herrnstein (b.1930–d.1994) and social scientist Charles Murray (b.1943–) argue there is a clear and consistent link between low intelligence and criminality. They note that since the 1940s, IQ tests have consistently placed the offender population with an IQ of between 91 and 93, while the general population is about 100. Herrnstein and Murray (1994) conclude: "Among the most firmly established facts about criminal offenders is that their distribution of IQ scores differs from that of the population at large. . . . The relationship of IQ to criminality is especially pronounced in the small fraction of the population, primarily young men, who constitute the chronic criminals that account for a disproportionate amount of crime" (p. 235).

Herrnstein and Murray (1994) acknowledge the possibility that high IQ could provide some measure of protection for those who might otherwise fall afoul of the law. They analyzed the National Labor Youth Survey, a longitudinal self-report study of young American males and found that "offenders who have been caught do not score much lower, if at all, than those who are getting away with their crimes" (p. 235). But how can we be confident in knowing the IQ of those "who are getting away with their crimes"? The self-report studies used by Herrnstein and Murray depends on the veracity of subjects to admit to criminality for which they have not been arrested. Self-report studies reveal that while persons readily admit to relatively minor criminal acts, such as shoplifting, they do not admit to crimes such as murder, rape, or robbery. It is reasonable to believe that persons with higher intelligence would be less likely to admit to criminality because they recognize, despite assurances of confidentiality, the harm that disclosure could cause. High IQ persons might ask themselves: "Why take a chance?" On the other hand, for young males who wish to conform to "street culture," admitting to not having committed crime is as embarrassing as admitting to being a virgin.

Race is key to Herrnstein and Murray's theorizing. Their argument sees race as a key precursor of IQ. Races genetically fated to lower than normal intelligence also exhibit a high tendency to commit crimes. Herrnstein and Murray did allow that not all low cognitive ability persons commit crime. However, race-based claims raise a number of questions, particularly around the notion of "race." Over the past several decades, sociologists and anthropologists have repeatedly issued a warning: The term race is biologically meaningless and unscientific. The old way of dividing races by hair texture, skin color, and facial features, is superficial as they may be responses to environment: "In the social sense, race is a reality. In a scientific sense, it is not" (Wheeler 1995: A15). Any theory using race as a variable is relying on a social construct, not a scientific one.

A recent shift in the IQ-crime debate has centered on the biogenic origins of intelligence. Both IQ and self-control, which have been shown to have close ties to criminality, have neurological underpinnings, the so-called *executive functions* of the brain.

## IQ-Crime Link: A Critique

Three positions dominate the debate on the IQ-crime connection—yes, no, and maybe. The use of IQ scores to predict crime is limited to those crimes most likely committed by persons with limited intelligence who have been arrested or convicted of a crime, pushing the IQ-crime connection close to a tautology. We could confidently assert that corporate crime, organized crime, crime by politicians, and computer hacks require superior intelligence. Harmful corporate activities—e.g., those that pollute our environment or expose consumers to unsafe products—rarely result in the criminal prosecution of corporate officers. Perhaps a high IQ predicts ability to avoid criminal penalties. We should also consider the definition of crime, an issue discussed in chapter 1. And, as suggested in box 5.2, there are even more basic questions about IQ tests and exactly what is being measured.

A low IQ may predict who gets caught and punished.

**Box 5.2    Consider This: What Do IQ Tests Measure?**

An overriding issue concerns exactly what IQ tests measure and whether environmental and cultural factors affect the outcome. If, as we suspect, the corporate offender's IQ differs from the street criminal's, what are the implications? IQ tests predict success in school. Middle- and upper-class children tend to score higher on IQ tests than do lower-class youths. Students in wealthy suburban areas consistently outperform those attending school in urban areas with high numbers of students qualifying for free lunch. There is concern that the questions on IQ tests do not adequately measure the capacity for learning or are culturally biased. Moreover, there is evidence that staying in school increases one's IQ on average about 3 points per year of education (Winship and Korenman 2011). This raises questions about the extent to which heredity impacts one's IQ score.

Charles Locurto (1991) asks a related question, "How do we know that an IQ score is a measure of intelligence?" Curt Bartol (1991) observes, "IQ scores and the concept of intelligence should *not* be confused" (p. 132). Perhaps all an IQ test tells us is how one performs on a particular paper-and-pencil test or whatever psychometric method is used to measure IQ. Until we have a direct method or technique for measuring innate intelligence, then all indirect tests of intelligence must be disputed as to their validity.

*Sources*: Bartol (1991); Locurto (1991); Winship and Korenman 2011.

# Behaviorism and Learning Theory

John B. Watson (b.1878–d.1958) first used the term **behaviorism** in 1913 when he authored "Psychology as the Behaviorist Views It." Watson (1914, 1930) was influenced by the work of the Russian scientist and Nobel Prize winner Ivan Pavlov (b.1849–d.1936). Pavlov's work is referred to as **classical conditioning**. Some stimulus-response connections require no learning—a dog will salivate when it sees food. Pavlov discovered that dogs could be conditioned to respond to a neutral stimulus—one that produces no response until the dog learns an association. By ringing a bell when giving food to his dogs, Pavlov conditioned them to associate the bell with food, and they eventually salivated at the sound of the bell alone; the ring became a conditioned stimulus. Classical conditioning casts the learning process as simplistic and straightforward, which later generations of behaviorists challenged.

For Watson, behavior is a physiological response to a given stimulus. In contrast to psychoanalytic theory, Watson saw no place in this process for the conscious or the unconscious. It remained for others, especially the U.S. behavioral psychologist B. F. Skinner, to explain the complex nature of these learning mechanisms. Julian Rotter and Albert Bandura would eventually link this perspective to crime.

## Operant Conditioning

B. F. Skinner (b.1904–d.1990) noted that **operant conditioning**, also called **instrumental conditioning**, involves the repeated presentation or removal of a stimulus following a behavior to increase or decrease the probability of the behavior. According to Skinner (1974), a reinforcer is a stimulus that increases the probability of a behavior. If the probability of a behavior goes up following the *presence* of some stimulus, then **positive reinforcement** has occurred (e.g., give a child a new toy for good behavior). If the probability of a behavior goes up after the *removal* of a stimulus, then **negative reinforcement** has occurred (e.g., studying for a big exam to avoid a bad grade). If the goal is to decrease a behavior, two punishment methods may be employed as well. A **positive punishment** *presents* a noxious or undesired stimulus after the offending behavior, which is intended to reduce an undesired behavior (e.g. spanking a child caught hitting a sibling); a **negative punishment** occurs with the *removal* of a desired stimulus following exhibition of the offending behavior (e.g., taking away a favorite toy when a child misbehaves). Table 5.1 summarizes these relationships.

Learning occurs through reinforcement from others (e.g., peers). Under controlled conditions, such as animal training, effective reinforcements need to occur as close to the event as possible—the dog who sits in response to a command is immediately given a dog biscuit. With children it is possible to provide positive reinforcement or administer punishment at the right moment of time—the child who misbehaves can be immediately reprimanded, sent to their room, etc. With adults (excluding prison inmates), it is more difficult to control the environment so that reinforcement or punishment occurs in close proximity to the target behavior.

Inappropriate responses or the failure to learn how to discriminate between competing norms (e.g., lawful and unlawful) are sometimes the result of the learning process. In some situations, conforming behavior is not adequately reinforced—or perhaps even punished. If the peer group rewards antisocial behavior, the actor may choose not to conform. Behaviorism rejects psychoanalytic theory as unscientific—id, ego, and superego

> Punishments and reinforcements both may be presented or removed, but the goal of the former is always less of the offending behavior, while the latter is intended to increase a specific behavior.

### Table 5.1   A Comparison of Operant Conditioning's Reinforcements and Punishments

| Status of Stimulus | Punishment (Behavior Ceases or Decreases) | Reinforcement (Behavior Continues or Accelerates) |
|---|---|---|
| Present | Positive Punishment | Positive Reinforcement |
| Absent | Negative Punishment | Negative Reinforcement |

Source: Adapted from Akers (1973:50).

cannot be observed. Inappropriate behavior is not the result of unconscious mechanisms but rather the result of the responses that were reinforced.

## Behaviorism and Crime

Most conventional crime involves substantial potential risk and relatively modest rewards—but the latter are typically immediate and the former often delayed or absent. Our criminal justice system's effectiveness as a conditioning agent, therefore, may be limited due to the question of timeliness. According to behavior theory, punishment is effective in controlling behavior only in the short term, unless the subject can be continually monitored and punished. Hans Eysenck (1969) noted the need for timeliness in order for criminal justice sanctioning to work and the reinforcements of criminal actions to be defeated. According to Eysenck, "an action followed by a small but immediate gratification will tend to be repeated, even though it is followed by a large but delayed painful consequence" (p. 689). That is, for a punishment to stop an offensive act, it must follow that act immediately and not be delayed, only then serving as a positive punishment, effectively cancelling the effects of the crime's positive reinforcement.

Behaviorism has several implications for understanding criminal behavior. We will explore three: Eysenck's *criminal personality theory*, Rotter's *cognitive learning theory* and Bandura's *modeling theory*.

*Eysenck's Criminal Personality Theory.*    Hans Eysenck (b.1916–d.1997) saw the *conscience* as controlling antisocial behavior. This is not the mechanism that Freud ascribed to the superego, but instead is the result of conditioning. Eysenck created **criminal personality theory**, the only psychological theory specifically designed "from the ground up" to explain criminality. Eysenck's theory is a mix of behaviorism, biology (chapter 3), and personality theories (chapter 4) to explain the links between aberrant personality characteristics and crime. A critic of sociological crime theories (Eysenck and Gudjonsson 1989), Eysenck saw crime as an interaction between environmental conditions and inherited nervous system features. Like many other psychobiologists, Eysenck (1973:171; 1977) believed that we should avoid a focus on the nature-versus-nurture controversy.

Eysenck suggested that certain inherited characteristics make crime more likely, even though criminality is not an inherited trait. He divided the control of behavior into: (1) that which is the result of the quality of conditioning and (2) that which is inherited, including elements of the nervous system, both the CNS and the ANS. He also believed that personality depends on four "higher-order factors"—(1) **ability**, innate intelligence (a quality called **g**) and three temperaments: (2) **extraversion,** where the excitable or lively person's energy levels are directed outside of him- or herself, manifesting as impulsive sociability; (3) **neuroticism**, a trait that is associated with anxiety, depression, and other negative psy-

Timeliness limits the ability of criminal justice to apply conditioning intended to reduce or stop crime.

chological states; and (4) **psychoticism**, in which case the person appears aggressive, impulsive, impersonal, cold, and lacking in empathy for others. Although g is important in understanding crime, Eysenck claimed that the three temperaments are far more critical. Two of these, extraversion and neuroticism, are related; the third, psychoticism, is unique. For Eysenck, extraversion reflected basic central nervous system (CNS) functioning. Neuroticism depended on nerve pathways outside the CNS; in particular, the ANS. Psychoticism had no specified neural links.

According to Eysenck's theory, two personality types exhibit the greatest proneness to crime. The first includes **neurotic extraverts**, or persons who—because of their biology—require high stimulation levels from their environments. Moreover, their sympathetic nervous systems are quick to respond without much counterbalancing from the parasympathetic system. The second type, the **psychotic extraverts**, are persons who—due to reasons of unknown physiological origin—are cruel, hostile, insensitive to others, and unemotional; they are not necessarily "out of touch with reality." These behavioral descriptors fit well with the discussion of psychopathy in chapter 4, as does the basic definition of psychoticism. By themselves, however, these personality types do not explain *why* crime occurs. Criminal behavior is thus the product of environmental factors (conditioning/learning habits) and biology (personality type intensifiers).

Eysenck's criminal personality theory is important for several reasons beyond its development as a psychological theory of crime. It represents an early example of an integrated crime theory. Specifically, it combines elements of biology (chapter 3's ANS and CNS functioning), intelligence (the g factor; see discussions of intelligence earlier in this chapter), and personality theory (chapter 4's psychopathy). In criminology, crime theories that combine ideas from multiple disciplines (e.g., psychology and biology) are relatively rare.

***Rotter's Cognitive Learning Theory.***    Human behavior is more complex than the relatively simple responses of other species, as it is often mediated by beliefs and symbols. The readiness to fight or die for a "cause," a strongly held belief system such as those associated with religious symbols, embody some of the most abstract complexities of human behavior. This recognition has led to **cognitive learning theory**, which is based on the idea that human behavior is motivated by what cannot be observed— internal to the person—such as beliefs and expectations. The way a person evaluates a situation determines the response (Gold 1980). Thus, based on past learning, a twisted cross (swastika) may have different meaning to a Jew (for whom it is a symbol of the Holocaust) than to a member of the Navajo nation (for whom it is a cosmic religious symbol).

According to Julian Rotter (b.1916–d.2014) such cognitions or expectations, although they cannot be observed, can lead to a certain outcome or consequence, an idea that formed the core of his **expectancy theory**.

When we look at an object or a symbol, such as a swastika, what our mind sees is filtered by our past learning, largely through the process of cognitive learning, which shapes how we process information, including visual cues.

Rotter (1954) believed that people weigh their actions' possible consequences in terms of recollections about what has happened in similar circumstances. The possible rewards—how much value we attach to the outcome—may determine whether people engage in certain behaviors. With respect to crime, Curt R. Bartol (1999:120) observed that when people engage in unlawful conduct, they expect to gain something. Violent persons, for example, may elect to behave that way because the approach has been used successfully in the past (at least they believe it has been successful). Humans use their cognitive powers to look into both the past and the future, to make decisions about likely outcomes, and to act on those decisions. It would appear, then, that their behavior is rational.

A rational criminal is not necessarily a smart criminal.

Rational, however, does not necessarily mean "smart" or even appropriate in a given situation (issues we explored in chapter 2's rational choice theory). But, what if a person lacks the experience to draw conclusions about the future? Albert Bandura provides an answer—modeling.

***Bandura's Observational Learning/Modeling Theory.*** Albert Bandura (b.1925–) is known for his experiments involving children watching an adult attack a plastic clown doll called "Bobo," sometimes kicking it and sometimes using small toys in their aggression toward the clown. The children were then placed in a room with attractive toys that they could not touch until they grew visibly agitated and frustrated. They were moved to still another room with a Bobo doll and the same toys the adult used to attack Bobo. (Recall the expression "monkey see, monkey do"?) Bandura found that nearly nine in ten children imitated the adult attack on Bobo and 4 in 10 reproduced the behavior when placed in a similar situation eight months later (Bandura and Huston 1961).

Bandura (1974: 859) called the process by which "people convert future consequences into motivations for behavior" **observational learning** or **modeling theory**, a process that need not involve direct reinforcement. Humans are capable of learning vicariously—through the experiences of others or through one's imagination. Bandura's research and theorizing largely involved aggression, and the theory is best couched in those terms. An individual who observes much aggressive behavior and is reinforced for acting aggressively learns to be aggressive. Bandura identified four steps in this process of observational learning/modeling:

1. *Attention*: Learners perceive what is happening and pay attention to the modeled behavior's important features, including what the model is saying and doing.

2. *Retention*: Learners encode the information into long-term memory for retrieval at a later time. Memory is a key cognitive element for successful observational learning.

3. *Reproduction*: Learners reproduce the model's behavior; they must have the basic motor skills and physical attributes to carry out the

behavior. If the child cannot pummel the doll, learning aggressive behavior is not possible; if the child cannot reach the pedals, learning to ride a bike is not possible.

4. *Motivation* (reinforcement): Learners comprehend and appreciate the positive reinforcements that accrue for the modeled behavior, the first step being to observe the model's reinforcement. Without motivation the behavior is not repeated.

Bandura saw the primary "teachers" as family members, members of one's subculture, and symbolic models provided by the mass media. Bandura was a frequent critic of the mass media, especially violence on television and in motion pictures. Research on Bandura's learning model has linked exposure to TV violence with increased aggression in children and adults, although this relationship is clearer for short-term effects and among those who were already aggressive (Freedman 1984, 1986).

Most behaviorist contributions to crime and justice issues have largely been indirect, through other theories such as Akers' social learning theory (see chapter 7) and Cornish and Clarke's choice theory (see chapter 2). The exception is the work of Bandura (1974), whose theory of aggression includes the influence of symbolic models, particularly the mass media (i.e., television and movies).

> Human behavior can be conditioned vicariously—without direct contact between the conditioner and the subject—by watching how others respond to the stimulus.

## Developmental and Life-Course Criminology

Criminals rarely emerge suddenly without any prior warnings. Over the past 20 years, this observation has pushed criminologists in different directions. In the early 1980s, criminologists debated the issue of *criminal propensity* versus *criminal careers*. The impetus was a longitudinal study conducted in Philadelphia by Marvin Wolfgang and his associates (1972), who explored delinquency in a single birth cohort (i.e., all persons sharing the same birth year). They reported that 6 percent of the juveniles accounted for 52 percent of all juvenile–police contacts and an astounding 70 percent of all juvenile contacts for felony offenses.

Criminologists disagreed over the theoretical and practical implications of Wolfgang's study. *Criminal Careers and "Career Criminals,"* a two-volume report by Albert Blumstein and associates (1986), summed up the position of the group that saw career criminals as chronic offenders who engage in a high volume of crime over a period of time. A **criminal career** is simply a description of the type, volume, nature, and length of a person's involvement in crime. Some careers are short, and others are long. Career criminal advocates focused on high-frequency offenders and examined the **onset** (beginning) and **desistance** (ending) of their careers, as well as the seriousness of criminal activity. They challenged the long-held belief that offending rates rise rapidly in the mid-teens, peak in the late teens or early 20s, and drop steadily throughout the 20s. Followers of

> The career criminal is a high-volume offender, whether that career is long or short.

the career criminal model maintained that offender frequency does not change, but rather the offender pool is less, owing to death or incarceration. Hence, anyone engaged in crime after age 20 is a career criminal and a threat to public safety, which lends support to the policy of putting career criminals in prison for lengthy sentences, if not life.

Michael R. Gottfredson and Travis Hirschi (1989) opposed the idea of a career criminal, proposing instead the **criminal-propensity thesis**— that some people are simply more prone to commit crime than others. Variations in the amount of offending follow the same age–crime curve for all types of crime-prone individuals. The greatest involvement occurs in the late teens, followed by declining involvement. Thus, the curve's appearance is the same for low-crime-prone persons and high-crime-prone ones. The magnitude—the peak offending level—is what differs. Whatever other forces are at work, claimed Gottfredson and Hirschi (1986), people outgrow criminality as they mature. Or, as they age, they become less adept at some crime, burglary, for example. It would be rare to find an elderly "mugger."

> The criminal-propensity thesis tells us that while some people are more prone to commit crime than others, all offending follows the same age-crime curve. Whether they commit much crime or very little crime, the age at which criminals *are most likely to offend* is roughly the same.

## Life-Course Criminology

In the 1930s, Sheldon Glueck (b.1896–d.1980) and Eleanor Glueck (b. 1898–b.1972) collected a wealth of information on two samples of youths, one delinquent and the other nondelinquent, matched in terms of general intelligence, ethnicity, and residence in underprivileged areas. Their cumulative work, which grew to over 250 published books, book chapters, and articles, described a wide range of youthful misconduct. They also examined links between chronic delinquency and such biogenic factors as psychopathy and body types. Robert Sampson and John Laub (1993) reanalyzed the Gluecks' qualitative and quantitative data, employing an integrated theory that drew heavily on social control (chapter 7) and labeling theories (chapter 8), with a strong appreciation for large-scale structural forces such as poverty and disadvantage (chapters 6 and 8).

Sampson and Laub (1993) used social control as an organizing principle to explore life-course social bonding; they included institutions of formal *and* informal social control. They described two essential forces at work: (1) **trajectories**, or long-term developmental pathways over the life course, and (2) **transitory events**, or short-term, specific life events that are part of trajectories and may mark movement from one status to another. These twin forces operate on individuals according to their age-graded status: (1) becoming juvenile delinquents, (2) making the behavioral transitions that accompany the transition from juvenile status to adulthood, and (3) becoming an adult offender.

According to Sampson and Laub, the family context associated with delinquency includes a lack of supervision, erratic or harsh discipline, and parental rejection. Structural background factors (including family SES, residential mobility, and household crowding) combine with individual differences (including early conduct disorders and difficult temperament) to influence the social bonding associated with family and school. They also acknowledged the relative stability of deviance over the life course, given that the best predictor of future delinquency is past involvement in delinquency. However, change in status—such as that created by a transitory event (e.g. a marriage, a divorce, a job change or an arrest)—is also an important feature of life-course development.

The key issue for Sampson and Laub was how many doors the past misconduct had closed for a given individual (see chapter 8's labeling theory). **Cumulative continuity** was their term for the idea that as a person fails in one arena of life (e.g., educational system), then they are far more likely to fail in another (e.g., occupational arena), leading to a type of forced stability. Transitory events lead to **turning points,** or changes in life-course trajectories (Laub, Sampson, and Allen 2001:100). For example, social capital emerged as a crucial force for change; those adults with strong ties to friends, family, and job have an investment in conformity even if they were seriously involved in delinquency as late adolescents and young adults. In the absence of transitory events—a new prosocial relationship or an epiphany or awakening after a particularly traumatic event in the person's life, such as the murder of a close friend—cumulative continuity pushes the offender deeper into crime.

Alternative views on the life-course of offenders emerged in the 1990s. In box 5.3 on the following page, we present the work of U.S. developmental psychologist Terrie Moffitt, who used psychological concepts to explore different types of delinquent offenders. The ties between developmental psychology and delinquency became the foundation for developmental criminology, our next topic.

## Developmental Criminology

Rolf Loeber and Marc LeBlanc (1990) believed that only by studying and describing within-individual differences in criminal careers, which they termed **developmental criminology**, can criminologists hope to understand why some youths become more deeply involved in criminal behavior than others. Developmental criminologists assume that the influence of causal factors throughout the cycle is a constant.

Loeber and D. F. Hay (1994) described three developmental pathways to offending:

1. **Authority-conflict pathway:** Children begin to engage in miscreant behavior before age 12, starting with stubborn conduct, moving to defiance, and settling into authority avoidance. While often a nuisance, adherents to this pathway pose minimal threats to society.

> Developmental criminology is the study of criminal behavior with an emphasis on what causes individuals to participate in crime or delinquency at different times or ages in life.

**B**
**O**
**X**

**5.3**

## Developmental Psychology and Delinquency

Moffitt, while studying a panel of New Zealand residents over time, observed two crime trajectories or pathways, from which she created a taxonomy, or a method of classifying, identifying, and organizing information about a phenomenon. **Life-course persistent (LCP) offenders** embark on paths that begin at a very early age. At age 4 and younger, LCP offenders engage in "acting out" behavior such as biting and hitting; by age 10 they are shoplifters and truants. Crime seriousness increases with age, so that by their 20s they are engaging in robbery and rape, and by their 30s they are committing fraud and child abuse. Moffitt found that many LCP offenders have neurological problems throughout childhood as well as attention deficit disorder and learning difficulties during their school years. Living in disorganized homes and violent neighborhoods exacerbates the growing antisocial tendencies of LCP offenders.

Most problem children are **adolescent-limited (AL) offenders,** who begin offending with the start of adolescence and cease causing trouble (desist) around age 18. These offenders differ in several ways from LCP offenders. First, they do not exhibit early and persistent antisocial behavior. Second, AL offenders learn to get along with others, something LCP offenders rarely master. Third, AL offenders do not have the same depth and duration of neurological problems. Fourth, although the frequency of offending for AL offenders may approach that of LCP offenders at certain ages, the antisocial behavior of LCP offenders far outstrips that of AL offenders during the teenage years. Fifth, AL offenders more so than LCP offenders become involved in expressions of autonomy from adult control, including vandalism, alcohol and drug offenses, truancy, and running away. Lastly, unlike the LCP offenders, AL offenders in their late teens can abandon their miscreant ways should they interfere with adult-like goals, such as getting a full-time job or going to college.

Moffitt's developmental taxonomy of delinquency blends neuropsychology and developmental psychology. Her work on different trajectories to delinquency and crime helps explain the threats posed by a small group of early-onset, long-term offenders. It also explains why most delinquents have the developmental skills to explore alternative pathways.

*Sources:* Moffitt (1993a, 1993b).

---

Developmental criminologists typically require longitudinal research, which includes trend or pattern analyses of crime, cohort studies (such as that employed by Wolfgang), and panel studies (like the one used by Moffitt) to test their ideas.

2. **Covert pathway:** This path consists of minor hidden behavior as the first step; however, the misconduct escalates quickly to property damage (e.g., vandalism and arson) and moderate forms of delinquency (e.g., burglary, car theft, and fraud).

3. **Overt pathway:** This path tends to manifest itself as aggression and violence; bullying and annoying behavior are the first step, followed by fighting and, finally, major aggressive acts, including assault and rape.

Identifying a child as an **experimenter type** or a **persister type** is important to developmental criminologists (Loeber, Keenan, and Zhang 1997). Both may start on their respective paths at an early age, but the former stops (desists), while the second continues. Given an emphasis on within-individual changes, classification requires more than one assessment over time—hence developmental criminologists' reliance on longitudinal research.

Overt and covert aggressive acts pose differential threats to the community (Loeber and Stouthamer-Loeber 1998). Behaviorally overt aggressors commit their acts in the open and in direct contact with victims; covert aggressors do not like confrontations, preferring to be sneaky, dishonest, or concealed. In developmental criminology terms, then, violent crimes are examples of overt aggression, whereas property crimes are acts of covert aggression. Emotional anger contributes to overt aggression; covert aggression entails far less emotionality. People who use overt aggression are hostile and exhibit cognitive deficiencies associated with violence-proneness, qualities missing in people who use covert aggression. Developmentally overt aggression generally begins early in life (see Moffitt's life-course persistent offenders), but not all overt aggressors begin early. **Late-onset offenders**, criminals who begin their careers well after adolescence, constitute a minority within the offender population and are rarely studied (Loeber and Stouthamer-Loeber 1998).

> It is rare but not unheard of that an individual becomes an adult offender having no involvement in delinquent misconduct.

Studies by developmental and life-course criminologists, employing longitudinal studies of youth, tend to find support for divergent crime pathways (Caspi et al. 1994; Moffitt, Lynam, and Silva 1994). It would appear that increased risk for neuropsychological disorders and disadvantaged childhood environments predict early-onset but not late-onset offending; this relationship was true for males, but not for females (Tibbets and Piquero 1999). Rather than more pathways, there may be fewer—or the pathways may be more complex than previously thought, differing for males and females.

DLC theories, as the combined developmental and life course criminology perspective has come to be labeled, highlight the mix of neuropsychological conditions, prenatal and perinatal events, and environments that produce offenders. The pathways describe what happens to various types of youth engaged in adolescent misbehavior and delinquency—those who go on to adult criminal careers and those who commit crime as delinquents but desist. As a set of integrated theories, the DLC perspective constitutes, as we shall see in chapter 10, a rich source of policies and practices.

> Developmental psychology plays a central role in the merger of perspectives known as developmental and life-course criminology (DLC).

## SUMMARY

- Early studies of the IQ-Crime connection were fraught with considerable controversy.
- IQ scores were used to promote eugenics.
- The link between IQ and crime depends on the accuracy of self-report studies.
- Low IQ may not predict crime but, instead, predicts "getting caught."
- Intelligence-based explanations of crime have clear roots in psychology and biology; however, some critics maintain that the sociological and general environmental bases of IQ testing are often overlooked.

- Behaviorism is based on learning theory and places emphasis on the objective measurable investigation of individual actions and reactions.
- Behaviorism rejects psychoanalytic theory and the concept of the unconscious.
- According to behaviorism, behavior that is rewarded will be continued.
- A reward is a positive reinforcer.
- Deviant behavior flows from misapplied reinforcements and inadequate punishments.
- The criminal justice system's effectiveness as a conditioning agent is limited due to the question of timeliness.
- Cognitive learning theory is based on the idea that human behavior is motivated by what cannot be observed.
- For criminals, being rational is not the same as being smart.
- Modeling notes that human behavior need not involve direct reinforcement because humans are capable of learning vicariously.
- Behavioral explanations of crime are a mix of psychological and biological factors.
- The criminological debate between criminal propensity and criminal careers led to the development of life-course criminology and developmental criminology.
- Trajectories refer to long-term developmental pathways to crime over one's lifetime.
- Transitory events are short-term, specific events in a given trajectory and may mark the movement from one status to another associated with turning points in the life-course.
- A minority of all delinquent youth become life-course persistent offenders.
- Most delinquents are adolescent-limited offenders.
- Developmental criminologists assume that the influence of crime causation factors is constant throughout the life cycle.
- Developmental criminologists see three pathways to crime: (1) authority-conflict pathway (i.e., defiant youth who pass quickly through this stage); (2) covert pathway (i.e., minor delinquents who escalate quickly to property damage and moderate forms of delinquency; and (3) overt pathway (i.e., aggressive and violent delinquents likely to continue their careers toward increasingly violent acts)
- Youthful offenders may be experimenters or persisters, which suggests to the developmental criminologist a need for longitudinal research.
- Developmental and life-course criminology is an integration of psychological, sociological, and biological explanations.

## KEY TERMS

ability (g)
adolescent-limited (AL) offenders
associative learning
authority-conflict pathway
behaviorism
career criminals
classical conditioning
cognitive learning theory
conceptual learning
covert pathway
criminal career
criminal personality theory
criminal-propensity thesis
cumulative continuity
desistance
developmental criminology
developmental psychology
expectancy theory
experimental psychology
experimenter type
extraversion
feeblemindedness

instrumental conditioning
IQ score
late-onset offenders
life-course persistent (LCF) offenders
modeling theory
negative punishment
negative reinforcement
neurotic extravert
neuroticism
observational learning theory
onset
operant conditioning
overt pathway
persister type
positive punishment
positive reinforcement
psychotic extravert
psychoticism
trajectories
transitory events
turning points

## CRITICAL REVIEW QUESTIONS

1. What is the connection between IQ testing and eugenics?

2. What are criticisms of the connection between low IQ and crime?

3. What is the connection between learning theory and behaviorism?

4. How might low intelligence influence criminal behavior? Why is this linkage a poor theoretical explanation?

5. What are the ties between early IQ testing and the bio-anthropological theories of the late nineteenth and early twentieth centuries?

6. Can you think of a way to create definitive links between intelligence and crime?

7. Do you believe that we should treat law violators with very low IQs differently from those who fully appreciate the nature of their illegal acts? Why or why not?

8. How does behaviorism explain criminal behavior? What are the criticisms of behaviorism's ties to crime and delinquency?

9. What specific part or element of behaviorism is its strongest contribution to crime theory? What is its weakest part or element?

10. How does behavior theory differ from psychoanalytic theory?

11. Explain the difference between a reinforcement and a punishment?

12. What is the basic view of cognitive behavior theory?

13. How can a process called modeling reinforce human behavior?

14. Explain the conflict between the criminal propensity position and the criminal career position? What grew out of each position?

15. Is life-course criminology sociological? If so, what is its role in understanding developmental criminology?

16. What is the contribution of developmental psychology to developmental and life-course criminology?

# Structural Theories

## LEARNING OBJECTIVES

- The social-ecological roots of social disorganization, an outlook on criminality with practical implications

- Society's formal structure provides unique insights into all behavior, including crime and deviance

- The theories used by criminologists to understand the crime and delinquency of groups called subcultures

- In the twentieth century, sociological theories shaped local and national policies, and these ideas still intrigue twenty-first century criminologists and policy makers

# Introduction

One way to look at crime is to step away from individual criminal acts and specific criminals and look at the range—breadth and depth—of crime and criminality across an entire sociopolitical area or community. Crime becomes part of the "big-picture," a macro-sociological orientation in which society and social processes hold the key to understanding criminality. If we wish to understand crime, we must recognize society's role in shaping the attitudes, orientations and behavior of its members, only some of whom are criminals. That is not to say that criminals are excused from responsibility because society "caused" them to commit crime. Society is not "blamed" for crime—crime emerges from the social cauldron found in some areas of the modern city.

A macro-sociological orientation focuses on social structure and social processes, exploring large scale populations, broad social trends, and social systems.

This chapter introduces two macro-sociological crime perspectives. First, social ecology employs the ecological model as a social lens through which to view a city's crime patterns. In this context, sociologists study all of the interrelated social and physical component parts of a community in which crime is an endemic problem, one that seemingly cannot be eradicated. Crime becomes a social phenomenon that exists apart from that community's current residents, and it continues long after they are gone and replaced by new residents. Second, structural functionalism stresses that every element in society is either part of the solution or part of the problem. When social conditions change dramatically, crime and other forms of social disorder can result.

Culture plays a significant role in the operation of both macro-sociological perspectives. **Culture** refers to a society's beliefs and moral values. Not everyone in a modern pluralistic society is equally committed to the same set of cultural prescriptive and proscriptive norms, beliefs, and values. This statement is especially true of the members of what are called subcultures, a topic to which we return later in this chapter. For their part, social ecologists view culture as a driving force in both the various manifestations of crime in a community and the mechanism by which it is transmitted from one generation to the next; structural functionalists see cracks in the integrity of a society's culture as creating conditions conducive to the emergence of crime, delinquency, and other forms of social disorder.

A pluralistic society is one where there are many different systems of beliefs—moral, religious, political, and social—as well as many different racial, ethnic, and political groups; conflict on some level is almost inevitable.

We begin our examination of sociological explanations with the ecological approach of the Chicago School, which itself was instrumental in founding U.S. criminology.

# Crime and Social Ecology

Early in the twentieth century, Robert Ezra Park (b.1864–d.1944) proposed a parallel between human societies and plant and animal kingdoms, one encompassing the principles of ecology. **Ecology** is the branch of biology that studies the relationships between organisms and their environment. To understand plant or animal life, one must master plant or animal ecology. Similarly, to achieve insights into human life, one must focus on human ecology.

Using the multicultural and racially diverse city of Chicago as a social laboratory, Park and his University of Chicago colleagues (Park, Burgess and McKenzie 1984) explored the city's "natural areas" where vastly different types of people lived. Ernest Burgess (b.1886–d.1966), one of Park's colleagues, divided Chicago into five **concentric zones** (giving it a bull's eye-like appearance) differentiating each zone according to land use, population types, and other physical, economic, and social characteristics. Burgess referred to the central business district as Zone I. Zone II surrounded the industrial and business base, which Burgess described as an **interstitial area,** a slum area with high levels of social deterioration. Zone II was the first home for most urban immigrants. Moving outward, the next area was Zone III, home to the city's working class, where living costs were higher and housing was better. Two characteristics distinguished Zone IV residents from those in Zone III: higher incomes and smaller families. Arrival in Zone V, the commuter's zone, signified economic success.

Over several decades in the early twentieth century, the inner-city community began to decline as an effective social control agent, while the interstitial zone exhibited few characteristics of a neighborhood and had little social cohesion. These inner-city slums had high concentrations of social ills (e.g., crime, poverty, illiteracy, mental illness, and alcoholism). They also had the highest levels of what Park and Burgess called **social disorganization,** defined as "any disturbance, disruption, conflict, or lack of consensus within a social group or given society which affects established social habits of behavior, social institutions, or social controls so as to make relatively harmonious functioning impossible without some significant intermediate adjustments" (Elliott 1967:280–81).

## Social Disorganization Theory and Crime

Clifford R. Shaw (b.1896–d.1957) and Henry D. McKay (b.1899–d.1980) used the social ecology model in general and **social disorganization theory** in particular to study Chicago's geographic distribution of crime and delinquency. They equated social disorganization with weak community controls, which led to geographic areas with high levels of law-violating behavior. They did not view people as inherently bad; rather, the problem was the residential area itself. Once a high crime rate became established, no matter who lived in these areas, the rate remained high. It was as if a crime pathogen had infected the very soil of the community, as one generation of residents passed along a tradition of deviance to successive generations.

The supporters of social disorganization theory view the social structure of a community and not that community's residents as holding the key to understanding its level of crime and delinquency.

To test their claim, Shaw and McKay collected massive amounts of quantitative data on delinquency. They studied court actions, arrest statistics, and commitment rates, which they overlaid on city maps. **The Chicago School** (as this group was known) complemented these numerical studies of crime, including *Juvenile Delinquency and Urban Areas* (Shaw and McKay 1942), with first-person accounts of criminal careers, such as *The Jackroller* (Shaw 1930) and *Brothers in Crime* (Shaw 1938). This latter approach became a significant part of the Chicago tradition of qualitative research. Autobiographies, or life histories, allowed the juveniles to tell their "own stories" as a part of a total case history. The veracity of the life histories was never at issue. As Shaw (1930) observed, "Rationalizations, fabrications, prejudices, exaggerations are quite as valuable as objective descriptions, provided, of course, that these reactions be properly identified" (p. 3).

The Chicagoans painted a picture of chronic social disorganization. They noted that as the distance from the Chicago Loop (the interstitial zone of transition) increased, the rates of crime decreased—whether looking at arrests, commitments, or court processing (Shaw and McKay 1942). Shaw (1938) reported that the community of the "brothers in crime" was neither unique nor unusual. He described it as simply another part of the physical deterioration that characterized the entire area, including the high level of truancy, delinquency, and crime.

A tautology is "circular reasoning, a logical argument constructed in such a way as to repeat the same idea twice, generally using slightly different words.

Three measurement problems plagued early tests of social disorganization theory. First, criminologists dismissed the theory as a *tautology* (see chapter 1), since Shaw and McKay's model had few independent measures of social disorganization. If an area was crime-ridden, this alone was evidence of a lack of social controls and social disorganization; socially disorganized areas were crime-ridden. As a result, social scientists began using a different definition: *Social disorganization* is "the capacity of a neighborhood to regulate itself through formal and informal processes of social control" (Bursik 1988:527).

Second, critics also noted the presence of the **ecological fallacy,** which involves making inappropriate *individual*-level inferences from *group*-level data. For example, suppose we find that for 200 communities the extent of participation in civic organizations relates to the level of reported crime. We may commit an ecological fallacy if we state that a given community has a greater likelihood of high crime because rates of participation in civic organizations are low or that increasing participation rates can reduce crime. Basically, what is true for the group may not be true for the individual. This practice has a parallel in auto insurance where a male under the age of 25 pays a higher rate, even if he is a careful driver, because as a group males younger than 25 have more accidents.

Third, obtaining, compiling, and analyzing the macro-level information needed to test social disorganization theory proved a difficult undertaking in an era without computers. The findings from smaller-scale studies, often including only a few neighborhoods, tended to support Shaw and McKay's predictions (Bursik 1988:532). However, questions remain about the validity and reliability of available crime statistics. Even in the 1930s criminologists questioned official statistics (Robison 1936). We do not know the extent to which neighborhood crime and delinquency rates are a consequence of local decision making. For example, one consequence of placing more police in a neighborhood may be more arrests and, therefore, a higher *reported* crime rate.

> Social disorganization theory has been criticized because of methodological issues related to measuring a community's level of social disorganization.

## The Legacy of Social Disorganization Theory

The Chicago School's work had several long-term effects on criminology. First, their efforts suggested important ideas about how the culture of crime passed from one generation to the next. Second, an entire approach to crime reduction, called environmental criminology, owes a major intellectual debt to social ecology. Third, during the 1980s, a new generation of criminologists rediscovered social disorganization theory and placed it in a more contemporary community context. Finally, in the twenty-first century criminologists began to use parts of social disorganization to explain the "disadvantage" experienced by residents of certain neighborhoods. Our look at this legacy begins with the cultural transmission thesis.

*Cultural Transmission.*    Two key findings reported by Shaw and McKay set the stage for later **cultural transmission theories.** First, Shaw and McKay (1972:174) described socially disorganized neighborhoods as brimming with attitudes and values conducive to delinquency and crime, particularly organized crime, which provided pathways to adult crime. Shaw and McKay saw *cultural transmission* as a general process whereby one generation conveys to the next various elements of its culture, from language to religion, and, in this case, crime and delinquency. They further suggested that conflict was inevitable in the mix of cultures found in Chicago. The values of the larger, more conventional society may have held little meaning for the youthful residents of these inner-city areas. The emergent cultural transmission theories, which include Edwin H. Sutherland's differential association theory (chapter 7), owe a great debt to the work of the Chicagoans. Ronald L. Akers' social structure social learning theory (chapter 7) uses the idea of differential social organization of the neighborhood of residence as a key to understanding why we find crime in certain areas and how the propensity for criminal activity is passed from one generation to the next. Moreover, the culture conflict described by the Chicagoans strongly influenced later conflict theorists (chapter 9), especially Thorsten Sellin. The views of the Chicago School led to efforts designed to break the crime link from one generation to the next: community-based organizations and the establishment of community centers promoting prosocial values.

Second, Shaw and McKay (1972:172) viewed the community as a source of divergent and often contradictory messages, including the following: children should obey laws, even if their parents and other adults do not; crime does not pay, but sometimes it does; people should obey the law, unless it runs counter to what their local neighborhood expects of them. How could society expect youth living in these environs to be anything but confused? Sutherland and Akers (see chapter 7) attempted to provide answers to these and other related questions.

***Environmental Criminology.*** An innovative approach to crime prevention discounts the usual variables such as poverty, broken families, and inadequate education. Beginning in the 1960s, social ecologists connected crime to land use. Social activist and journalist Jane Jacobs (b.1916–d.2006) theorized about the connection between the use of residential and commercial land. In analyzing the quality of interactions along residential streets, Jacobs (1961) noted that interaction between residents increased surveillance, which, in turn, increased safety and reduced crime. The diversity of land use, especially the establishment of commercial use buildings close to residential housing, was the key to understanding high crime levels. When property owners used their land strictly for commercial purposes, they essentially abandoned their property for long periods, creating opportunities for crime. This was the beginning of *environmental criminology*. Proponents of this approach study crime and criminals by looking at: (1) the specific and unique places where crime is likely to exist, and (2) the ways that individuals, groups, and even organizations respond to the perceived and actual threats at these locations.

In a 1972 work entitled *Defensible Space: Crime Prevention Through Urban Design*, architect and city planner Oscar Newman (b.1935–d.2004) coined the term **defensible space**, which he defined as "a residential environment whose physical characteristics—building layout and site plan—function to allow inhabitants themselves to become the key agents in ensuring their own security" (Newman 1975:4). He saw defensible space as having four elements. First, **territoriality** means that one's home is a valued possession to be protected. Second, **natural surveillance** reflects the residents' ability to keep a close watch over the area. Third, **image** refers to the capacity of an area's physical design to impart a sense of security for residents and a barrier against potential "invaders." Finally, **milieu** addresses those other features that might influence security, such as the proximity of a park or shopping mall (Newman 1972:50). Newman saw the physical design of an area as enhancing or inhibiting the inhabitants' feelings of control and sense of responsibility. At about the same

Environmental criminology includes the observation and measurement of crime and victimization in certain locations, along with how those working and living at those locations respond to illegal activities.

time, C. Ray Jeffery (b.1921–d.2007), in *Crime Prevention through Environmental Design* (1971), expressed the idea that physical design, combined with high levels of citizen involvement, could make an area more resistant to criminals. Jeffery also advocated for a more effective criminal justice system—one that emphasized police effectiveness in detecting and arresting criminals as well as an equally effective and efficient court and corrections system.

Contrary to what Newman believed, however, researchers have reported that we cannot rely on physical factors alone to preserve the local order and promote feelings of security. Rather, territoriality tends to provide more insights into crime and fear than do the remaining defensible space features (Taylor, Gottfredson, and Brower 1984). For example, Gerald Suttles (1968) used territoriality to study "defended neighborhoods" as recognized ecological niches in which inhabitants form cohesive groups and seal themselves off through a forbidding reputation. A reputation for territoriality, and not necessarily the neighborhood's physical qualities, provided effective crime control, a point amplified in box 6.1.

*Refining Social Disorganization.* During the 1980s, Robert J. Sampson (b.1963–) and W. Byron Groves (b.1953–d.1990) developed a community-level version of social disorganization. Besides economic status, ethnic heterogeneity, residential mobility, family disruption, and

---

### Box 6.1    Consider This: Does It Matter Who Provides Guardianship?

In the Italian section of New York's Greenwich Village "street corner boys" traditionally enforced the social order, making the streets safe. The formidable reputation of the local organized crime figures backed their self-appointed role. In one Brooklyn neighborhood, a Lucchese crime family stronghold, informal social control, devoid of the restraints of due process, provided justice that was swift and final: On a dark night, a man following a woman did not realize that he was being watched. Several large men foiled his attempt at a knifepoint robbery by quickly carrying him up a set of stairs. An observer recalls: "I could make out the small roof wall on the front of the building—it was made of brick—and then I saw the guy launched right over it into the air. He hung there for just a second, flailing arms like a broken helicopter, and then he came down hard and splattered all over the street" (Pileggi 1990:40).

As ex-FBI agent Joe Pistone (2004) notes: "Neighborhoods that are dominated by wiseguys are considered to be under the protection of these wiseguys. There are far fewer robberies, rapes, or muggings in wiseguy neighborhoods than even the safest precincts of the city" (p. 76). Moreover, that would extend to some Chicago suburbs, where unsanctioned drug sales resulted in mutilated corpses. Despite their effectiveness, no one has seriously suggested we turn over neighborhood crime control to the organized crime families or the Hell's Angels, but in Japan, a *quid quo pro* policy leaves effective control over street crime in entertainment areas to the strict and often violent local organized crime groups called *yakuza*.

*Sources:* Abadinsky (2013); Pileggi (1990); Pistone (2004); Tricarico (1984).

urbanization, Sampson and Groves (1989) tied community social disorganization to the strength of social network systems in those communities. These systems include *informal controls* (e.g., friendship ties), *formal controls* (e.g., participation in religious or civic groups), and the *collective supervision* related to troublesome local concerns (e.g., youth groups). In sum, neighborhoods that "have their act together" also have less crime:

> When residents meet with each other and interact, they form social ties or acquaintanceships. In well-functioning neighborhoods, there will be a large number of social ties between residents; while in poorly functioning neighborhoods there will be a lot fewer of them. . . . Social ties are the glue that helps bind neighborhood residents together. . . . Residents living in neighborhoods with close social ties tend to watch out for each other and their property. (Uchida, et al. 2014: 3)

Paul Bellair (1997) explored serious crime rates in 60 urban neighborhoods, examining the level and type of social interaction found in each neighborhood. He reported that neighbors' getting together once a year or more had the strongest positive impact on burglary, motor vehicle theft, and robbery rates. This finding suggests that residents' general willingness to provide supervision and guardianship in the neighborhood is important: know your neighbors. Sampson and Groves (1989) found that communities in Great Britain with few friendship networks, unsupervised teenage groups, and low organizational participation had disproportionately high crime and delinquency rates.

According to Anthony A. Braga and Ronald V. Clarke (2014), streets and not neighborhoods should be the unit of investigation when looking for a connection between social disorganization measures and crime. Why, for example, do certain streets have a higher concentration of crime than other streets in the same neighborhood? In their study of Seattle, David Weisburd, Elizabeth Groff, and Sue-Ming Yang (2014) found that one percent of streets accounted for 23 percent of city crime. They looked at indicators of social disorganization (litter, weeds, graffiti, dilapidated homes, junk, abandoned cars) as well as the number of high-risk juveniles (motivated offenders), suitable targets (workers and residents), and easy accessibility (nearby highways). Social disorganization explained the crime discrepancy between streets in the same neighborhood.

## Social Disorganization in the Twenty-First Century

Over 100 years after its introduction, social disorganization theory continues to influence criminology. Consider, for example, the idea of **concentrated disadvantage,** whereby certain geographic areas are characterized as creating living conditions for residents that reduce the chances of success or positive life outcomes. Such conditions are often described as neighborhood disadvantage (Sampson, Morenoff and Gannon-Rowley 2002; Topalli et al. 2014). Growing up in such neighborhoods has both long-term and short-term implications. Researchers report that even when residents remove themselves from the neighborhood, they do not entirely escape the impact of exposure to concentrated disadvantage, including the manifestations of a wide range of mental and physical conditions, psychological adjustments, antisocial attitudes, and engagement in criminal conduct (Sampson 2012, 2013).

Sampson has also studied how social control is achieved in neighborhoods lacking community ties, ones characterized by high levels of social disadvantage (Sampson 2002; Sampson and Raudenbush 2001; Morenoff, Sampson and Raudenbush 2001). The mechanism at work is **collective efficacy**, which refers to the ability of a neighborhood as a whole to control the behavior of individuals and groups living and working in that area, thereby creating a safe and orderly environment in which crime, violence and other undesirable behaviors are less likely to occur (Sampson, Raudenbush and Earls 1997). It is this "collective capacity for social action, even if rooted in weak personal ties" that may yield the strongest insights into often observed variations in neighborhood crime rates (Morenoff et al. 2001: 542).

Collective efficacy, which mediates between concentrated disadvantage and crime, is present or absent depending on a community's ability to exercise informal control, as well as its collective capacity for action (Sampson et al. 1997; Wikström and Sampson 2003). Areas with high levels of concentrated disadvantage are typically low in collective efficacy. Collective efficacy can even overcome a community's low levels of personal and social ties, an idea that contradicts the "urban village" concept so closely tied to traditional social disorganization theory (Sampson 1999).

Clearly, the final word on social disorganization theory's legacy has not yet been written. During the second decade of the twenty-first century, revised social disorganization has been linked with varying degrees of success to campus property crime, homicide investigation outcomes, and the consequences of gang membership, to name a few (cf., Barton, Jensen and Kaufman 2010; Fox, Lane and Akers 2010; Papachristos, Hureau and Braga 2013; Regoeczi and Jarvis 2013). Research on neighborhood disadvantage and collective efficacy may call into question social disorganization's urban village concept, but central elements of social disorganization continue to inform criminologists. The "criminology of place," which can be described as a law of crime concentration at certain physical locations, is now a well-established and highly studied phenomenon (Weisburd et al. 2014).

> Social disorganization's notion of the "urban village" suggests that the residents of a given neighborhood must rely on each other for personal and private needs, including crime control and, further, that disorganized areas lack this coalescing and crime-fighting force.

## Crime and Social Structure

Beginning in the late nineteenth century sociologists called *structural functionalists* explored the ways in which different parts of the community interacted with each other. While the term structural functionalist may sound daunting, its meaning is rather simple: the continued existence of a social structure such as the family, or a school system, indicates that it is functional; that is, it provides a continuous benefit to society. In the Darwinian sense, a social structure that provides no benefit will not survive.

Structural functionalists view society as consisting of various institutions and groups that, given their constant contact, shift, move, and alter their impact on one other. The result is a unified social system. A given practice or tradition persists over time because it is functional—that is, it provides something beneficial to society. Anything that threatens to destroy society is dysfunctional and, therefore, likely to cease or be eliminated. We might ask, therefore, what is the benefit of the continued existence of crime? In the absence of crime, those employed by or writing and teaching about criminal justice would need to find other employment, as would locksmiths, alarm installers, and related workers. Absent crime, how many TV programs would remain? More to the point, the presence of criminals in society helps remind the rest of us that there are limits to the kinds of behavior that are lawful and acceptable, as well as what happens to those who fail to abide by the established limits. Crime—and by extension criminals—play important roles in any "civilized" society, an idea first articulated over 100 years ago.

### Anomie and Society

The French sociologist Emile Durkheim (b.1858–d.1917) considered structural elements to be central to any analysis of societal ills. As a society develops, Durkheim (1961[1925]) claimed, unstable relationships evolve. More sophisticated societies experience greater difficulties in socializing members, promoting a feeling of "us." It helps to have a "them" in the equation. Cohesiveness requires a unifying mechanism, the state actively promotes devotion to country—in place of family or tribe— through symbols such as flags, oaths, and anthems. The state's emphasis on rule and laws, along with the processes and institutions for their enforcement, is also crucial. Cohesiveness is further promoted by the existence of criminals—the good (us) against the bad (them).

In Durkheim's view, crime and deviance were caused by unrestrained ambition, let loose by disturbances in the social equilibrium that held society and its members in check.

Can a valued behavior such as ambition be the cause of crime? For Durkheim, the answer is yes: unrestrained ambition—individualism at its worst—causes deviance. How much wealth is "enough"? The absence of a societal goalpost can generate deviant adaptations, such as corporate crime, in pursuit of "success" that is unlimited and open-ended. Societal disturbances or transitions, even ones that seem beneficial, could upset the balance and alter or even diminish the community's ability to control social behavior. The problem centers on disturbances in the collective order or **social equilibrium** that set people adrift; patterns are upset and people no longer have the comfort of knowing their place in society. When this happens, society cannot immediately improvise an acceptable new balance (in biological terms, homeostasis). It takes time for the collective conscience to reclassify people and things, to create a new social equilibrium. In the interim, unbridled individualism, absent social restraints on behavior, becomes the norm, as old values and norms become irrelevant.

Such disturbances are problematic, whether they are negative (e.g., an economic depression or failure in war) or positive (e.g., economic prosperity or success in war). Durkheim called the resulting societal condition **anomie,** meaning a relative absence or confusion of norms and rules. For Durkheim, anomie explained deviance in times of war and rapid industrialization and urbanization. The breakdown in social controls throws many people's lives out of whack. The society devolves to a condition of "normlessness," or anomie, a feeling of being adrift without customary social guideposts or constraints on behavior. Readjustments eventually restore social controls, homeostasis returns; until that time, however, there is a period of time during which society can expect high levels of deviance.

While Durkheim's original theory is rarely tested, his concept of anomie has been used to examine modernization, industrialization, and crime on the global stage (Howard, Newman and Pridemore 2000; Zhao and Cao 2010). Anomie also provides insights into changes in crime rates within certain political regimes, as has been observed in an increasingly Westernized and capitalized China with subsequent changes to its society (Cao 2007). Durkheim's **anomie theory** predicts increases in crime and other social disturbances as significant social, economic, or political changes occur in a country.

## Anomie and Crime

Durkheim envisioned entire nations, cultures and societies being forever changed by the anomic state. His work focused on large-scale destabilizing forces, ones that upset the social equilibrium with often catastrophic consequences. Later generations of sociologists and criminologists took his ideas and fashioned them into theories that explained exactly how anomie produced criminal tendencies. The first to make this leap from the macro-level forces to individual reactions was Merton.

***Strain Theory: The Americanization of Anomie.***    Robert K. Merton (b.1910–d.2003) "Americanized" anomie in 1938. Writing during the Great Depression, he argued that "good" can cause "evil." In this case, unrestrained ambition was a prime cause of crime in the United States. Merton (1938) argued that U.S. society considers economic success as an absolute value without equal; moreover, the resulting pressure to achieve economic success eliminates effective social constraints on the means employed to this end. He referred to this as "pathological materialism."

The resulting "end-justifies-the-means" doctrine becomes a guiding tenet for action when cultural structure unduly exalts the end and social organization unduly limits possible avenues to approved means.

Merton viewed adherence to "American culture" and its stress on economic success as generally equal across society, while access to **legitimate opportunities** for economic success was restricted. Specifically, legitimate opportunities are far more available among advantaged classes and far less available among the disadvantaged. According to Merton, anomie results when people confront a contradiction between culturally defined economic goals and societally restricted means of achieving economic success. Normlessness arises out of this contradiction or *strain* between goals and means—hence the name **strain theory**.

How do individuals respond to this **anomic trap**? Most simply "grin and bear it"—that is, they make the best of the situation and suffer in silence. These **conformists** accept both the goals (ends) and the means, and they strive to achieve success within the rules even if this necessarily limits their goals. Others become **ritualists**, rigidly adhering to and accepting their station in life. Three adaptations to anomie, however, have implications for criminology, including:

- **Rebels** reject the goals and attempt to overthrow the existing social order and its cultural values, joining a revolutionary group or a countercultural commune, for example.
- **Retreatists** abandon all attempts to reach conventional social goals in favor of a deviant adaptation (e.g., abusing alcohol and drugs).
- **Innovators** use illegal means to gain societally defined success goals. Routine criminality, however, cannot gain economic success. Innovation, then, refers to skilled criminality exhibited by professional criminals and members of organized crime.

Critics questioned Merton's emphasis on economic success. Ruth Kornhauser (1978) reported that although anomic theory predicts that delinquents will have higher aspirations than expectations, they often possess low expectations *and* low aspirations. Her assessment: Delinquents do not want or expect much, and so they do not experience the anomic trap. Initially, anomie was not viewed as an explanation for crime by elites, including white-collar and corporate crime, or nonutilitarian crime, such as vandalism and violent offenses. Recent thinking about anomie suggests that it exists even in the corporate world (Passas 1990).

***Anomie and Delinquent Subcultures.***   Albert K. Cohen (b.1918–d.2014) applied Merton's theory to subcultural responses to the anomic trap. A **subculture** is an identifiable subgroup within a larger culture, whose values may differ from those of the larger culture. Cohen (1955:13) focused on lower-class delinquent subcultures as constituting "a way of life that has somehow become traditional among certain groups in Amer-

*Legitimate opportunities represent the lawful means to obtain desired socially defined goals.*

*Merton Americanized Durkheim's ideas about the influence of anomie and applied it to the economic conditions of Depression-era society, especially its lower-class communities, focusing on the different ways individuals experiencing the strain respond to the contradiction between economic success and limitations on how it can be achieved.*

ican society. These groups are the boys' gangs that flourish most conspic-
uously in the 'delinquent neighborhoods' of our larger American cities."
In this context, gangs are primarily male lower-class phenomena and status depends on repudiation of the mainstream culture's conventional
norms. No physical attributes distinguish a gang boy from a Boy Scout.
The difference is in the culture each endorses.

Cohen's **reaction formation thesis** suggested that delinquent subcultures take the larger culture's norms (ones he described as middle-
class values) and turn them upside down in a process psychoanalysts call
reaction formation. Certain unresolved destructive urges remain, as well
as conflict with the internalized middle-class norms. The delinquent's
conduct, which exhibits little regard for profit or personal gain, is correct
"by the standards of his subculture, precisely because it is wrong by the
norms of the larger culture" (Cohen 1955:26, 28). Rather, the goal is status. According to Cohen, delinquents see society's rules as not merely
something to evade but also to *flout*. Doing so with active spite, malice,
contempt, ridicule, challenge, and defiance allows delinquents to gain status with their peers.

The lower-class male delinquent (Cohen wrote about delinquent
boys) is at a distinct disadvantage as he progresses into adulthood. Certain cultural characteristics are necessary to achieve success in our society, and the upbringing of a middle-class boy is more likely to develop
these characteristics, such as the ability to postpone gratification, skills
for achievement, industry and thrift, control of physical aggression, and
cultivation of manners and politeness.

Walter B. Miller (b.1920–d.2004) argued that street-corner adolescents in lower-class communities *do not flout* conventional middle-class
norms. Instead, they conform to behavior defined as acceptable by *their*
community. The delinquent subculture, according to Miller's (1958)
**lower-class culture thesis**, did not rise in conflict with the larger, middle-class culture; it does not deliberately violate middle-class norms.
Rather, lower-class culture is simply *different*. The focal characteristics
are (1) **trouble,** law-violating behavior; (2) **toughness,** physical prowess
and daring; (3) **smartness,** the ability to "con" and act shrewdly; (4)
**excitement,** a tendency to seek thrills, risk, and danger; (5) **fate,** the idea
of being lucky or unlucky; and (6) **autonomy,** the desire to be independent from external control.

Trouble for men often involves fights, police encounters, or sexual
promiscuity; trouble for women frequently means sexual activities with
disadvantageous consequences, including rape and unwanted pregnan-
cies. For both genders, the excessive consumption of alcohol plays a facil-
itative or enabling role. Miller contended that members of the lower class
rarely seek to avoid troublesome behavior based on a sense of commitment to social order norms or laws. Instead, they try to avoid any negative

consequences associated with engaging in such behavior. Although trouble-producing behavior is a source of status, trouble avoidance is necessary to forestall legal complications. Individuals may, in an attempt to resolve this conflict legitimately, become part of highly disciplined organizations, such as the military or law enforcement.

Miller emphasized that lower-class attachments to peers and commitments to their norms prevent lower-class youth from moving into middle-class (i.e. conventional) society. The larger society stifles their upward mobility unless they can break free. Because the lower class does the dirty work of an industrial society, members are encouraged to indulge their whims in liquor, sex, and violence. Crime and delinquency are the costs of a smooth-running industrial machine.

Richard A. Cloward (b.1926–d.2001) and Lloyd E. Ohlin (b.1918–d.2008) integrated Merton's strain theory with the Chicago School's ideas about the cultural transmission of criminality and Albert Cohen's work on negativistic subcultures, creating **differential opportunity theory**. Cloward and Ohlin (1960) explain how delinquent subcultures arise, develop various law-violating ways of life, and persist or change over time. They distinguish three types:

1. *Criminal subculture.* Gang activities devoted to utilitarian criminal pursuits (e.g., racketeering).

2. *Conflict subculture.* Gang activities devoted to violence and destructive acting out as a way of gaining status.

3. *Retreatist subculture.* Activities in which drug abuse is the primary focus.

Each of these subcultural adaptations arises out of a different set of social circumstances or opportunities. Cloward and Ohlin (1960) state that the dilemma of many lower-class people is that they are unable to locate alternative avenues to success or goals: "Delinquent subcultures, we believe, represent specialized modes of adaptation to this problem of adjustment" (p. 107). The criminal and conflict subcultures provide illegal avenues to success through illicit income or violence, while the retreatist "anticipates defeat and now seeks to escape from the burden of the future" (p. 107). Criminal behavior is not viewed as an individual endeavor but as part of a collective adaptation. Cloward and Ohlin further note that

> many lower-class adolescents experience desperation born of the certainty that their position in the economic structure is relatively fixed and immutable—a desperation made all the more poignant by their exposure to a cultural ideology in which failure to orient oneself upward is regarded as a moral defect and failure to become mobile as proof of it. (pp. 106–107)

Cloward and Ohlin point out that the societal distribution of both legitimate *and* illegitimate means of success is not equal. Failing with legitimate opportunity structures, despondent youth cannot simply turn to a wellspring of **illegitimate opportunities**. For the average adolescent, a career in professional or organized crime can be as difficult to attain as a legitimate career. Cloward and Ohlin understood that both systemic injustice and system blaming occur when youth perceive little opportunity for success, when they see a discrepancy between formal ideology— expectation of economic success—and unfair practices that deny them the ability to achieve this goal. The former may promise equality of access, while the latter reflects the realities of prejudice and discrimination.

> The societal distribution of both legitimate *and* illegitimate means of success is not equal.

Cloward and Ohlin point to the **double failures,** people who are unsuccessful in both legitimate *and* illegitimate pursuits, likely to populate and repopulate our prisons. They suggested that such people are "more vulnerable than others" to retreatism, including joining hedonistic, drug-using subcultures. Retreatism may also manifest itself in other ways. Failed criminals may unconsciously retreat to prisons because of their inability to succeed using either legitimate or illegitimate means. Cloward and Ohlin's (1960:184) work, however, recognizes that some double failures adopt conventional lower-class lifestyles, becoming conformists.

> Double failures help us understand why our prisons are so full of people who cannot seem to succeed either as law-abiding citizens or as criminals.

***General Strain Theory.*** Robert Agnew (b.1953–) expanded the goals of American youth to include short-term aspirations such as popularity with the opposite (or same) sex, good school grades, and athletic achievements; this helps to explain middle-class strain. For adults, the failure to achieve expected goals causes strain that, in some persons, leads to anger, resentment, and rage—emotional states that can precipitate criminal behavior (Agnew 1985, 1992). In **general strain theory**, Agnew suggests that social injustice or inequity might be at the root of strain. A sense of being treated unfairly (others are the source of adversity) and not simply an inability to reach goals creates strain. Some children sense that the deck is stacked against them and that there is no reason to even try to be "normal" or law-abiding. Delinquency, then, becomes a natural reaction to the stresses of adolescence, and the source of that stress becomes far less important than the injustices embodied in the stress itself. Agnew's focus, then, was not on Durkheim's macro-sociological forces or even the mid-range strains described by Merton and the anomie-tradition gang theorists. Rather, it was Agnew's belief that we can understand anomie by adopting a micro-level perspective that is social-psychological in orientation.

The difference between traditional strain theory and general strain theory is crucial to understanding Agnew's insight into the process. The imagery in traditional Mertonian strain theory is like a person running *toward* something—in most cases, societally defined success goals, such as money, fame, cars, and jewelry. Agnew's general strain theory, in contrast, suggests that some children are running *away from* something, such as undesired parental punishments or negative relationships at school. Thus, adolescents are *"pressured into delinquency by the negative affective*

Whereas Mertonian anomie theory links criminality to the employment of illegal means to obtain a valued status or object, Agnew's general strain theory suggests that delinquency ensues when young people seek to avoid an undesired person, place, or thing.

*states—most notably anger and related emotions—that often result from negative relationships*" (Agnew 1992:49; emphasis in original). The fact that Agnew has provided a social-psychological explanation of the emotional condition most likely to precipitate delinquency resulting from general strains moves this form of anomie theory further from both Durkheim's macro-level and Merton's mid-level explanations.

Agnew identified three major types of strain:

1. *Strain as the failure to achieve positively valued goals.* This form of failure includes a series of subtypes, including (1) strain as a disconnection between aspirations (goals) and expectations, irrespective of whether those goals are long in the future and idealized in form or more near term; (2) strain as a result of a gap between expectations and actual achievements, which can lead to emotional responses such as anger and resentment; and (3) strain as the conflict between just or fair out-comes and actual outcomes, meaning that the youth feels that he or she has put a great deal into the effort, but, unlike others, has not receive a reward that is commensurate with that effort.

2. *Strain as the removal or loss of something valued by the individual.* This type of strain follows the actual or anticipated loss of something valued (e.g., the loss of a close friend, death of a relative, or suspension from school, if school is valued.)

3. *Strain as the presence of a negative stimuli.* Delinquency may follow when a youth attempts to avoid or escape what he or she defines as a negative situation, ends or reduces the source of that which they wish to avoid, or seeks revenge against the source. This form of delinquency captures the essence of the movement away from something—in this case a negative stimulus that the child wishes to avoid, sometimes at any cost. Agnew included child abuse, general victimization, and adverse school experiences among the negative stimuli likely to elicit a delinquent response from the child.

In all its major forms, actual and anticipated strains may create a *predisposition* for delinquency or function as a *situational event* that instigates a delinquent act. These strains are, in Agnew's opinion, so strong that they can overcome the effects of other forces in a youth's life, such as the labels applied to children by society and the presence of delinquent or prosocial peers.

As youth attempt to avoid problems caused by the strain, four factors predispose them to delinquency (Agnew 1992:61). First, their normative coping strategies are at their absolute limit. Such children simply do not believe that they have any alternatives, and this state of frustration is likely to create additional negative emotions, including anger and resentment. Second, chronic strain lowers the threshold for tolerance of adversity, meaning that youth are unable to deal with increasing levels of discomfort. Third, repeated or chronic strain may change anger and resentment into outright hostility and avoidance. Finally, chronic strain increases the likelihood that the youngster will be prone to fits of anger that focus the blame for bad outcomes on others, particularly towards those they see as the source of the perceived injustices and against those peers who are seen as being rewarded inappropriately. Delinquency, then, becomes almost a "natural" consequence of the strains in the lives of some youth.

Researchers provide a measure of support for Agnew's theorizing. It appears that general strain theory's *desire for autonomy* (also stated by Miller above) has a direct effect on school-based delinquency but not on other types of delinquency; the schools themselves may be the source of many of the perceived negative strains (Chen 2010). In terms of race and delinquency, Agnew's theory has also provided insights into why race-based insults and slights, including outright discrimination, lead to anger and depression in Black males (Simons et al. 2003) and Hispanics (Perez, Jennings, and Gover 2008). Other negative consequences of general strains, such as alcohol abuse, also function as predicted by general strain theory, irrespective of the youth's race (Akins, Smith, and Mosher 2010). General strain theory seems to perform better when tested than does classic strain theory (Akers and Sellers 2013:192).

## SUMMARY

- Culture represents the sum total of a society's beliefs and moral values, including its law attitudes toward crime and criminals.
- Social ecologists see culture as a driving force in both crime in a community and the mechanisms by which it is passed from one generation of that community's residents to the next.
- Structural functionalists key on breakdowns in a society's culture that create conditions leading to crime, delinquency, and other forms of social disorder.
- The Chicago School of social ecology identified concentric zones emanating from the central business district of Chicago; the slum area or interstitial zone was ripe with crime and misconduct.
- Park and Burgess, two members of the Chicago School, suggested that a city's crime and delinquency rates were related to the presence of social disorganization in the local community.
- Shortly after it emerged, social disorganization theory was largely dismissed for being a tautology, subject to the ecological fallacy, and nearly untestable because of the difficulties in obtaining the data necessary to complete such a test.
- The legacy of the Chicago School's social disorganization theory includes the cultural transmission thesis, which gave rise to learning

theories of crime as well as environmental criminology that includes the key concept of defensible space and its four elements.

- Refinements to social disorganization theory began appearing in the 1980s; local community signposts for combating disorganization and crime include informal controls such as friendship ties, formal controls such as participation in civic groups, and collective supervision of local trouble such as youth groups and gangs.

- The idea that growing up and living in certain areas creates long-standing issues for people, also called concentrated disadvantage, is a modern incarnation of social disorganization theory.

- In the face of crime and other forms of social disorder, disadvantaged neighborhoods must resort to collective efficacy—whereby the entire neighborhood works to control the behavior of residential groups and individuals.

- One meaning of Durkheim's anomie is normlessness, or the feeling of being adrift without customary social guideposts or constraints on behavior.

- The anomic state, where the old ways of doing things no longer seem to apply, is likely to ensue when large-scale changes occur—whether they are to the betterment of the community (e.g., economic prosperity, victory in war) or to its detriment (e.g., economic collapse, defeat in war).

- Disruptions in a collectivity's social equilibrium often translate into crime and delinquency.

- Strain theory represents the Americanization of anomie theory by Merton; it emphasizes that while we all seek the culturally defined trappings of success, society often restricts the legitimate means to obtain them—people may choose criminal or nonconventional means to overcome these barriers.

- Strain theory has been criticized as placing too much emphasis on social class, particularly lower-class responses to society's barriers to legitimate means.

- Cohen's reaction formation thesis, W. B. Miller's lower-class culture thesis, and Cloward and Ohlin's differential opportunity theory are subcultural theories of crime and delinquency that owe a considerable debt to Merton's theory.

- Cloward and Ohlin's theory contributes the idea of limited access to even illegitimate means to achieve success plus the concept of "double failures."

- Agnew's general strain theory, a micro-level anomie offshoot, tells us that youth become delinquent because they feel a sense of social injustice or inequity and are, by their criminal acts, moving away from the source of their injustices.

## KEY TERMS

| | |
|---|---|
| anomic trap | image |
| anomie | innovators |
| anomie theory | interstitial area |
| autonomy | legitimate opportunities |
| Chicago School, the | lower-class culture thesis |
| collective efficacy | milieu |
| concentrated disadvantage | natural surveillance |
| concentric zones | reaction formation thesis |
| conformists | rebels |
| cultural transmission theories | retreatists |
| culture | ritualists |
| defensible space | smartness |
| differential opportunity theory | social disorganization |
| double failures | social disorganization theory |
| ecological fallacy | social equilibrium |
| ecology | strain theory |
| excitement | subculture |
| fate | territoriality |
| general strain theory | toughness |
| illegitimate opportunities | trouble |

## CRITICAL REVIEW QUESTIONS

1. What is the basic assumption of the ecological approach to the study of crime? What are the major criticisms of this approach?

2. What did the Chicago researchers see as the links between a city's physical and social development and its incidence of crime and other social ills?

3. How would you characterize ecological theories in general? Which ones seem to provide the greatest insights into contemporary urban crime problems?

4. How might some neighborhoods that sociologists characterize as disorganized actually be quite well organized?

5. What do you see as social disorganization theory's most significant shortcoming? Explain why you made this selection.

6. What do you think is the greatest strength of environmental criminology? What is its greatest weakness?

7. Social disorganization theory was "redefined" in the late twentieth century. What is this new definition and how does it help us understand the emergence of crime and other forms of problematic conduct in certain neighborhoods?

8. What is "concentrated disadvantage," and what are its ties to social disorganization?

9. How does the term the "urban village" help us understand the operation of collective efficacy as a crime-fighting strategy?

10. How does Durkheim's theory of anomie explain criminal behavior?

11. How did Merton Americanize the theory of anomie?

12. In your opinion, which of Merton's adaptations to the anomic trap poses the greatest threat to a well-ordered society? Why did you pick this one and not one of the others.

13. What is Cloward and Ohlin's greatest contribution to our understanding of the ties between anomie and crime? Explain your selection.

14. According to Cloward and Ohlin, what are the three categories of response to differential opportunity?

15. What is the most important form of anomie theory: Durkheim's anomie theory, Merton's strain theory, or Agnew's general strain theory? Explain your choice.

16. How do the views of Cohen and Miller about delinquent subcultures differ?

17. Support or refute the following statement: "Subcultural versions of anomie theory contribute little to our understanding of crime and delinquency generally."

# Social Process Theories

*LEARNING OBJECTIVES*

- How social processes create or work against crime problems in society
- How offenders learn crime propensities, including the various mechanisms involved in the learning process
- How society's control mechanisms, ranging from individual to group controls, collectively and individually stand as a bulwark against crime propensities
- Various expansions on the social control theme, including effective (and ineffective) parenting and too little self-control

# Introduction

The theories in chapter 6 primarily emphasized large-scale social structural conditions conducive to the creation of crime and the emergence of criminals. The theories in this chapter are also primarily sociological in origin, but they emphasize social processes as causal mechanisms. In this context, then, a **social process** is any identifiable, repetitive pattern of interaction between humans in a group or social context. The term acknowledges that humans are social beings, living and acting in groups. Moreover, the social processes leading to crime, like all social processes, are based on social interactions that occur repeatedly.

A social process is any identifiable, repetitive pattern of interaction between humans in a group or a social context.

Some social process theorists in criminology differ in their views on basic human assumptions. Some contend that social forces produce crime by endorsing or failing to stop the learning mechanism behind criminality—that humans are largely blank slates upon which society "writes" the lessons of life, some of which lead to crime. Other criminological theorists see breakdowns in the control mechanisms associated with social institutions as the chief culprits. In agreement with Classical Criminology's hedonistic view, they see humans as prone to evil. It is up to society—from the family to the schools and legal system—to control the evil inclination. Criminality results when these controls fail.

# Learning Theories

If there are no "born criminals," what explains the presence of criminals among us? Perhaps crime, like reading, writing, and arithmetic is learned behavior. If so, how is crime learned? Edwin Sutherland addressed this question early in the twentieth century.

### Differential Association Theory

Edwin H. Sutherland (b.1883–d.1950) proposed **differential association theory** to explain how criminal behavior is learned. This learning, he argued, requires a close personal relationship between "teachers" and "students." Sutherland did not believe it possible to learn criminal behavior through the mass media (e.g., movies, books, newspapers, or, more recently, television, video gaming, and the Internet). Such mechanisms, he claimed, cannot provide the required social context for learning.

According to Sutherland, criminal behavior ensues when the motives, drives, and rationalizations direct the individual to view the law unfavorably. Sutherland's (1947) Chicago School (chapter 6) roots were showing when he stated:

> In some societies an individual is surrounded by persons who invariably define the legal codes as rules to be observed, while in others he is surrounded by persons whose definitions are favorable to the vio-

lation of legal codes. In our American society, these definitions are usually mixed and consequently we have *culture conflict* in relation to the legal codes. (p. 7, emphasis added)

The conflict, said Sutherland, is between definitions we learn from those close to us that are at odds with the legal codes. The principle of differential association explains how one set of definitions comes to dominate our thinking.

*Defining Differential Association.*    Sutherland's **principle of differential association** maintains that an individual turns to crime when he or she is exposed to an excess of definitions favorable to law violations in contrast to unfavorable ones. These people view crime favorably "because of contacts with criminal patterns and also because of isolation from anticriminal patterns" (Sutherland 1947:8). In other words, a person starts out in balance, and the scale tips in favor of anti- or prosocial behavior based on the weight of associations.

Sutherland observed that such associations vary in terms of frequency, duration, priority, and intensity. **Frequency** and **duration** are "modalities of associations." How often one has these contacts and how long the contacts last are self-explanatory. What Sutherland meant by priority, and especially by intensity, however, has proven to be more problematic for those interested in testing the theory. Sutherland believed that early childhood socialization was critical; we learn many of the most important definitions of "right" and "wrong" as children and hold them throughout our lives. The associations someone has first in life—those with the highest **priority**—may be the most important ones. Sutherland (1947:7) further stated that **intensity** "is not precisely defined but it has to do with such things as the prestige of the source of a criminal or anticriminal pattern and with emotional reactions related to the associations."

In sum, differential association theory views criminal behavior as resulting from the strength (i.e., frequency, duration, priority, and intensity) of an individual's criminal associations and is a cumulative learning process. A balance scale that starts out level provides a metaphor for differential associations. Criminal and noncriminal associations accumulate over time. Criminal activity ensues when the scales reach a tipping point, and definitions favoring law violations tilt the scale toward criminality.

*Measuring Differential Association.*    Shortly after Sutherland's death, criminologists began critiquing his theory. They questioned the theory's claims and its empirical testability. For example, some critics note that it lacks sufficient operationalization for testing. Sutherland failed to operationalize important concepts (e.g., "definitions" and "an excess of definitions"). Secondly, the theory assumes that humans respond exclusively to social stimuli. Sutherland, some critics argue, based the theory on an "oversocialized" view of human beings (Wrong

> The principle of differential association maintains that people become criminals because of an excess of definitions favorable to the violation of law compared to definitions favorable to following the law.

1961) that did not account for personalized motives. Finally, the theory may be inherently tautological. Criminal-norm learning is central, but the theory views behavior as evidence of those norms; independent evidence of learning is often missing in tests of the theory.

Despite assertions that the theory could not be subjected to testing, empirical studies did just that within a decade of his death. The dependent variable for these early studies was nearly always delinquency. As a rule, this body of work supported the principle of differential association as researchers reported that juveniles with delinquent peers also tended to commit—or at least report—more delinquent acts than those who had no such contacts. Later cross-sectional studies also supported Sutherland's basic tenets (Jensen 1972; Tittle, Burke, and Jackson 1986), as did longitudinal studies of drug use (Sellers and Winfree 1990) and experimental evaluations of correctional treatment programs intended to help offenders learn ways of conforming to lawful standards (Andrews 1980; Empey and Erickson 1972).

Sutherland's impact on criminology is undeniable. Besides differential association theory, he authored one of the most successful criminology textbooks in history—with various coauthors it spanned eight decades (from the 1920s to the 1990s). He also inspired later generations of criminologists to consider, as described in box 7.1, exactly what was meant by differential associations.

## Social Learning Theory

Sutherland's emphasis on crime as *learned* behavior led Robert L. Burgess (b.1936–) and Ronald L. Akers (b.1939–) to develop **differential association-reinforcement theory**. Burgess and Akers (1966:140) restated the principle of differential association in operant conditioning terms: "Criminal behavior is a function of norms which are discriminative for criminal behavior, the learning of which takes place when such behavior is more highly reinforced than noncriminal behavior." They also added nonsocial factors to Sutherland's social factors. Burgess and Akers believed the metaphorical scale's balance depended not only on the definitions for or against following the law but also on the level of reinforcement accorded one set of definitions over the others.

Akers' theory fills in the gaps found in Sutherland's theory by adding operant conditioning as the mechanism that explains how learning occurs.

In 1973, Akers renamed the theory as **social learning theory,** an explanation that "has persisted as one of the central theories within criminology" (Bradshaw 2011: 3). Through the final three decades of the twentieth century, social learning was one of the most tested criminological theories (Akers and Sellers 2013; Sellers, Winfree, and Akers 2012). It has also been shown to be one of the most successful theories in the empirical realm (Pratt et al. 2010).

***Defining Social Learning.*** Social learning theory addresses the how, the what, and the where of learning. As for *how,* the answer lies in

**Box 7.1    Consider This: Making Sense of the Differential in Differential Associations**

After his death in 1950, sociologists and criminologists began to rethink Sutherland's theory, suggesting that other forces were at work. Daniel Glaser combined aspects of differential association, control theories, rational choice theory, operant conditioning, and strain theory in his **differential anticipation/expectation theory.** He described three mechanisms by which anticipations shape behavior:

1. Procriminal and anticriminal "social bonds," or punishments and rewards for law-violating behavior that conform to the expectations of others.

2. Differential learning, by which one is exposed to the attitudes, orientations, and behavior associated with the gratifications of criminal and noncriminal activities.

3. The perceived opportunities for success or failure in criminal pursuits.

Glaser's theory predicts a person will commit a crime if the expectations of gratification derived from the three mechanisms above exceed the unfavorable anticipations identified by those sources. Engaging in a crime depends on the consequences expected, prior learning experience, and the quality of the bonds established with others.

C. Ray Jeffery's **differential reinforcement theory** ties psychological learning processes (i.e., behaviorism and operant conditioning) to differential association theory: "criminal behavior is operant behavior; that is, it is maintained by the changes it produces on the environment" (Jeffery 1965:295). Social *and* physical environmental changes are important; the latter include material gains. According to Jeffery, the environment in which the act occurs is critical. If, the actor's past criminal act has been reinforced and aversive consequences have not controlled or prevented it, the crime is likely to be repeated. For example, an armed robbery may produce the reward of money but also aversive consequences of physical injury, arrest, conviction, or imprisonment. The robber will stop only after associating the crime with aversive consequences or punishments. Moreover, punishment only works if applied in a consistent manner and soon after the act occurs—a combination often missing in the contemporary criminal justice system.

These theoretical variations on differential association are important primarily as transitional hypotheses and partial theories.

*Sources:* Glaser (1978); Jeffery (1965).

Skinnerian *instrumental conditioning* (see chapter 5). Human behavior takes two forms: (1) **operant behavior**, which is voluntary and mediated by the brain (i.e., food-seeking); and (2) **respondent behavior**, which is automatic and reflexive (i.e., blinking). Operant behavior depends largely on instrumental conditioning, acquired (or conditioned) by the "effects, outcomes, or consequences it has on the person's environment" (Akers 1985:45). Instrumental conditioning has two associated processes (see chapter 5):

1. Punishments, including punishments received (e.g., when a law violator receives a prison sentence) and rewards lost (e.g., when a law violator has property confiscated), decrease illicit behavior.

2. Reinforcements, including rewards received (e.g., when a law violator scores "the big one") or punishments avoided (e.g., guilty law violator avoids a conviction at trial), continue or even increase criminal activity. Social reinforcements can be symbolic and abstract, such as gaining ideological, religious, or political goals; nonsocial reinforcements may be physiological, unconditioned, and intrinsically rewarding, such as the feelings associated with sexual intercourse or the use of illicit drugs. Akers believed that social reinforcements are more plentiful in one's environment and therefore play a larger role in learning than do nonsocial reinforcements.

Social learning occurs in two ways. The first is by **imitation** or **modeling:** Observing what happens to others, people can be vicariously reinforced and may imitate the rewarded actions. They may also develop new behavior without other forces at work simply by modeling what others do. The **principle of differential reinforcement** represents a second method: Given two or more forms of behavior, the one retained and repeated is the one most highly rewarded.

Akers' theory addresses the content—the *what*—of learning. The importance of techniques is elementary. Unless one knows how to commit a crime, motivation and intent are meaningless. **Discriminative stimuli** are environmental and internal signals that tell us whether a particular behavior is likely to be rewarded or not. The **motivating definitions** for discriminative stimuli take two forms: (1) those that put deviance/criminality in a positive light; and (2) those that allow the offender to neutralize negative aspects of the crime. The latter are similar to Gresham Sykes and David Matza's (1957) techniques of neutralization (see the section on subterranean values and drift theory later in this chapter). They *"counter or neutralize definitions of the behavior as undesirable"* (Akers 1985:50; emphasis in original) and may originate through negative reinforcement, providing a means to escape the social disapproval of others and oneself.

Akers tells us that learning takes place—the *where*—primarily among **differential associations**. This emphasis is behavioral (i.e., associating directly and indirectly with people who engage in various types of legal and illegal behavior) and attitudinal (i.e., coming to know the normative beliefs and orientations of these people). One's associations provide sources of reinforcements and punishments. Those that occur most often and in the greatest number—and that enjoy the greatest probability of reinforcement—tend to be the ones that guide behavior. Akers saw this element as representing not peer pressure, but rather peer influence (Akers and Sellers 2013).

***Measuring Social Learning.***    Social learning theory outlines a process that describes how people move from nonoffender status to offender status and back again (Akers 1998; see also Winfree, Sellers, and Clason

1993). The reinforcers and punishers assume roles that are more promi-nent once an initial act is committed, and imitation becomes less impor-tant. People's personal definitions solidify after repeated exposure to reinforcers and punishers. The commission of a specific act in a given sit-uation depends largely on the individual's learning history.

Feedback is also important, such as when one's own actions influence personal definitions. The first, tentative criminal acts are generally free of feedback. Afterwards, both responses to the behavior and emerging per-sonal definitions become cues for future behavior. People initially have both deviant and nondeviant peers. After instrumental conditioning, the balance may shift to one group over the other (Akers and Sellers 2013).

Finally, Akers (1998) acknowledged the role of social structure (see chapter 6). Society, community, and even individual characteristics—race, gender, religion, and class—create the individual's learning context. Akers assumed that "social learning is the primary process linking social structure to individual behavior" (p. 322).

Critics of this application of operant conditioning to Sutherland's crime-learning process express several concerns. First, the theory does not specify the workings of punishers and reinforcers. Some critics observe that social learning theory fails to state what is rewarded and not rewarded, as well as what is considered rewarding and not rewarding (Chambliss 1988). Akers (1985) concurred: "The theory is . . . incapable of accounting for why anyone or anything is socially defined as undesir-able. . . . The theory does not say how or why the culture, structure, and social patterning of society sets up and implements certain sets and schedules of reactions to given behavior and characteristics" (p. 43).

Second, social learning, like differential association, may be tautolog-ical. Some learning theorists attribute crime to deviant norms and pro-ceed to take the forbidden behavior as evidence of those norms, the very definition of a tautology (Goode 1984:30).

Third, the theory is rarely applied to serious law-violating behavior. Most tests involve relatively minor forms of social deviance (e.g., youthful cigarette smoking or illicit drug use); largely missing are tests that involve serious delinquency or crime (Curran and Renzetti 1994:196). Moreover, the absence of social learning theory-based research into "crime in the suites," law violations by political and corporate elites, constitutes a criti-cal shortcoming (Bradshaw 2011:3).

## Control Theories

Criminologists generally acknowledge the roles played by informal control mechanisms, such as family, friends, and neighbors, and formal control mechanisms, such as schools, police, and the courts: the weaker the for-mer, the greater the reliance on the latter (Black, 1976). The strength of the criminal justice system is rarely sufficient to do more than react to crime, let alone prevent it. Social control theorists are not interested in why people commit crime because the answer is obvious: criminal behavior offers many rewards. Instead, they ask: "Why don't more people commit crime? Control theorists provide several interesting answers to this question.

### Early Control Theories

In the 1950s and early 1960s, criminologists examined the social control factors associated with delinquency. Sociologist Albert Reiss (b.1922–d.2006), a well-known police researcher, observed that youthful probation revocations are more likely when juveniles receive poor psychiatric evaluations. Reiss (1951) attributed both poor psychiatric conditions and probation revocations to failures in **personal control**. Low-control youths meet their personal needs in a manner that conflicts with community rules. However, Reiss found little empirical support for this contention.

Perhaps the reason youth turn to crime is the influence of a weak **stake in conformity.** Jackson Toby (b.1925–), a sociologist who specialized in youth crime, contended that, although every youth is tempted to break the law, some—particularly those doing well in school—risk a great deal by giving in to temptation. According to Toby (1957), being caught means possible punishments and possible changes to one's desired future career. Poor school performers risk only punishment: Their futures are less bright, so their stake in conformity is lower. While not a complete theory, Toby's ideas about social control and conformity reappear in the work of later theorists, particularly Travis Hirschi. Toby speculated that there is more delinquency in urban areas than in suburban areas because low-stake urban youths are exposed to similarly disposed peers (e.g., youth gang members); in contrast, suburban low-stake youths, with fewer similarly disposed peers, are "merely unhappy" and not necessarily delinquent.

Reiss and Toby barely acknowledged the family as a source of control. In contrast, family sociologist F. Ivan Nye (b.1918–d.2014) saw ties between family, social controls, and youthful misbehavior. According to Nye (1958), there are three types of social control: (1) direct controls, such as family-level punishments and restrictions; (2) indirect controls, such as affectional identification with one's parents and noncriminals generally; and (3) internal controls derived from one's conscience (Freud's superego).

Nye found impressive support for his theory: Misbehavior was greatest among those youths with poor family relationships and weak social controls. However, as critics, principally Toby (1959), have pointed out, Nye failed to study serious delinquency. Plus, actively delinquent youths may have been more willing than others to report poor family relationships, thus creating a bias that resulted in support for the theory. Nye's main contribution to control theory was his idea about the different sources of control.

*Containment Theory.*    Walter Reckless (b.1899–d.1988) took the search for social controls to a new level with **containment theory**. Reckless (1961) saw several forces pulling people away from conventional society or pushing them toward misbehavior,

- **Social pushes** include poor living conditions, minority-group status, poor lifestyle opportunities, and family conflicts.

- **Social pulls** are generated by criminal and delinquent subcultures (i.e., youth gangs) or bad companions.

- **Biological pushes** or **psychological pushes** result from inner tensions, unhappiness, hostility, and aggressiveness.

Reckless, a University of Chicago-trained sociologist, saw outer and inner containment as the only restraining forces with sufficient strength to control these pushes and pulls. Containment stood between any individual and a life of crime. **Outer containment** comes from the family and other support groups; it involves, among other things, a consistent moral front, reasonable norms and expectations, effective supervision and discipline, and group cohesiveness. **Inner containment** comes from personal strengths such as self-control, good self-concept, the ability to tolerate frustrations, and the ability to internalize societal norms. These ideas were to play important roles in the creation of later generations of control theory.

*Subterranean Values and Drift Theory.*    Sociologists Gresham M. Sykes (b.1922–d.2010) and David Matza (b.1930–) studied the mechanisms that permit delinquents to accept society's norms and, simultaneously, to violate them. They found that delinquent youth are fully aware of and generally support society's norms. How then do they explain why they violate these norms? Sykes and Matza (1957) found that delinquents use various **techniques of neutralization** to deny that a crime or rule violation had taken place. Delinquents are not necessarily committed to their misdeeds, nor do they see themselves as outside the law. Rather, they justify their misdeeds in a way that, although not valid for the larger society, works for them. Sykes and Matza insisted that the types of justifications they found are not to be dismissed as post-crime rationalizations.

- *The denial of responsibility.* The offender may point to the absence of intent, suggesting that it was an accident or that the injured party "got in the way." At other times, forces outside the youth's control are to blame, including uncaring or abusive parents, a failed educational system, and an indifferent community.

- *The denial of injury.* The perpetrator suggests that no one was hurt. This technique plays well for victimless crimes, such as drug abuse or underage consumption of alcohol and cigarettes. In the case of pranks or vandalism, the youth may point out that no real harm occurred: no harm, no foul.

- *The denial of a victim.* If no injury occurs, it follows that there can be no victim. Alternatively, even if an injury occurred, the perpetrator may claim that it was a righteous act of retaliation based on race, gender, sexual orientation, or economic status. For the latter, the youth defines an act of thievery as redistribution of the wealth. The key is to transform the victim into someone deserving of injury.

- *The condemnation of the condemners.* The delinquent shifts the blame to the person doing the complaining. The offender views the condemner as guilty of bad behavior and hypocritical. If the condemner is a police officer, all police are brutal and corrupt; if the condemner is a schoolteacher, all schoolteachers are lazy and incompetent. The intent is to shift attention from the delinquent's behavior.

- *The appeal to higher loyalties.* Faced with obeying either society's rules or those of their peers, perpetrators often come down on the latter's side. They do not reject society's norms; rather, other norms take precedence.

Sykes and Matza (1957) believe control does not derive directly from the larger societal norms; rather, those norms must pass through the delinquent adolescents' contextual filter: "Values or norms appear as qualified guides for action, limited in their applicability in terms of time, place, persons, and social circumstances" (p. 666). The delinquent youth is not expressing support for criminal behavior as such, since its victims could be the youth's mother or sister. They are simply "justifying" their own actions in a given set of circumstances.

Matza and Sykes (1961) also discussed the role of **subterranean values** for adolescent leisure-time activities. Certain values set delinquents apart: "Juvenile delinquency appears to be permeated by a cluster of values that can be characterized as the search for kicks, the disdain for work and a desire for the big score, and the acceptance of aggressive toughness as proof of masculinity" (p. 715). They argued that these values, often thought to be uniquely juvenile, have parallels in the dominant culture, particularly in leisure-time activities. For example, the search for emotive excitement is a subterranean value that parallels middle-class thrill seeking. One set of values represents living on the edge; the other is far more centrist in the middle-class value system. Both may enjoy the physiological rush that comes from placing one's life in danger. The delinquent may do it by illegal freerunning on restricted high-rise apartment buildings or base-jumping from an electrical tower, while the more normative youth may bungee jump or zipline at a local amusement park.

Matza included these techniques and subterranean values in what has come to be called **drift theory**. Consider the following question: Do juvenile delinquents move on to become adult criminals, or do they mature into law-abiding citizens? Matza (1964) viewed delinquents as

---

Neutralization theory tells us that rather than being committed to lives of crime, delinquents need some mechanism—neutralization techniques—that afford them a measure of insulation from the rejections society typically accords law breakers.

---

Illegal freerunning (urban acrobatic moves that include vaulting, flipping over or spinning past obstacles) and base-jumping (parachuting from buildings and towers) allow delinquents to employ the same core value—seeking excitement—associated with somewhat tamer and legal activities such as ziplining and bungee-cord jumping.

moving, or drifting, between criminal and conventional actions but behaving most of the time in a noncriminal mode. Such youths often feel ambivalent about their episodic criminal conduct. Matza believes that juveniles experience less alienation than adults and are not yet committed to an oppositional subculture. He is also highly critical of most delinquent subculture theories, which paint a picture of nonstop delinquent behavior, especially for gang youths (see chapter 6). Most of the time, delinquents engage in law-abiding activities. In fact, Matza does not see the delinquent subculture as a binding force on its members: "Loyalty is a basic issue in the subculture of delinquency partially because its adherents are so regularly disloyal. They regularly abandon their company at the age of remission for more conventional pursuits" (1964:157–58). Many if not most delinquents abandon adolescent misbehaving (i.e., "kid stuff") in favor of adult prosocial or conventional behavior. This observation has important policy implications that argue against a "zero tolerance" approach to relatively minor misbehavior.

## Social Bond Theory

Social bond theory emerged in the turbulent 1960s, and it would become one of the longest-lived and most researched control theories in criminology (Akers and Sellers 2013). Sociologist Travis Hirschi (b.1935–) saw a strong bond as essential for *deterring* people from a life of crime. In essence, Hirschi (1969) saw the **social bond** as the sum total of the forces in a person's social and physical environment that connect him or her to society and its moral constraints. For example, a lack of attachment to others frees an individual from moral constraints, a concept that has direct ties to Durkheim's anomie (chapter 6) but which is now expressed in individual terms rather than at the societal level. Absent such bonds, people are free to deviate—to act without "moral" restraint. According to Hirschi, weak bonds do not predict deviance, but they make it possible or probable. As he concluded: "The bond of affection for conventional persons is a major deterrent to crime" (p. 83).

Hirschi (1969) endorsed the position that humankind's natural propensity is to engage in hedonistic pursuits (an element in the Classical view). He saw the social bond as curbing this natural human propensity for misbehavior. In a claim similar to that made by earlier control theorists, Hirschi stated that youths with strong bonds to social institutions, including family and school, are less inclined to engage in delinquency.

Hirschi's social bond has four elements, all of which are tied to conventional norms, rules, activities, and significant others.

- *Attachment* is affection for and sensitivity to social group members. Without attachment, there is no internalization of norms and values. The child who exhibits no affective or emotional bonds to others, and who is not particularly sensitive, may feel, in Hirschi's

(1969:18) words, "free to deviate." Researchers measure attachment by the level of parental supervision or discipline, the quality of child–parent communications, or attitudes toward school and school authority.

- *Commitment* refers to investment in conventional norms and rules; this concept recasts Toby's stake in conformity. Attachment and commitment reflect personal attitudes or orientations. Researchers measure commitment by two methods. First, children's engagement in adult activities, including smoking, drinking, and sex, indicates a lack of commitment. Second, educational or occupational aspirations and expectations—two strain concepts—also find their way into social control tests as measures of commitment to conventionality.

- *Involvement* is behavioral and measures the level of conventional activity, a modern version of the age-old dictum "idle hands are the devil's workshop," which includes an opportunity element (Curran and Renzetti 1994:200).

- *Belief* contrasts with Sykes and Matza's neutralization techniques. For Sykes and Matza, conventional moral beliefs are paramount; youths must neutralize their deviations to engage in misbehavior. According to Hirschi, belief in the correctness of norms is variable; he questioned whether everyone feels bound to adhere to the dominant moral beliefs. He hypothesized that delinquency is more likely when a youth attaches less significance to conventional moral beliefs.

> Social bond consists of four elements (i.e., attachment, commitment, involvement, and belief); if any one of the four is weak, delinquency is likely to ensue.

The strength of delinquent peer bonding derives from the actor's ties to conventional groups. We would expect delinquent behavior when bonds to the delinquent peer group overcome familial bonds. If any one of the four social bonds is weak—even if the other three are strong—there is a heightened probability of misconduct.

Social bonding is one of the most influential crime theories of the twentieth century (Akers and Sellers 2013). A recent meta-analysis of parental attachments, especially to one's mother, were found to be important predictors of delinquency (Hoeve et al. 2012). As we shall see in chapter 10, the theory is rich in its implications for criminal justice policies and practices.

## Self-Control Theory

In the late twentieth century, Hirschi and Michael R. Gottfredson (b.1951–) questioned the value of the *career criminal* concept, challenging many contemporary crime control policies and intervention strategies based on the career criminal concept, such as selective incapacitation and "three-strikes" legislation (see chapter 10). They also challenged much of the *developmental and life-course criminology* discussed in chapter 5, ideas that have been linked to the frequency of offending. Instead, Gottfredson and Hirschi (1990) proposed a "general theory of crime," one they claim is consistent with the observed stability of crime propensity and versatility, now called either **self-control theory** or **event-propensity theory** (Gottfredson and Hirschi 1989; 1990).

Gottfredson and Hirschi see self-interest as motivating human behavior and reflecting a universal desire to secure pleasure and avoid pain—ideas that would resonate with virtually any of the classical deterrence theorists examined in chapter 2. Sounding almost Freudian, they describe criminality's origins in child rearing. These early beginnings "suggest that criminality is more or less naturally present, that it requires socialization for its control" (Gottfredson and Hirschi 1989:61). Crime and analogous acts (e.g., drinking, smoking, drug use, illicit sex) collectively and individually offer short-term pleasures (e.g., money, altered states of consciousness, thrills, and excitement) for little effort. Unrestrained individuals, or those with little commitment to conventionality and equally low concern for the long-term consequences of their behavior, are thus attracted to crime. They exhibit low self-control, a precursor for crime and delinquency.

*Defining Self-Control.* Self-control's causal elements are straightforward: Parental management and child-rearing practices are central because they are instrumental in children establishing self-control as early as age 10 or 11. Adequate parental management includes (1) the monitoring and recognition of deviant behavior in a child, (2) appropriate punishment in response to inappropriate behavior ("let the punishment fit the crime"), and (3) emotional investment in the child (Gottfredson and Hirschi 1990). Gottfredson and Hirschi conclude that inadequate parental management results in low self-control, which influences an individual's choices when faced with an opportunity for immediate gain through little investment. Low-self-control persons, who share some or all of the characteristics described in box 7.2 (on the next page), exhibit a wide variety of inappropriate behaviors, including crime, because such activities hold the promise of immediate pleasure for minimal effort.

Critics focus on several claims made by Gottfredson and Hirschi. While it is claimed that self-control is a general theory of crime, much crime does not fit the theory. Ken Polk (1991), for example, has observed that there is no "typical" homicide, and whatever exists is far from the two forms described by Gottfredson and Hirschi (homicides as the result of a heated argument and pursuant to a burglary). Moreover, white-collar and corporate crimes simply do not fit the self-control model (Ermann and Lundman 1992; Polk 1991). Organizational offending must take into account factors not acknowledged by Gottfredson and Hirschi, including the actions of political, economic, and bureaucratic systems (Reed and Yeager 1996:377).

Other challenges to the self-control theory derive from its conceptual similarity to other perspectives on crime causation. For many criminolo-

Selective incapacitation removes high-threat offenders from society, thereby reducing new crime; "three-strikes" laws confine repeat offenders in prison for life after a third felony conviction.

According to event-propensity theory, low self-control is a precursor for crime and delinquency.

BOX 7.2

## Characteristics of Low Self-Control Individuals

Low-self-control individuals—the unrestrained—share the following six common characteristics:

1. *A need for immediate gratification.* Short-term, immediate rewards (pleasures) are the goal; deferred gratification—postponing pleasures and rewards to a more appropriate time or renouncing them entirely—is a foreign concept to low self-control individuals.

2. *Simplicity.* They avoid complicated tasks and decisions, preferring to seek easy answers and easy work.

3. *Physicality.* They prefer to keep physically active.

4. *A need for risk taking.* Tending to be impetuous and impulsive, they are supreme risk takers, seeking excitement and danger over sameness and safeness.

5. *Self-centeredness.* They tend to emphasize personal needs, wants, and desires while ignoring those of even significant others, such as relatives and friends.

6. *Anger.* They have a low frustration tolerance and exhibit a tendency to resort to aggressive coping strategies when faced with frustrating situations or events.

In summary, Gottfredson and Hirschi claim ineffective parenting determines whether children will seek out crime and analogous behavior largely before they enter their teenage years. The presence of the six characteristics reveal a bedrock of low self-control that is well established and largely immutable in children by the time they are 10 or 11 years of age.

*Source*: Gottfredson and Hirschi (1990).

---

Low self-control, especially impulsivity, is a variable found in many crime theories, from psychology's psychopathy to biocriminology's genetic traits.

gists, the theory resembles a personality theory (chapter 4). Larry Siegel (1992:237) captured the essence of this position: "Saying someone 'lacks self-control' implies that they suffer from a personality defect that makes them impulsive and rash." How does this characterization differ from the "criminal personality"? Biocriminologists (chapter 3) also question the claim that parental management and not biological and genetic influences determine self-control; self-control appears to be part of a constellation of "executive functions" performed by the brain's prefrontal cortex (Beaver, Wright, and DeLisi 2007). Research using twins suggests that genetic and nonshared environmental factors strongly influence self-control levels (Wright et al. 2008b).

During the 1990s, dozens of studies explored the utility of self-control theory. Travis Pratt and Frank Cullen (2000) conducted a meta-analysis of 21 empirical studies of self-control theory, all published between 1993 and 1999. They reported that low self-control was an important predictor of crime and analogous behavior, irrespective of the sample employed. However, the constructs fare poorly in longitudinal research. When compared with social learning theory, self-control theory receives less empirical support.

As a group, the theories in this chapter provide insights into the actual social processes by which people learn to violate laws. The answers they provide are quite different, as are the assumptions they make about both the sources of control and learning, as well as the processes that are at work. Whatever their individual weaknesses or shortcomings, the theories are among the most strongly supported theories in criminology, both by empirical studies and by the endorsements of criminologists themselves (Akers and Sellers 2013; Sellers, Winfree, and Akers 2012).

## SUMMARY

- A social process is any identifiable, repetitive pattern of interaction between humans in a group or in a social context.
- Learning theories tell us that humans are basically *tabula rasa*, or blank slates, upon which society, through various "teaching" mechanisms, writes its rules and guidelines for living as a social being.
- Sutherland's differential association theory suggests that criminals learn their behavior—and accompanying motives, drives and rationalizations—by the same learning mechanisms at work in society at large.
- The principle of differential association maintains that an individual turns to crime when he or she is exposed to an excess of definitions favorable to law violations rather than unfavorable.
- A person's differential associations vary in frequency, duration, intensity, and priority.
- Glaser's differential anticipation/expectation theory and Jeffery's differential reinforcement theory provided transitions between Sutherland's differential association theory and Akers' social learning theory.
- Human behavior takes two forms: operant behavior, which is voluntary and brain mediated (instrumental conditioning is central to operant behavior) and respondent behavior, which is automatic and reflexive.
- Punishments refer to something bad received (e.g., criminal sent to prison) or something good lost (e.g., criminal has home confiscated as ill-gotten gains); in either case, the result is a decrease in illicit behavior.
- Reinforcements refer to something good received (e.g., criminal scores "the big one") or something bad avoided (e.g., guilty offender is found not guilty at trial); in either case, the result is an increase in the behavior.
- Social learning occurs by imitating or modeling the behavior of others and through the principle of differential association.
- Critics of social learning theory attack the use of operant conditioning to fill in the gaps in differential association theory and call the theory, like differential association, a tautology.
- Generally, empirical support for social learning theory is moderate to high, while criminologists themselves see it as one of the discipline's most important theories.

- Control theories see people as prone to bad deeds, largely due to the absence of effective social controls that emanate from multiple sources, including family, schools, and other social institutions.

- Reiss's personal control hypothesis, Jackson's stake in conformity, Nye's family-based control hypotheses, Reckless's containment theory, and Sykes and Matza's subterranean values, along with Matza's drift theory, created a solid theoretical foundation for later social control theorizing.

- Hirschi's social bond consists of four elements: attachment, commitment, involvement, and belief.

- If any of the four elements of the social bond are weak, then the probability of delinquent conduct increases.

- Critics of social bond theory point to issues with the involvement element (i.e., it often does not perform as predicted), an overreliance on the ideas that humans are innately aggressive or characterized by violent tendencies, and the inability of the theory to predict serious delinquency.

- Whatever its weaknesses, social bond theory is also a highly regarded and often tested theory in criminology.

- Self-control or event-propensity theory tells us that unrestrained individuals (i.e., persons with low self-control) are attracted to crime.

- Critics point to problems with the conceptual and operational definitions associated with low self-control, including questions about the six characteristics of low self-control people.

- Critics suggest self-control theory is a personality or biogenic theory cast in different terms.

- Self-control theory, like social bond theory, remains a very popular and highly respected criminological answer to why humans give in to their baser instincts.

## KEY TERMS

biological pushes
containment theory
differential anticipation/
  expectation theory
differential associations
differential association theory
differential association-
  reinforcement theory
differential reinforcement theory
discriminative stimuli
drift theory
duration
event-propensity theory

frequency
imitation
inner containment
intensity
modeling
motivating definitions
operant behavior
outer containment
personal control
principle of differential association
principle of differential reinforcement
priority
psychological pushes

respondent behavior     social pulls
self-control theory     social pushes
social bond     stake in conformity
social learning theory     subterranean values
social process     techniques of neutralization

## CRITICAL REVIEW QUESTIONS

1. List and discuss the key elements in differential association theory. How is this theory related to the Chicago School's cultural transmission theory?

2. List three major criticisms of differential association theory. Which one, in your mind, is most damaging? Explain your choice.

3. How did Glaser and Jeffery modify differential association theory to produce their respective theories?

4. What are the two forms of human behavior? Explain the role of instrumental conditioning, along with its two associated processes.

5. List and discuss the key elements in social learning. How is this theory related to the Chicago School's cultural transmission theory?

6. What is social learning theory's explanation for how learning takes place? What are the important elements in that process?

7. According to social learning, when is someone most likely to commit a crime?

8. List two major criticisms of social learning theory. Which one, in your mind, is most damaging? Explain your choice.

9. Describe how the early social control theorists answered the question: Why don't more people commit crimes?

10. Which of the early control theorists offers the most complete theory on crime or delinquency? What is the basis for your selection?

11. What are the five techniques of neutralization? Can you see why some supporters of differential association and social learning theories view these techniques as the substance of what is learned by offenders? Explain your answer.

12. What are the ties between drift theory and subterranean values?

13. List and describe the four elements of the social bond. According to this theory when is one likely to become a delinquent?

14. List and describe the six common characteristics of a low-control individual. Explain why some critics view these characteristics of low self-control as factors in making the theory a tautology.

15. How does self-control theory differ from bonding theory?

# Labeling Theory and Reintegrative Shaming Theory

## *LEARNING OBJECTIVES*

- The processes by which society defines certain people as criminals
- The significance of criminal labels for those doing the labeling and those being labeled
- The role of shaming in controlling crime is complex, and it can result in various outcomes, depending on whether the goal is to bring those persons being shamed back into the community or to isolate them further
- How shaming and labeling work for and against society's interests

# Introduction

What is the community's role in "creating" criminals? Two theoretical perspectives address this question. The first is labeling theory or the societal reaction perspective; it is one of the most intuitively comprehensible crime theories and elements of it can be found in ancient texts dating back thousands of years. While modern labeling theory's roots date to the 1930s, the perspective rose to prominence in the 1960s and 1970s, mainly due to the work of U.S. sociologists. They believed the key to understanding law-violating behavior is found in the responses of social institutions—such as the family, schools, and criminal justice system—to conduct viewed as outside acceptable societal boundaries. Labeling theory stresses the power of social institutions to limit a person's life choices by stigmatizing adults as criminals or minor children as delinquents. When those who are stigmatized realize that they have few paths left except law-violating ones, they may take on the criminal identity completely, the final stage in the labeling process.

Reintegrative shaming is the second perspective; like labeling, it has a long history and a relatively new "rediscovery." Behind this practice is the idea that societal punishments should focus on the offender's behavior rather than on the offender, the goal being to return the individual to the community. There is anthropological evidence that reintegrative shaming was widely practiced in preliterate cultures. Since the 1980s, it has assumed a central role in both criminology and criminal justice policies and practices. The theory offers an explanation of why some societies have higher crime than others *and* why some people are more likely than others to engage in crime. In communities employing shaming processes that stigmatize, ex-offenders are pushed to the community's fringes. In communities practicing reintegrative shaming, lawbreakers rejoin the community as fully functioning members. Criminals who undergo stigmatizing shaming are more likely to re-offend than those experiencing reintegrative shaming.

> While both labeling and reintegration shaming have ancient origins, their use by criminologists is relatively new.

These two perspectives share a focus on the community's role in creating the very conditions that laws exist to control: crime and delinquency. Both acknowledge that communities have immense power to harm and to heal. How the respective theories view this power and the processes of creating criminals and delinquents, as well as the resolution of those spoiled identities, takes each one in rather different directions.

# Labeling Theory

Before examining how communities designate acts and actors as problematic for good social order, we need to understand the significance of symbols for social interaction.

## Symbolic Interactionism

Symbols are an essential part of any culture—we communicate through symbols. Words have no intrinsic meaning, only the meaning that we impute. The letters "r-e-d" symbolize a color for those understand English, while the letters "*r-o-j-o*" serve the same purpose for those who understand Spanish. Simply put, a **symbol** is a thing that stands for something else, usually a material object that represents an abstract idea.

Consider the symbolism in the following example:

> If someone sets fire to a structure for profit (insurance fraud), the act is arson. But if the building is a church, mosque, or synagogue, it is a **hate crime**—a criminal act precipitated by the victim's religious beliefs, race, gender, sexual orientation, or other protected status. Crimes are sanctioned for their harm to society but hate crimes are punished more severely. The motive for arson is money, but the symbolism of religion is the target in the hate crime.

To understand why society distinguishes the punishment for the same behavior—setting a fire—depending on the motivation for the crime, we must turn to **symbolic interactionism**. This perspective explores how individuals render the world meaningful (Mead 1934; see also Matsueda 1992). While the term may appear daunting, it is actually simple and literal: people interact through symbols, in particular, through language symbols.

According to symbolic interactionists, human beings gradually internalize the expectations of the groups with which they socialize, largely in reaction to rewards and sanctions. For example, we praise children who act politely, and chastise those who do not. "Polite," however, is a socially determined characteristic whose elements differ from society to society. Consider the propriety of wearing shoes or a head covering, for example, when entering someone's home or place of worship. In essence, we evaluate our own conduct from the group's perspective (Quadragno and Antonio 1975). For criminal labels, the focus is not on the criminal behavior of any given social actor, but on how others, including the criminal justice system, view that behavior or actor. No behavior is inherently deviant; rather, deviance is a property given to the behavior by others who have direct and indirect contact with those engaged in it (Erickson 1966).

Symbols have the power to galvanize social action. W.I. Thomas and Florian Znaniecki (1918) observed that objective reality is less important to our definition of a social situation than is our subjective belief about it. If we believe something to be true and act accordingly, it does not matter if that belief is true. Thus, the *innocent* but convicted will be treated the same as the *guilty* and convicted. Symbolic interactionists are less interested in "truth" than in the societal reaction to beliefs.

> The origins of labeling theory are to be found in symbolic interactionism, a branch of sociology that is concerned with how we make sense of the world around us.

## Societal Reaction: From Tagging to Labeling

Frank Tannenbaum (b.1893–d.1969) was among the first to articulate the idea that social institutions cause society to label some people as criminals. As Tannenbaum (1938) observed, what a youth views as a lark or an adventure, the community may define as a nuisance or evil. Such divergent views can create rifts between the parties involved. If definitional differences persist, a shift occurs within the community, from the deed-as-evil to the person-as-evil, a process Tannenbaum described as the **dramatization of evil**. This redefinition occurs through the intervention of an institution created for the task—the criminal justice system. Exposed by police, courts, and correction to various dramatization rituals, the child receives the delinquent tag and must live in a new and unexplored environment, the world of crime and criminals (Tannenbaum 1938).

> The delinquent tag serves to dramatize a youth's misconduct, which ties the evil behavior to the youth and helps society see the person as evil.

Successive generations of symbolic interactionists addressed society's power to redefine social situations. Erving Goffman (b.1922–d.1982) described how people respond to **spoiled identities**—both the community at large and those whose identities were spoiled—through the process of **stigmatization**. Goffman (1963:43–44) distinguished **prestige symbols**, which convey "a special claim to prestige, honor or desirable class position," from **stigma symbols**, which draw "attention to a debasing identity," negatively altering how society views that person, spoiling his or her identity.

> In the process of labeling, prestige symbols convey a positive image, while stigma symbols attach a negative identity to the person being labeled.

Consider the following examples of both prestige and stigma symbols. Honor societies traditionally award pins or keys to their members as an indication of their special status. Universities and colleges bestow honorary degrees on persons they wish to designate as having led exemplary professional or personal lives. Conversely, in many states, convicted and released sex offenders have their pictures, offense records, and current addresses posted on public Web sites. These prestige and stigma symbols send strong messages to society: *These people bear watching!*

The processes by which symbols become part of the defining criteria for a person's identity are also important. Prestige ceremonies, including pinning or graduation rituals, have clear implications. Harold Garfinkel (b.1917–d.2011) noted that **status degradation ceremonies**, including arrests and trials, provide ritualistic denunciations of certain designated individuals. According to Garfinkel (1956), the publicness of such ceremonies is essential so that the community knows whom to avoid.

> Status degradation ceremonies provide public denunciations of those among us who have been identified as being members of a lower social type and, therefore, undesirable, untrustworthy and devalued persons.

## Deviance as Social Status

Howard Becker (b.1928–) advises:

> Deviance is not a quality of the act the person commits, but rather a consequence of the application by others of rules and sanctions to an "offender." The deviant is one to whom that label has successfully been applied; deviant behavior is behavior people so label. (Becker 1963:9)

According to Becker, negative societal reactions result in tarnished and even damaged self-images, deviant identities, and a host of negative social expectations. How would members of your community react to terms like *ex-con, parolee, child molester,* and *serial killer?*

We all play many community roles, including teacher or student, child or parent, and worker or boss. Which one defines how others view us or, as importantly, how we see ourselves? In Becker's view, the **master status** is our defining social position. The criminal label can become a master status, overriding all others (Becker 1963). For example, consider the fallout if the police arrested your favorite professor on child molestation charges. At that point, all his education, rank, status, and professional standing would become irrelevant. The professor would be an accused pedophile, a damning master status, likely to elicit high stigmatization no matter whether there is a trial, guilty verdict, or legal sanction. Indeed, even if the charge is found to be false, an aura of stigma is likely to remain.

> A master status can override all other social positions associated with an individual and become the primary social lens through which others view that person and how that person sees him- or herself.

Not all stigma symbols are of equal social significance; they may not have a negative impact on the person labeled. Even a successful status degradation ceremony may not result in a new master status. Consider the following hypothetical situation. A faculty member at your college or university decides that the local community is not doing enough to help the homeless. Moreover, the police are targeting the homeless for arrest and removal from the streets. Because of strongly held beliefs, your professor decides to join a noisy picket line outside a city council meeting where the council is considering revising its anti-loitering ordinance and increasing the sanctions. The police order the picketers to disperse. The picketers refuse, engaging in civil disobedience, and the police take the protestors, including your professor, into custody. The charge is creating a public disturbance and resisting arrest. At trial, your professor enters a plea of no contest, pays a $10 fine, and serves 10 days of community service at the local homeless shelter. Rather than viewing the professor as an outcast and a criminal, colleagues and students praise the individual as a "victim of conscience."

## The Labeling Process

The damaged self-image and its meaning for the individual can result in a **self-fulfilling prophesy**—what people believe to be real becomes real in its consequences (see Merton 1957; Thomas and Thomas 1928). Edwin Lemert (b.1912–d.1996) and Edwin Schur (b.1930–) provide two versions of how this movement from "normal" to criminal occurs.

***Lemert's Primary and Secondary Deviation.*** An initial foray into a criminal activity, unless it involves an extremely heinous crime, may be nothing more than what Lemert (1951) called **primary deviation**, a condition in which the actor has little commitment to a deviant career. Some individuals do not stop here, but the decision may not be entirely their own.

The accusations may appear on the newspaper's front page, while exonerations are typically back page material. Many ex-convicts find it difficult to secure employment, or at least meaningful and rewarding jobs, increasing the attraction of crime and the likelihood of subsequent labeling.

According to Lemert (1951), labeled persons may reorganize their behavior according to society's reactions and respond to society in terms of that negative label. Lemert called this condition **secondary deviation**. Moving from primary to secondary deviation generally follows a seven-step process:

1. Primary deviations bring out penalties, usually of a mild nature, which often

2. stimulate further primary deviations, which

3. elicit stronger penalties and rejections by a wide range of groups and individuals,

4. causing further deviations, possibly including hostilities and resentment toward those doing the penalizing, which

5. creates a crisis in the tolerance quotient, expressed in formal action by the stigmatizing body,

6. meaning harsher reactions to misdeeds, further strengthening the deviant act as a reaction to the stigmatization and penalization, and, ultimately,

7. yielding psychological acceptance of the deviant status and reorganization of one's social-psychological makeup around that deviant role, or secondary deviation. (p. 77).

If the initial act is especially troubling to the public—a rape or homicide, the accused may skip several steps, resulting in a far faster journey to secondary deviation.

***Schur's Elements of Labeling.***    Schur (1971) believed that successful labeling requires four elements. First, **stereotyping** is essential in helping people make sense out of what is new and unfamiliar. A stereotype is a simplistic mental image resulting from the presence of certain cues that constitute biased generalizations about a group or individuals that are often unfavorable or exaggerated. For example, a conservatively dressed, middle-aged couple passing a car thumping with loud music might denigrate both the car's occupants and their music as "trash." Schur was concerned with far more damning forms of stereotyping, ones that begin with police observations of or encounters with youths and culminate in the use of prejudicial stereotypes at sentencing.

Second, labeling can continue after the fact. This is the case when the media describe a person accused of a horrible act as "a former mental patient"—as if to say: "Now we understand why that person did it." Schur (1971:152) used the term **retrospective interpretation** to describe the

The movement from primary to secondary deviation reflects the idea that the labeled person now sees him- or herself as different and fully adopts the deviant role.

We generally think of stereotyping as applying negative labels, but its denotative meaning is an oversimplified opinion—a shorthand method of associating certain inner, personal values or characteristics with external cues.

process of looking to the past for previously unseen causes of present undesired behavior. The implication is that society should have suspected that the person was a deviant from prior clues, such as a stint in a mental hospital. Even unseen clues, like the presence of a brain tumor, allow society to "understand" the deviance, albeit after the fact. In fact, few such persons actually commit crimes, but society rarely lets facts get in the way of a good retrospective interpretation. This mechanism allows us to make sense of an otherwise unfathomable behavior by providing a medical, psychological, or social explanation that, even if incorrect, helps us label the deviance.

Schur's (1971) third element consists of **negotiations** between the labeled and the labelers. Superficially, the parties involved are negotiating the formal charge, the plea, and the eventual sentence; in fact, they are negotiating the label. Stereotypes and retrospective interpretation play major roles in the negotiation process. The negotiation process includes how the police defined the youth at detainment or arrest, as well as what the probation officer can piece together about the youth's life before the offense. Occasionally the youth may promote a negative stereotype by acting belligerent and unresponsive with authorities, an indication of Schur's fourth element described below.

Role engulfment differs from Lemert's secondary deviance. Secondary deviance includes *both* the impact of labeling on the individual's self-concept and the "secondary expansion of deviance problems at the situational and societal levels" (Schur 1971:69). Role engulfment, a narrower facet of secondary deviation, relates to society's response to individuals now recognized as deviants, criminals, or delinquents. **Role engulfment** is the social-psychological process by which the individual assumes the master status; it is the sum total of stereotyping, retrospective interpretation, and negotiation. Because legitimate roles are no longer available to the individual, the only alternative is total engulfment in the deviant role, to the exclusion of all others. Schur believed that this step stabilizes one's self-concept. As "philosophers of the street" say: "If you got the name, might as well play the game"—exploit the label, for example, using it to intimidate.

> Role engulfment occurs when the labeled person assumes the new master status, which stabilizes his or her self-concept.

## Labels and Their Consequences

Official labels have a clear impact on recidivism, or the return to crime. Persons labeled as juvenile delinquents and criminals are far more likely to re-offend than persons that avoid such public stigma (Barrick 2007, 2014). According to contemporary labeling researchers, the implication of deviant labels is not a straight line from being labeled to being a recidivist. The impact of the criminal label may be indirect, operating through factors standing between the initial label and recidivism. These are the intermediate "costs" associated with being labeled, ones that often occur even prior to re-offending. For example, an official label may limit a person's friendship and socializing networks, something called **social exclusion**. Social exclusion is a form of marginalization, a practice that relegates excluded individuals to society's fringes. They may find that previously close friends and even relatives are less likely to desire or tolerate social engagement (Restivo and Lanier 2015; Wiley, Slocum, and Esbensen 2013). There is evidence that for juvenile offenders a strong affective family bond can diminish the harmful effects of an official designation as delinquent (Jackson and Hay 2013).

> Social exclusion is the successful application of a negative label and subsequent limitations, if not outright restrictions, of that person's social networks.

Second, labeling can restrict a person's access to legitimate opportunities. Youth subjected to law enforcement actions, including arrest, may find that school officials block their return to school. Even if they return, the odds of academic success will be much lower (Bernburg and Krohn 2003; Hjalmarsson 2008; Sweeten 2006). Being convicted of a crime as an adult, especially a felony, brings even more significant costs. The label of criminal can severely restrict one's options for securing lawful employment. Some occupations—including many health care and law-related occupations that require licensing—are usually closed to those with felony convictions. Even where these legal barriers are not present, individuals convicted of a crime may find that potential employers are far less inclined to hire them (Schwartz and Skolnick 1962; Pager 2003). Being sentenced and incarcerated have the most severe impact on future employment. For females even suspension or expulsion from school limits one's employment prospect (Davies and Tanner 2003).

> Secondary sanctioning refers to the sum total of all negative outcomes that accumulate following the initial act of public labeling.

Early labeling as a delinquent by police has the potential to limit if not block a youth's legitimate opportunities (Bernburg and Krohn 2003; Bernburg, Krohn and Rivera 2006). Akiva Liberman and associates classify the labeled person's subsequent negative experiences, such as poor employment prospects and reliance on welfare, as **secondary sanctioning**. Faced with such impediments, ex-offenders may see few alternatives to a return to crime. They are arrested and sanctioned more often than those who had no such early contact with the police because of the "intensified gaze, or declining intolerance, of the criminal justice system" (Liberman, Kirk, and Kim 2014: 348). The police place them in their "usual suspects" file, thereby increasing their chances of arrest.

> The police are a prime example of a public agency that practices deviance amplification.

The significance of initial police contacts on the labeling process cannot be overstated. Whether they are the "victims" of social exclusion or secondary sanctioning, most official labeling processes start with the police (see box 8.1).

## Rethinking Labels

Several new conceptualizations of labeling arguments emerged in the late 1980s. For example, the **status characteristics hypothesis** states that certain personal characteristics, such as race, sex, and social class, determine whom social control agencies label (Paternoster and Iovanni 1989).

B
O
X
8.1

## Labeling: A Deviance Amplification System?

Over 50 years ago, before labeling theory took on near iconic status in criminology, Wilkins described **deviance amplification** as a system by which misbehavior is magnified and made worse. Less tolerance leads to more acts being defined as crimes, which leads to more action against criminals, which leads to more alienation of deviant groups, which leads to more crime by deviant groups, which leads to less tolerance of deviants by conformists—and the cycle continues. Those whom the system has condemned and excluded can hardly be expected to feel a part of it. The continued criminal acts of the "outliers" (outlaws), and the amplifying effects of self-perception, typically result in even harsher responses by conforming groups.

For example, Jock Young proposed that in drug cases police are important deviance amplifiers. As the police occupy a socially isolated position in the community, they are susceptible to behavioral stereotypes, including drug use. Given their inherent power, officers negotiate the evidence—the reality of drug-taking behavior—to fit preconceived stereotypes. Given repeated police interaction with members of the drug culture, the latter's misbehavior transitions to a self-fulfillment of the drug-user stereotypes. As Young saw it, due to police actions, these stereotypes go from fantasy to reality.

Deviance amplification is far from a forgotten idea of the 1960s and 1970s. Police contacts are viewed as crucial to the labeling process generally, but especially for juveniles. There do appear to be intermediary forces at work, such as social exclusion, weakened social bond, blocked opportunity, deviant identity, and delinquent group involvement. But these intermediaries are found far more often in the case of children having contact with the police compared to those who have no contact.

*Sources*: Liberman et al. (2014); Restivo and Lanier (2015); Wiley, Slocum, and Esbensen (2013); Wilkins (1965); Young (1971).

Researchers using the status characteristics hypothesis studied "label applications" by different agencies within the criminal justice system, including police, prosecutors, and courts in arrests, trials, and postadjudicatory dispositions. Their findings suggest that, given certain contexts and stages in the criminal justice process, a person's race, ethnicity, gender, or social class may influence the labeling process (Barrick 2007; Chiricos et al. 2007). For example, a black male accused of harming a white female may stand in greater legal jeopardy than if his victim had been another black male (Vito and Keil 1988). In addition, the importance of social class and race increases during the later stages of processing for juvenile suspects (McCarthy and Smith 1986).

Another trend involves the integration of differing theoretical frameworks with the goal of better understanding the specific contextual aspects of labeling. As Roger G. Morris and Alex R. Piquero (2013) revealed, for some offenders sanctions cause *less offending*, while in other persons these same sanctions bring about *more offending*. These are the contradictory predictions made by deterrence theory—less offending with sanctions—and labeling theory—more offending with sanctions. What Morris and Piquero's work revealed was the specific context in which sanctioning worked one way or another: Arrest substantively amplified subsequent delinquency among *the most chronic trajectory group* (i.e., those with the most prior offending); arrest was less crime-inducing among *the medium-risk group* and had no effect on *the low-risk group*. That is, for the most delinquent group, sanctioning operated according to labeling principle; for the least delinquent group, sanctioning operated according to deterrence principles.

Criminologists have also taken Robert Merton's (1988) ideas about cumulative advantage, turned them around, and included them in labeling theory. Merton noted that those who are born with "a silver spoon in their mouths" tend to succeed simply by reason of their initial position of advantage. Others, lacking in these resources and often subjected to negative forces in society, are disadvantaged. The negative forces can include arrest, trial, and confinement; collectively, they create **cumulative disadvantage**—the sum total of all negative life experiences to which a person is exposed and that further restrict or limit their potentialities as humans throughout their lifetime. These experiences would include what Liberman and associates (2014) described as *secondary sanctioning*, along with social exclusion (Bernberg and Krohn 2003; Restivo and Lanier 2015).

It is important to note, however, that many youth gang members who have never been formally labeled nevertheless have well-formed deviant identities (Akers, 1968). Those aspiring to a criminal career may actively seek out a criminal label, as in the case of the professional safecracker or "box man," rather than have it ascribed to them (Mankoff 1971). For some of the most violent of all offenders—terrorists and revolutionaries—an official designation may mean that they have finally received sought-after recognition for their (mis)deeds (Appleby 2010; Schwartz, Dunkel, and Waterman 2009). Gang jackets and tattoos, such as those of outlaw motorcycle club members, are reminders that some persons value the deviant labels. The bottom line is that the labels of criminal and delinquent are not viewed uniformly by all those to whom they are applied, as illustrated by box 8.2. One of the authors (Abadinsky) was an adolescent gang member and cherishes the label as indicated by his continued interaction with his former gang associates who now have an additional label: senior citizen.

## Reintegrative Shaming Theory

Anthropologists sometimes describe situations where cultures must respond to two countervailing sets of rituals. Inclusionary rituals help hold together the communities. When someone violates a group norm, the community finds a way to bring the offender back into the fold. Any other course of action would have devastating consequences for both the group and the individual, who might be a relative of valued community

---

Cumulative disadvantage refers to the sum total of all negative life experiences that have the potential to restrict or limit the ability to succeed.

### Box 8.2    Consider This: The Value of a Bad Reputation

Labeling theory must consider the "value of a bad reputation." In the Hobbesian world inhabited by criminals, members of an organization with sufficient martial (dangerous and frightening) capacity can offer services typically reserved for government, such as contract enforcement and adjudication of disputes. Members of criminal organizations are also in a position to enforce extralegal social norms. In Chicago, when the police failed to adequately respond to complaints about reckless driving by youngsters in a particular neighborhood, several residents went to see their neighbor, Joseph ("Joey the Clown") Lombardo. This ranking member of the Windy City's crime family (the "Outfit") resolved the problem with a few carefully chosen words to the young men. One of the authors (Abadinsky) has a law enforcement-source photo of a Harley Davidson motorcycle with the following plaque attached: "This motorcycle belongs to a Hell's Angel—fuck with it and find out."

*Source*: Abadinsky (2013); Reuter (1987).

members or someone who performs an essential role in the community's survival. To push that person to the group's fringes or beyond, to exclude him or her entirely, would be counterproductive to the community. Hence, they must find some way to punish the person without driving him or her away. The offender suffers more than a symbolic punishment, depending on the significance of the norm violated, but the ultimate goal is the reintegration of the offender.

Other cultures place less emphasis on inclusiveness as a community value and greater emphasis on the roles of law and sanctions. Short of killing the transgressor, appropriate punishments may involve the imposition of real or symbolic stigmata that signify the rule-violating nature of the person and the associated act, as in the case of branding offenders or requiring that they wear other symbols associated with their transgressions. When the community wishes to make a stronger statement, the offender may be banished, which is usually irreversible. Whether the sanctions are physical stigmata or banishment, their intent is clearly exclusionary, the removal of the offender symbolically or physically from the community.

At their core, these rituals are about shame. Exclusionary rituals use shame to isolate offenders, identifying them as objects of distain and hatred. Inclusionary rituals use shame to embrace the offender, demonstrating an entirely different set of emotions, including warmth, friendship, and love.

> Exclusionary rituals use shame to isolate offenders; inclusionary rituals use shame to show the value and worth of offenders to the community.

## Crime, Shaming, and Social Disapproval

Shame is a very old idea. Nearly all the world's religious and cultural traditions refer to shame's behavior-shaping role. **Shame** is an internal emotional response to embarrassing actions, ideas, words, or thoughts that, when made public, threaten to diminish a person's value or standing in the family or community. Darwin viewed shame as a key self-monitoring activity. He saw blushing, an external marker for shame, as resulting when humans perceive the evaluations of themselves by others as either positive or negative.

Other early twentieth-century sociologists and psychologists explored the capacity of shame to control behavior. For example, William MacDougall (1908) saw shame's capacity to control human behavior as second to no other emotion. Charles Horton Cooley (1922) viewed pride and shame as central "social self-feelings," with shame closely tied to his concept of social fear. Embodied in Cooley's **social fear** is the anticipation of the shame and loss of social standing associated with being found out as a criminal. This concern motivates the offender to take whatever steps are necessary to avoid having his or her conduct made public, which, oddly enough, can include the commission of additional crimes to hide the original.

Thomas Scheff (1988) made the distinction between shame cultures and guilt cultures. However, he also believed that "shame is *the* social emotion, arising as it does out of the monitoring of one's own action by viewing one's self from the standpoint of others" (p. 398; emphasis in the original). Perceiving that they are doing something right, human beings sense deference and a feeling of pride for conformity to exterior norms; perceiving that they are doing something wrong, they sense disrespect and shame for violating exterior norms. Shame has the capacity to achieve conformity through informal but pervasive rewards (e.g., deference from others and inner pride) and punishments (e.g., lack of deference and inner shame).

> Shame is an internal emotional response to embarrassing actions, ideas, words or thought that have the potential to devalue a person's perceived value.

## Reintegrative Shaming

John Braithwaite (b.1951–) provides the theoretical grounding for shame's contemporary role in maintaining social order. He noted that African and Asian cultures use shame as a means of maintaining social control over a host of behaviors. Braithwaite (1989:100) further stated that **shaming** involves "all social processes of expressing disapproval which have the intention or the effect of invoking remorse in the person being shamed and/or condemnation by others who become aware of the shaming." **Disintegrative shaming** blames offenders and denies them reentry into the group. Shaming processes are reintegrative if they first establish the deed's wrongfulness (as opposed to the person's evilness) and then provide an equally public and ritualistic means to restore the offender to the group.

The key to **reintegrative shaming** is the ritualistic reinforcement of a person's status within the group. The last step is **gestural forgiveness**, where members of the harmed community ceremonially welcome the shamed person back into the group. For example, after an offender has served his or her sentence, made public amends to the victim or the victim's family and to the community, a representative of the community must physically and publicly embrace the ex-offender, signifying that person's return. This step is missing in disintegrative shaming, as are affective contacts between those doing the shaming and the shamed person.

## Communitarianism and Shaming Processes

Braithwaite describes two sets of processes in shaming, one operating at the societal (macro) level and the other at the individual (micro) level. Braithwaite suggests that contemporary urban communities with high levels of mobility typically exhibit low interdependency among residents. In Braithwaite's (1989:100) terms, these communities lack **communitarianism**, or interdependencies generally characterized by high levels of mutuality and trust.

High communitarian communities view dependency as a positive social force. Such communities view the characteristics of dependency and dependability as integral to a healthy community (Braithwaite 1989, 2000). Low-communitarian communities widely practice shaming that is stigmatizing or disintegrative. The result is that groups of stigmatized individuals form mutually reinforcing criminal subcultures, groups that provide the learning environments for illegitimate activities. Low levels of communitarianism and the growth of criminal subcultures further erode the existing communitarianism, exacerbating the crime problem.

Communities high in communitarianism typically practice reintegrative shaming. For example, the Japanese not only practice *amaeru* (to be succored by others) but also *amayakasu* (to be nurturing to others) (Wagatsuma and Rosett 1986). A contemporary restorative program in China, *bang jiao*, literally means "help education." Although it begins with stigmatizing encounters, it concludes with reintegrative ones (Lu 1998; Wong 1996; see also Braithwaite 1999). Other Asian and traditionalist cultures with similar levels of communitarianism practices parallel rituals of reintegration (Braithwaite 1989; 1999). Public shaming is important for effective social control, and public ceremonies help promote a shared understanding of acts defined as criminal or immoral. However, moralizing and shaming should occur informally within the offender's social network. Heavy reliance on public forums invites disintegrative shaming, since interdependency at this level may be lower, yielding lower communitarianism.

At the individual level, disintegrative shaming has the most negative impact on individuals who already possess little connectivity to conventionality—young, unmarried, unemployed males with low educational and occupational aspirations. Such individuals lack the interdependencies that negate stigmatizing shame and foster reintegration. Disintegrative

> Reintegrative shaming uses inclusionary rituals to embrace the return of the offender to the community; disintegrative shaming uses exclusionary rituals to push offenders to the community's fringes, maintaining their devalued status.

shaming further weakens their already attenuated ties to conventionality. Absent effective social controls, they join subcultures that endorse antisocial, criminal values. Thus, in Braithwaite's view, disintegrative shaming results in continued and perhaps even increased crime because of its stigmatizing power.

### Looking for Evidence of Reintegrative Shaming

Carter Hay (2001) looked at parental reintegrative practices and shaming. For reintegrative practices, he examined situations where a parent showed a child respect, thought that the child was good even if behaving badly, and eventually forgave the child. Shaming occurred when the parent tried to convince the child that the act was immoral or unfair, made him or her feel guilty or ashamed, or made the child "make up" for the bad deed. Parent–child interdependency was, as the theory predicted, strongly related to parental use of reintegrative practices and, to a lesser degree, their use of shaming. However, Hays' research generated more questions than answers about the influence of shaming. For example, his data supported the idea that reintegrative sanctioning of children leads to high parent–child interdependency, rather than the reverse relationship as predicted by the theory. In addition, the negative effects of shaming on offending were independent of where the offenders were in the reintegration process, a finding also not supportive of reintegrative shaming. Hay proposed that stigmatization may be important but that shaming's moralizing effects may be overstated: an unknown force is the source of harmful stigmatization.

Perhaps the most comprehensive test of reintegrative principles occurred in Australia. Lawrence Sherman and associates (1998) conducted an experimental study called the Re-Integrative Shaming Experiment (RISE), which followed 1,285 offenders and their victims, the former assigned randomly to either traditional processing or involvement in the RISE. Treatment consisted of face-to-face restorative sessions with the victim, based on the group conferencing model. The offender had to consent before seeking the victim's consent. The researchers reported mixed results. The RISE property-crime experiments seemed to cause a decrease in violent offending that was not statistically significant. For other crimes, there were no effects on recidivism; however, victims felt better about their participation when contrasted with nonparticipants (Strang 2002; Tyler, Sherman, and Strang 2007).

Barriers to tests of reintegrative shaming theory's macro-level constructs are significant (Braithwaite 1989; Hay 1998). Large-scale surveys across communities, cultures, or societies would be prohibitively expensive. Moreover, measures of the levels of reintegrative shaming do not currently exist. Mitchell Chamlin and John Cochran (1997), proposed an alternative involving the linking of social altruism levels to crime rates in a sample of several hundred U. S. cities. **Social altruism** is a community's willingness to "share scarce resources to the aid and comfort of their members, distinct from the beneficence of the state" (p. 204). In a test of the theory's macro-level claims, Chamlin and Cochran hypothesized that crime would vary inversely with altruism levels, a prediction consistent with communitarianism. This linkage was present for both property and personal crimes, leading them to speculate that "communities that effectively teach their members to respect and engage in behaviors that promote the welfare of others enjoy relatively lower rates of crime" (p. 221).

Contemporary concerns about reintegrative shaming's utility for criminology fall into two categories. First, criminologists debate whether this is a new theory or a new of looking at old ideas. Braithwaite argues that disintegrative shaming creates fertile ground for other social forces to act, leading to crime. It is difficult to describe reintegrative shaming as an entirely new theory, as it has ties to subcultural (chapter 4), control and learning (chapter 5), and labeling theories.

Second, reintegrative shaming appears to some to be a theory about predatory crime or perhaps only *mala in se* offenses. A central reintegrative shaming assumption is that the consensus surrounding a rule-breaking act generates the shame: no consensus yields little shame. What about crimes for which there is less consensus? Certain drug offenses, for example, may be difficult to cast into a reintegrative shaming framework. Thus, the theory's scope may be limited to explaining predatory offenses against persons and property (Hay 2001).

## SUMMARY

- Modern labeling theory originated during the 1930s.
- Labeling theory acknowledges the power of social institutions to limit a person's life choices by stigmatizing adults as criminals and minor children as delinquents.
- Reintegrative shaming is a very old perspective on punishment and forgiveness.
- Symbolic interactionism explores how individuals render their world meaningful.
- Tannenbaum's idea of the dramatization of evil explains how society transfers and affixes the evil of a deed to individuals, creating the status of "person-as-evil."
- Goffman explained that the successful application of stigmata result in change in the master status of an individual, creating an often irreversible spoiled identity.
- Garfinkel described status degradation ceremonies (e.g., arrest, court appearances, and sentencing) as providing public denunciations of people identified as undesirable, untrustworthy and devalued persons.

- Becker saw deviance as the consequence of the application of a label to a person, which by that act changes their master status.
- Lemert's contributions allow us to understand how some people avoid a deviant label while others do not.
- Schur's four elements of the label (stereotyping, retrospective interpretation, negotiations, and role engulfment) explain the precise mechanisms at work to move a person from primary to secondary deviation.
- Social exclusion is one of the "costs" associated with a negative label; the deeper the penetration into the justice system, the more encompassing the level of social exclusion.
- Secondary sanctioning reflects the sum total of the costs of the labeling episodes, including the first arrest.
- Deviance amplification refers to the process whereby the actions of an official agency, often the police, increase the negative aspects of the behavior controlled by that agency, further devaluing those engaged in it.
- The status characteristics hypothesis extends labeling by suggesting that certain personal characteristics determine whom social control agencies label.
- The context of sanctioning determines whether sanctions cause less offending (deterrence theory) or more offending (labeling theory).
- Early labeling of youthful misbehavior contributes to the cumulative disadvantage affecting the life-course of some people.
- Current evidence tends to favor labeling theory, unlike 30 years ago when it was largely dismissed as untestable.
- Shame is an internal emotional response to embarrassing actions, ideas, words, or thoughts.
- Social fear is the idea that the anticipation of a loss of social standing if a crime is revealed can lead to other crimes to conceal the first.
- Scheff considered shame a better means of social control than guilt.
- Shaming itself is neither positive nor negative.
- Reintegrative shaming seeks to reinforce the offender's status within and importance to the group.
- Disintegrative shaming blames offenders for their action and denies them reentry into the group.
- Communitarianism is behind reintegrative shaming's macro-level processes.
- Disintegrative shaming has the greatest negative impact on individuals who already possess little connectivity to conventionality (e.g., young, unmarried, and unemployed males with low educational and occupational aspirations); they should be the targets of integrative shaming.

• Reintegrative shaming theory tests are generally positive, but limitations on both the studies and the findings suggest more work is required.

## KEY TERMS

| | |
|---|---|
| communitarianism | secondary sanctioning |
| cumulative disadvantage | self-fulfilling prophecy |
| deviance amplification | shame |
| disintegrative shaming | shaming |
| dramatization of evil | social altruism |
| gestural forgiveness | social exclusion |
| hate crime | social fear |
| master status | spoiled identities |
| negotiations | status characteristics hypothesis |
| prestige symbols | status degradation ceremonies |
| primary deviation | stereotyping |
| reintegrative shaming | stigma symbols |
| retrospective interpretation | stigmatization |
| role engulfment | symbol |
| secondary deviation | symbolic interactionist |

## CRITICAL REVIEW QUESTIONS

1. How similar are labeling and reintegrative shaming theories? How do they differ?

2. What are symbols? How does symbolic interactionism help us understand their role in social settings?

3. Compare and contrast Tannenbaum's dramatization of evil, Goffman's stigmatization, and Garfinkel's status degradation ceremonies.

4. Define each of the following terms and give examples: prestige symbols and stigma symbols. How do they help us understand status degradation ceremonies?

5. What is the value of Becker's use of the term master status in the study of crime and delinquency? Do you agree with his ideas about perceived and actual behavior? Explain why you feel the way you do.

6. Compare and contrast Wilkins' deviance amplification with Schur's labeling process.

7. What is meant by the phrase "self-fulling prophesy"? How is this idea reflected in the labeling process?

8. Define primary and secondary deviations. How do they differ from one another? What do they contribute to our understanding of the labeling process?

9. What are Schur's four elements of labeling? Which one do you think is the most important? Why? Which one do you think has the most

application to everyday life, even outside of the study of crime and justice? Why?

10. Define "social exclusion" and "secondary sanctioning." What does each term contribute to our understanding of labeling?

11. "The police are clearly an instrument of "deviance amplification". Attack or defend this statement, describing how you arrived at your position.

12. Since the 1990s, there have been several attempts by criminologists to expand and rethink the labeling process. Which one is most helpful to you? Why?

13. "Not all labels are bad. Not all labels stick, even the bad ones? Having a bad label may not be a bad thing" Dissect these statements and explore them in terms of what you have learned about labeling theory.

14. Shaming seems to be a natural phenomenon. Why do you think it works to curb behavior, even crime, in some situations but not in others?

15. Describe the key elements of reintegrative shaming theory. What are the opposing forces, ones that could move shaming in the opposite direction?

16. What is the importance of communitarianism for reintegrative shaming? Do you think the concept makes it likely or unlikely that reintegrative shaming could be adopted in the United States?

17. Characterize the status of support for reintegrative shaming theory.

# Conflict Theories

## *LEARNING OBJECTIVES*

- Conflict is multilayered and contextual: An individual, group, value, idea, or relationship may create conflict
- When responding to the threat of conflict or actual conflict, the more powerful group may criminalize the behavior of the "offending" party—the weaker group
- Social facts—language, religion, culture—that define who we are as a community can and often do create conditions that are divisive and even destructive
- Laws embody the interests and values of powerful groups in society, sometimes to the detriment of less powerful groups
- Whether a law receives full enforcement or whether those convicted of violating it are given a severe penalty may depend on the offenders' symbolic threat to those making enforcement and sanctioning decisions

# Introduction

Conflict theories, like the structural theories in chapter 6 and the process theories in chapter 7, owe a considerable debt to basic sociological concepts and ideas. For example, in contrast to classical criminology, which assumes society is based on a consensus of moral values, conflict theory asserts that society is built on conflict between disparate groups (Moore and Morris 2011). For all conflict theorists, this process is described as a struggle for **power**, which is the ability of a group to carry out its wishes or policies, attain its goals or intentions, and influence the behavior of others, whether those others share the same vision, goals, intentions, or desires. In the United States, the ability of powerful business interests to influence legislation allows them to keep corporate taxes relatively low, especially when compared to other Western nations. The very richest Americans quietly shape tax policy that allows them to shield billions from taxation (Scheiber and P. Cohen 2015). Power allows those who hold it to influence the definition of crime and the enforcement of laws, so corporate executives' law transgressions are rarely punished with prison sentences, a disposition typically reserved for those at the bottom of the economic ladder.

> Central to all conflict theory is the exercise of power, which is the ability of a group to carry out its wishes or policies, attain its goals or intentions, and influence the behavior of others, whether those others share the same vision, goals, intentions, or desires.

Social scientists examine how the groups with power use and abuse it against those without it, the result sometimes being conflict. **Conflict** is a social condition in which two or more social, political, or cultural groups—each having unique identities, interests, and goals—compete or struggle for the same physical space, resources, power base, or social position in a community, nation, or geographic region. Criminologists are interested in the connection between conflict and crime. Often, the group with power invokes the formal legal process to criminalize their opponents' behavior. The goal is to recast *outsiders* as *outlaws* and to place them and their conduct beyond the law's protection, solidifying and strengthening the power-group's position.

> Conflict theories refer to situations in which there is a struggle for power.

*Oppression* and *coercion* constitute the means by which those with power maintain and extend it. **Oppression** refers to the imposition of excessive and severe burdens on others; **coercion** refers to compelling a requirement or set of conditions on others, often, but not exclusively, through legal authorities. Those who are most powerful in a society control the laws and other key social institutions, including the society's religious, educational, legal, and economic systems through which they can assert and maintain power.

> *Oppression* and *coercion* are two of the primary means by which the powerful maintain their authority.

# Origins of Conflict Theory

Modern conflict theory is deeply rooted in nineteenth and early twentieth century Germany. One adherent was Max Weber (b.1864–d.1920), a German lawyer, economist, and sociologist who studied conflicts between social classes. He was interested in authority relations—why people take or relinquish power and authority and why they feel that others should obey them. Weber (1947[1918]; 1978[1925]) described a system whose purpose was to insure the fair and equal application of legal principles and procedures to all under its dominion as **rational-legal authority**. Even in this ideal state, conflict was inevitable and acceptable, originating in business, religion, government, and law.

German sociologist Georg Simmel (b.1858–d.1918) emphasized the role of **group interests**—the needs, goals, status, power, influence, and other concerns related to the collective's continued existence—in the sociology of conflict. Simmel (1955) argued that when individuals recognize they have interests or needs in common with others, they form groups. These groups collectively seek to further their interests and fulfill their needs. They develop group loyalty and form emotional attachments. Those who infringe on the interests and needs of the group become its enemies, and conflict ensues.

> The desire of one group to protect its interests (needs, goals, status, power, and influence) can lead to conflict with another group trying to achieve the same objectives.

The views of German political philosopher and economist Karl Marx (b.1818–d.1883), known as **Marxism**, are central for an understanding of economic conflict. Marx (1956) saw conflict as deriving from the evils of **capitalism**, the political, economic, and social theory that promotes private ownership and control of a nation's commerce and industry. Working alone and with Friedrich Engels (b.1820–d.1895)—ironically, the son of a wealthy German merchant—Marx described industrialized nations as divided societies in which **capitalists** own the means of production and the **proletariat** (workers) provide the labor. For Marx, power derived from ownership of property and control over the means of production. Capitalists use their power to subjugate the workers, guaranteeing consolidation of wealth by the former. In a capitalist system, a class struggle, also called a **class war**, exists between capitalists and the proletariat. Seeking to maintain dominance, capitalists use their power to mobilize the resources of government—the police and military break strikes—and organized religion—the churches divert the proletariat's attention from current hardship with the promise of a heavenly afterlife.

As capitalism advances, the economic gap between capitalists and exploited workers grows; the result is an increasingly alienated proletariat. Lest we think that these ideas are no longer relevant, consider that the gap between rich and poor is growing in the United States: between 1961 and 2013, the wealth of the richest 1 percent grew six-fold, while the "wealth" of those at the bottom went into negative territory (Urban Institute 2015). As the politicians debate raising the minimum wage in the United States, 15 percent of families hold 85 percent of the nation's wealth (Domhoff 2014).

> Marxists blame capitalism for creating a class-based conflict between the capitalists who have power (and control the means of production) and the relatively powerless working class.

The remainder of this chapter focuses on two primary forms of conflict. *Economic conflict* looks at the use of the economic system to oppress certain classes of people. It is embodied in Marxist criminology, a perspective or paradigm that defines crime in terms of power and oppression. *Social conflict*, the second perspective, explores the use of power as an instrument of social control by identifiable groups; it includes culture conflict and group conflict theories. Those with power seek to keep it, often using forms of oppression and coercion that are virtually identical to the weapons of Marxist criminology's boogeymen, the capitalists. Elements of both perspectives have found their way into twenty-first century mainstream crime theorizing, the latter tending to focus on the characteristics of specific societal groups, including racial and ethnic minorities.

# Economic Conflict and Crime

Marx wrote little about crime and criminals, although he did author treatises on capital punishment (1984[1853]) and criminal law (1964[1862]). Indeed, Marx would likely not be interested in the myriad of biological, psychological, and sociological theories that seek to explain crime. He would see them as an effort to divert attention away from the *real* cause of crime, the exploitation and resulting alienation of the proletariat. The root cause of crime is found in capitalism as critiqued by Marx in his most famous work, *Das Kapital* (1867). For his part, Engels (1958[1845]) wrote that crime was a reflection of the inherent inequities created by capitalism.

> Wealth and power inequities cause alienation and demoralization, particularly among the proletariat, which lead to crime.

## Modern Marxism and Crime

The Dutch criminologist Willem Adriaan Bonger (b.1876–d.1940), often considered the first Marxist criminologist, saw capitalism as promoting greed and self-interest, what he called **excessive egoism.** Bonger believed that those with power criminalized only the greed of the poor, allowing the wealthy (i.e., themselves) to pursue their desires with impunity. Bonger saw capitalism as standing at the problem's core: The poor commit crimes out of need or a sense of injustice when they perceive capitalism's inequities. Poverty alone does not cause crime, but when merged with other negative social forces, including individualism, racism, and materialism, it creates conditions conducive to the rise of criminality.

Bonger saw socialism as a solution to this problem. Socialism, he declared, promotes the general welfare of all citizens, alleviates the legal bias enjoyed by the rich, and undermines the evil influences of capitalism (Bonger 1969[1916]). Socialism's selfless altruism should promote the growth of public-spirited communities, as opposed to the destructive egoism of capitalism. A test of Bonger's ideas, found in box 9.1, suggests he was far ahead of his time in thinking about how capitalism influences crime.

By the middle of the twentieth century, Marxists described ties between capitalism and three specific crime types. First, there are revolutionary *crimes of the proletariat* directed at capitalists. Second, there are

B
O
X
9.1

**A Comparative/Cross-National Test of Bonger's Theory of Criminality and Economic Conditions**

Olena Antonaccio and Charles R. Tittle tested two hypotheses derived from Bonger's theory of criminality and economic conditions.

- The degree of capitalism among societies should be related positively to crime rates in those societies, with the most capitalist societies having the highest crime rates and the least capitalistic having the lowest crime rates.

- Demoralization serves as a mediating link between capitalism and crime, with the degree of demoralization positively related to crime rates.

The researchers included information from 100 nations; the data were from sources generally viewed as providing both reliable and valid information—the World Bank, International Labor Organizations, the United Nations Statistics Division, and the United Nations Office on Drugs and Crime. Antonaccio and Tittle selected homicide as the study's single dependent variable, since previous studies have concluded that this statistic has the most validity and reliability of all crime figures for cross-national comparisons. They used four indicators of capitalism: (1) social security taxes as a percent of income, (2) private health expenditures as a percent of total health spending, (3) the extent to which unions existed in a given nation relative to the others, and (4) an index of income inequality. To this cluster of variables, they added an index of corruption for each nation, as derived from national polls of experts and general surveys reported by the World Bank.

The researchers reported that capitalism is a significant predictor of homicide rates—generally, the higher the level of capitalism, the higher the level of homicide. Corruption, their single indicator of egoism and demoralization, failed to moderate capitalism's effects. Other factors, including gender ratio and religion, impacted homicide rates independently of the degree of capitalism. Specifically, they found that in nations dominated by Eastern religions that promote traditional norms and values, encourage communitarianism, and de-emphasize individualism such as Islam, Buddhism and Confucianism, the capitalism-homicide link was the reverse of that found for nations dominated by the remaining religions. In nations dominated by Eastern religions, the *higher* the level of capitalism, the *lower* the level of homicide. Antonaccio and Tittle concluded that ideas from other theories, but especially social structural and social control theories, have the potential to expand the utility of Bonger's theory.

*Source*: Antonaccio and Tittle (2007).

reactionary *crimes of the lumpenproletariat* that victimize the working class. The **lumpenproletariat**, German for "rabble," is a parasitical group that serves as "storm troopers" for the titans of industry (e.g., used as strike breakers). Third, *crimes of the capitalists—real* crime—are acts of greed and avarice harmful to the common good (e.g., unsafe products, industrial pollution, price-fixing, and food contamination).

These mid-century Marxists viewed crime as capitalism's inevitable by-product. They condemned criminologists who were interested in only minor forces in crime causation and who failed to see the larger social context of crime—the bigger picture in which capitalism leads to a class system of severely differentiated wealth. The resulting social system is one in which the behavior of the weak has a greater chance of being defined as criminal than do the actions of the powerful. The alienated and demoralized underclass reacts in ways defined by capitalists as deviant. Some abuse alcohol and other drugs, while others seek more destructive means to escape capitalism's crushing power. The resulting demoralization generates criminal behavior.

## Twentieth Century American Marxist Criminology

The 1960s and early 1970s saw much political and social upheaval in the United States. During this tumultuous period, American Marxist criminologists, such as Richard Quinney (b.1934–) and William Chambliss (b.1933–d.2014), expanded the basic arguments about the ties between the state, law, and crime. A later generation of Marxist criminologists, including Barry Krisberg (b.1945–) and John Hagan (b.1946–), emphasized power relationships as central to understanding crime.

***Crime and Demystification.*** According to Quinney (1973:vi), crime is best understood as a product of "how the capitalist ruling class establishes its control over those it must oppress." The dominant institutions of a capitalist society—the schools, political organizations, mass media, religions, and the like—mislead, misdirect and openly lie to the proletariat and others about capitalism's exploitative tendencies, resulting in a generalized false consciousness, the inability to see things as they really are. Quinney urged the **demystification** of false consciousness about crime that is fostered by the state and enables oppression to continue. As Chambliss and Robert B. Seidman (1982:315) further observed, the legal order practices high levels of mystification through its accompanying rituals, costumes, and incomprehensible language. While these accoutrements of legal practice may have had a place and purpose at some time, their use today removes the law from everyday life and makes it incomprehensible to all but law's high priests, the attorneys.

Modern Marxist criminologists demystified crime by defining its many forms. The work of Quinney (1973) and Chambliss (1989a, 1989b) led to the consideration of three types of crimes that could be found in a capitalist states: (1) crimes of the working class, (2) crimes of the elite, and (3) crimes of government. Working-class crimes take two main forms. First, *crimes of accommodation* do not challenge the social order; rather, they take place within it. For their part, predatory crimes of accommodation mimic capitalism, in that offenders get property from their victims (e.g., robbery, theft, burglary, and auto theft). Alternatively, violent crimes of accommodation—including homicide, rape, and assault—reflect capitalism's reliance on institutionalized brutalization. Second, *crimes of resistance* are working-class reactions to the ruling elite's exploitation and include both predatory and violent crimes. A revolutionary group could engage in crimes of violence against the state, such

> Demystification is the process of ridding something of its inherent mystery or obscurity, as in revealing the true nature of life's social, legal, and economic conditions, counteracting the false consciousness created by capitalists.

as bombing court buildings or other governmental facilities. Revolutionaries commit predatory crimes, such as bank robbery and kidnapping, to
finance the revolution and hit capitalists where it hurts the most.

*Elite crimes* take three forms. First, elites seek to protect their interests, property, and profits. To accomplish these goals they engage in
*crimes of economic domination*, such as bid rigging and price-fixing,
intended to solidify their control of the means of production. Corporations, as proxies for the elite, also commit *crimes of repression* directly
against the public. This second form of elite crimes includes such acts as
selling faulty or dangerous products even after they are aware of the dangers, such as exploding air bags or faulty ignition switches (Michalowski
1985; Pepinsky and Jesilow 1984).

The third form of elite crime are complicated. *Crimes of control*
involve the actions of the police, courts, and corrections—the instruments of social control for the ruling class. Capitalists call on these crime
control agents, and sometimes the military, to act against workers and the
unions seeking to improve working conditions (Spitzer 1975). For example, until 1929 strikes were criminalized and were routinely crushed by
private police, public law enforcement, and the National Guard.

*Governmental crimes* are as complex as they are important and
include behavior that violates legal guarantees and civil rights (Balkan,
Berger, and Schmidt 1980; Chambliss 1989a). Those who commit these
crimes do so on behalf of the state. According to this view, governments
commit crimes when they engage in military operations that violate other
nations' sovereignty (Chambliss 1988; Clinard and Quinney 1967). In the
aftermath of 9/11, much legal criticism has focused on the U.S. government's alleged violation of the human rights—use of torture—of both
detainees in various secure facilities and combatants in the field (McColgin 2011).

***Crime and the Law.***    Modern American Marxists view the law as
supporting capitalism's interests, whether it is criminalizing conduct that
is a threat to its interests or avoiding the criminalization of conduct that is
viewed as instrumental to its continued existence. Chambliss expanded
on the idea of state control in his analysis of late medieval English property and vagrancy laws. As feudalism declined and was replaced by capitalism, formal laws also emerged, especially laws designed to protect the
interests of early capitalists (Balkan, Berger, and Schmidt 1980). Chambliss (1976) observed that English vagrancy laws reflected the interests of
the economic elites. A compelling indirect force in the creation of
vagrancy laws was the bubonic plague, which decimated the labor force.
The elites were forced to use the English vagrancy law of 1349 to force
work from beggars, setting low wages for their labor and limiting their
movement through the countryside (Chambliss 1964). Moving forward
600 years or more, selective enforcement of vagrancy laws has the effect

The crimes of the
working class are
crimes of *accommo-
dation* and crimes of
*resistance.*

Elite crimes include
economic domina-
tion, crimes of
repression, and
crimes of control.

of increasing the transitory nature of migrant work, which lowers the cost of labor. According to this interpretation, the police only enforce vagrancy laws when the supply of labor is greater than needed in a given area and there is a need to shift workers to other locations, guaranteeing a constant supply of cheap labor (Spradley 1970).

Chambliss (1976) further noted that theft laws protect property, capitalism's cornerstone. However, no systematic laws protected private property in England before 1473. As feudalism gave way to commerce and trade, landowners lost control of the lawmaking process to the emerging economic elites. The new elites could not rely on existing laws because they were too unsophisticated and narrowly defined, only prohibiting theft by servants. The act of stealing by a carrier transporting goods from one city to another was not a crime. In the Carrier's Case of 1473, an English court found a carrier guilty, and thereby designated a new definition of larceny—theft from a carrier's bundles, "which was central to the well-being of the emergent class of capitalist traders and industrialists" (p. 86).

The use of laws to exploit workers was not limited to medieval times. In the United States during the nineteenth and early twentieth centuries, the Supreme Court thwarted federal legislative efforts to prevent the exploitation of children. In 1918 and again in 1922, the Court ruled unconstitutional federal laws intended to restrict the use of child labor. In the first case, a father fought for the right of his minor children—one under age 14 and the other under age 16—to find employment in North Carolina's cotton mills (*Hammer v. Dagenhart et al.* 1918). In the second case, a North Carolina furniture manufacturer successfully fought the imposition of federal taxes intended to restrict the use of child labor (*Bailey et al. v. Drexel Furniture Company* 1922a). In both instances, the Court ruled that the federal government had no business restricting the rights of parents or the exercise of free trade (*Bailey et al. v. George et al.* 1922b). Labor's value to capitalism was more important than the welfare of children.

> As Marxist criminologists see it, law serves the interests of the powerful.

***Crime and Privilege.***     Krisberg's (1975) *Crime and Privilege* helped create a **New Criminology**, which criticized traditional (i.e., "old") criminology as serving the power elite's interests. According to Krisberg, crime studies should be framed by a broader concern for **social justice**—a condition of equality, self-determination, and liberation that strives to eliminate human suffering.

> New Criminology framed crime studies in terms of social justice.

Krisberg (1975) wrote that **privilege** is "the possession of that which is valued by a particular social group in a given historical period" (p. 20). The specific things that are valued—be it land or wealth—may change with time and place, but class, power, and status remain essential and interrelated aspects of privilege. New Criminologists see conflict arising from misuse of privilege systems. Thus, from initial police contacts to processing through the courts and correctional system, privilege systems associated with race, class, and economic statuses determine the fate of those accused of crimes. The poor, the lower classes, and minorities do not commit more crime, but they are more likely to suffer negative processing at the hands of the "(in)justice system." New Criminologists also number women among society's "disprivileged." Although women commit quantitatively less crime than men, they "are often subjected to harsher conditions than men" (p. 25), including disrespect and brutality at the hands of criminal justice officials.

When the privileged engage in rule violations, observed Krisberg (1975), they rarely find themselves accorded the status of criminal, a notion that fits well with Bonger's earlier characterization of capitalists in general. As noted before, even when they are on the receiving end of justice processing, the penalties are generally far lighter than those accorded the crimes of the disprivileged, when—*and if*—elites find themselves in a court of law. Indeed, many harmful deeds of the powerful may not even be defined as "crime" and perpetrators are more likely to be fined than incarcerated.

***Power, Authority, and Crime.*** John Hagan (1989) viewed power as relational; that is, power is meaningful only in terms of how it connects social actors to one another and, ultimately, to crime. He described two such relationships. First, **instrumental power relationships** help us understand how elites achieve certain goals, even when those goals involve criminal acts. Corporate criminals' power resources—enormous capital and political influence—allow them to engage in unsafe disposal of toxic waste, among other illegal practices, with little concern for legal repercussions. While street-level criminals also have power resources at their disposal, including semiautomatic weapons or brute strength, they have greater concerns for legal intervention. Second, **symbolic power relationships** are ones in which society views certain individuals or groups as less vulnerable to control agents because they have comparatively more power. The corporate criminal may appear more reputable and credible than the street-level criminal: *crime in the streets* versus *crime in the suites*.

Power relationships may occur simultaneously and complement each other. Consider, by way of example, the domestic marijuana grower. Many in society view them as drug purveyors, living off human weaknesses. Law enforcement agencies hunt these individuals, who face major sanctions as manufacturers, growers, and distributors of an illegal substance. Domestic marijuana growers may have instrumental power, including vast financial resources and increasingly high-tech farming methods. However, their symbolic power relationships are typically low, owing to how society generally views their work.

Hagan defined class in relation to ownership and authority. Some social actors, including the owners of businesses and those in positions of

Some modern Marxists see two types of power relationships: *instrumental* power relationships, which are the direct means used to achieve a goal, and *symbolic* power relationships, which shape how society views those wielding power.

occupational authority such as corporate executives, have greater resources that can result in crimes with greater impact. Those with little authority and no business ownership commit relatively unimportant crimes—important to only a few, such as the immediate victims or their friends and families (Hagan 1989). Consider that the executives of General Motors who failed to reveal automobile defects that claimed the lives of 124 persons were not incarcerated. In 2015 GM, the corporation, not its executives, was penalized $900 million (Ivory and Vlasic 2015).

# Social Conflict and Crime

Two U.S. criminologists saw conflict as creating the conditions for crime in two very different ways. First, Thorsten Sellin's (b.1896–d.1994) culture conflict theory focused on **conduct norms,** societal rules requiring certain people to act in a specific manner in a given situation (Wirth 1931). Sometimes, for various reasons, the conduct norms of some groups are at odds with those endorsed by others, and conflict ensues. Second, George Vold (b.1896–d.1967), influenced by Simmel, believed that social conflict created crime through the operation of group interests.

> Sellin's conduct norms require people to behave in a certain way given a particular set of circumstances.

## Culture Conflict Theory

Sellin (1938) saw conduct norms as expressions of group cultural values. In a homogeneous society, they express group consensus—there is general agreement about what is right or wrong. In more heterogeneous societies, disagreements may exist about what is right and wrong, as well as what is to be valued and what is to be condemned. **Culture conflict**—the mental and physical clashes that occur when the values and beliefs of two groups collide—are inevitable because "differences in mode of life and the social values evolved by these groups appear to set them apart from other groups in many or most respects" (p. 63). Culture conflict has at least two separate and distinct sources, which Sellin identified as *primary culture conflict* and *secondary culture conflict*. As current world and national events reveal, what Sellin wrote in the 1930s is just as relevant for criminologists today as it was for his contemporaries.

*Primary Culture Conflict.*   Sellin believed one of the three forms of **primary culture conflict** would emerge whenever one culture brings its legal norms to bear on people socialized in a different culture. The first is **cross-border culture conflict,** which can occur when two distinct cultures share a physical border with one another, creating opportunities for those with different conduct norms to clash directly and openly. The extent to which the differences include religion, ideology, language, and political systems often exacerbates the problem. Long-standing enmity toward the *cultural outsider,* a stereotypical representation of those living across the political barrier, makes the likelihood of open conflict even greater, especially if the land on which the border sits is part of the dispute. Consider current world events. One reason for the Islamic State's (ISIS) political and military success in Southwest Asia has to do with their exploitation of the long-standing conflicts between Sunni and Shia Muslims. Predominantly Hindu India and largely Muslim Pakistan have a border dispute that has erupted into open warfare; acquisition of nuclear weapons by both countries has only worsened tensions on the Indian subcontinent. Over the millennia, conflicts that have at their core a religious element have proven hard to defuse and often become extremely violent.

The second form is **colonialism-derived culture conflict**. The term **colonialism** refers to a philosophy, process, policy, and practice whereby one nation establishes **hegemony**, a claim of political dominance, over a geographic area. This claim is generally followed by the settlement of its own citizens in that area with the intent of using or even exploiting the region in perpetuity. These actions led to colonialism-derived culture conflict, which is especially oppressive when the colonizing power declares the indigenous culture to be inferior. During the **Colonial Era**, Britain, France, Portugal, Spain, and the Netherlands variously warred and cooperated with each other from 1500 to 1800, planting their flags and placing their citizens in faraway places, generally ignoring the rights of the original inhabitants to rule themselves and their lands (Wolny 2005). When indigenous residents resisted, the colonial power swiftly and decisively defined those actions as criminal and responded with often brutal police and military force. The European powers maintained colonies into the 1960s, or until they found the political, economic, and social costs of keeping them outweighed their benefits (Englebert 2000; Lange, Mahoney, and vom Hau 2006). France, for instance, found the cost of maintaining control over its colonial empire in Indochina too high—in terms of finances and French lives lost. The French withdrew in ignominious defeat, replaced by the U.S., which itself suffered a humiliating exit from Vietnam in 1975.

The third form of primary culture conflict is **immigrant-status culture conflict**, which can occur whenever immigrants leave one culture to live in another. Sellin described a Sicilian father who avenged his family's honor by killing the "despoiler" of his daughter. Sellin viewed the father's reactions as an example of primary culture conflict: The father could not understand why the police viewed him as a criminal, since in the eyes of his cultural peers the killing was an expected and demanded act of retribution (Sellin 1938).

As box 9.2 on the following page points out, all three forms of Sellin's primary culture conflict are important for our understanding of certain kinds of offenses in the United States in the twenty-first century and around the globe.

Primary culture conflict takes three forms, cross-border culture conflict, colonialism-derived culture conflict, and immigrant-status culture conflict.

**Box 9.2    Consider This: Primary Culture Conflict in the U.S.**

Consider the following three examples of the ways that primary culture conflict have impacted the U.S. over the past 100 years.

*Cross-border primary culture conflict:* Recall the long border shared between the United States and Mexico. Conflict along this border, from water and land disputes to smuggling to illegal immigration, existed even before the 1848 Treaty of Guadalupe Hidalgo that formalized the boundaries after the Mexican–American War. Recent efforts by the federal government to build a physical barrier across the region in the name of homeland security and border integrity have done little to reduce the level of conflict. Not surprisingly, then, illegal migration from Mexico emerged as a major campaign issue in the 2016 presidential campaign. The fact that we share an equally long border with Canada to the north—the longest demilitarized border in the world—only adds fuel to this particular cultural fire.

*Colonialism-derived primary culture conflict:* The relationship between Native American tribes and the U.S. government highlights this particular form of culture conflict. The U.S. government's treatment of the nation's indigenous peoples can be linked to physical genocide (e.g., General Philip Sheridan's infamous quote that "the only good Indian was a dead Indian") and cultural genocide (e.g., the creation of Indian Schools to "assimilate" Indian children into the U.S. mainstream, forbidding both indigenous languages and religious practices). This form of culture conflict continues; the U.S. government continues to exercise control over Native American tribes, including law enforcement, through the Department of the Interior's Bureau of Indian Affairs. The quasi-independent status of Indian reservations permits casino gambling without much government oversight.

*Immigrant-status primary culture conflict:* The Amish, a group that immigrated to North America in the early eighteenth century, refused to participate in universal education beyond the eighth grade. In 1972 (*Wisconsin v. Yoder*), the Supreme Court ruled that the benefits of universal education did not offset the Free Exercise Clause of the First Amendment. On the other hand, in the United States female genital circumcision—removal of all or part of the clitoris—is legally defined as **female genital mutilation (FGM)**, a criminal act. Immigrants from African nations where the practice is widespread run the risk of primary culture conflict—arrest and prosecution. Since 1996, 24 states and the federal government have adopted legal measures targeting FGM.

*Sources*: Armstrong (2000); World Health Organization (2016); Little (2003); Nyangweso (2014).

***Secondary Culture Conflict.*** Sellin's **secondary culture conflict** occurs whenever a group emerges within a dominant culture that has significantly different values and conduct norms (see chapter 6 on delinquent subcultures and chapter 7 on subterranean values). According to Sellin (1938:105), such developments are normal and natural outgrowths of social differentiation, creating many "social groupings, each with its own definitions of life situations, its own ignorance or misunderstanding of the social values of other groups." He did not view the law as a consensus of all views; rather, it was a reflection of the dominant culture's conduct norms. When an emergent group's behavior conflicts with those norms, the dominant culture can declare the behavior a crime.

## Group Conflict Theory

Vold (1958) saw the group as a source of conflict, and his theory incorporates a *pluralistic* view. Like Sellin, Vold saw society as consisting of many different groups whose interests are often overlapping and compatible. However, some interests are unique to particular groups—distinct and incompatible. For example, ranchers in the western U.S. who graze their cattle for free on public land might find themselves at odds with both the government and naturalist groups seeking to keep the areas pristine. These ranchers view themselves as "freedom fighters" and defenders of the Constitution, while other groups may define them as troublemakers at best and criminals at worst. Conflict results when groups seek to expand or to protect their interests; as the level of disagreement grows, in-group loyalties intensify.

When does group conflict rise to the level of criminality? According to **group conflict theory**, groups in positions of authority have their values woven into the law to protect that which they hold dear. Hence, the likelihood of criminalizing the behavior of power-groups is low, but it increases for those with less power but conflicting values.

*Power, Laws, and Group Conflict.*   Vold (1958), similar to some modern Marxist criminologists, saw the legislative "state house" as a key battleground. While one group may wish to criminalize behavior that threatens its interests and needs, another group may view such efforts as threatening its well-being. In the resulting conflict, the group with the most power, money and votes wins—or there is compromise. In the end, the law intrudes on the losers' interests.

Group interests and differences in political power help us understand why legislatures outlaw certain substances such heroin and cocaine, while harmful substances such as tobacco and alcohol—which kill more persons than all of the illegal drugs combined—are freely available (Abadinsky 2014a). The poor, lacking the ability to influence lawmakers, often find their behavior—usually *mala prohibita* or victimless crimes—criminalized. For example, numbers betting—illegal lottery common in lower-class residential areas—promises quick riches for little money invested. As a result, it clashed with middle-class values of hard work and thrift, and local and state governments criminalized it. Late in the twentieth century cash-strapped state governments found virtue in gambling and the legal lottery has proliferated, as has casino gambling. Moreover, by legalizing gambling in the form of lotteries, the interests of multiple groups are satisfied: the poor have access to the promise of wealth; anti-gambling interests see the activity as controlled, monitored, and restricted; and legislators gain a revenue stream without taxation. Lottery opponents decry government advertisements promoting gambling aimed at lower-income populations (Abadinsky 2013) and see lotteries as a regressive form of taxation aimed at the poor (Clotfelter and Cook 1991).

The poor, lacking the power to shape laws, often find some of their behavior outlawed as *mala prohibita* crimes.

*Crime as Minority Power-Group Behavior.* According to Vold (1958), crime is the behavior of minority power-groups, collectives that lack sufficient influence to promote or defend their interests and needs (see Sellin's secondary culture conflict). Finding themselves disconnected from the law-making process, they are more likely to violate existing laws that conflict with their interests and needs ("If it's not my law, why should I do as it says?"). For example, inner-city gang members may feel disenfranchised from the power structure represented by the dominant majority. They may engage in behavior that the law prohibits, such as underage drinking and illicit drug use. The youth gangs conflict with the police who represent the majority's interests. Police actions (representing the majority's interests) against gangs solidify in-group loyalties. It is important to note that Vold's minority-power groups were not simply minority racial or ethnic groups *per se*, but rather groups that were in relative positions of powerlessness.

## Contemporary Conflict-Based Crime Theorizing

By the mid-1980s, American criminology all but gave up Marxist ideas of crime control (Anderson 2002; Russell 2002). There were also few tests of culture conflict theory (Lee 1995), and tests of social conflict theories were rare (Akers and Sellers 2013). At about the same time, theory-based discussions about conflict and crime began to refocus on specific population subgroups such as racial and ethnic minorities (Liska and Chamlin 1984; Smith 1986) and women (Hagan 1990). With respect to women in particular, Hagan's (1989) **power–control theory** saw wives in patriarchal families as having little power compared with husbands, just as daughters have less freedom when compared with sons. According to Hagan, these differences should decrease in families with egalitarian structures, in which the spouses share power or in which the father is missing. Tests of Hagan's theory on delinquency yielded generally positive results (Hagan and Kay 1990; Singer and Levine 1988). However, they reported that irrespective of family type—patriarchal versus egalitarian families—girls were far more controlled than were boys (Morash and Chesney-Lind 1991; Blackwell 2000).

These emergent **neo-conflict theories** owed much to the split in conflict theorizing: *economic* conflict versus social or *cultural* conflict. It also had links to the work of Swedish sociologist Gunnar Myrdal (b.1898–d.1987), who in 1944 published *An American Dilemma: The Negro Problem and Modern Democracy*, wherein he catalogued the barriers to full participation by blacks in U.S. society. Myrdal's (1944) assessment of U.S. race relations in the 1940s was unflattering and predictive: "White prejudice and discrimination keep the Negro low in standards of living, health, education, manners and morals. This, in its turn, gives support to white prejudice. White prejudice and Negro standards thus mutually 'cause' each other" (p. 75).

## Social Threat Thesis

During the late 1960s, the United States experienced heightened racial tensions; moreover, African-American crime rates came under scrutiny. At about this time, criminologists and sociologists started to consider the perceptions held by whites concerning the "threats" represented by various racial and ethnic groups. Herbert Blalock (b.1926–d.1991) wrote in *Toward a Theory of Minority Group Relations* (1967) that majority groups escalate punitive efforts to protect their base of power as the size of any minority group increases until it reaches 50 percent, when such efforts cease and power sharing becomes far more likely. Blalock observed that the white-majority enacted three forms of discrimination to keep blacks in their (economic) place, including political discrimination (e.g., poll taxes and literacy tests), symbolic segregation (e.g., Jim Crow law, which enforced separate but "equal" practices), and "threat-oriented" ideologies (e.g., the white belief that black males are predisposed to violence, which justified punitive criminal sanctions levied against them). Blalock's *economic threat thesis* characterized the increasing proportion of minority group members as a threat to the economic power-base of the majority.

In *Criminality and Legal Order* (1969), Austin Turk (b.1934–d.2014) argued the following: "The greater the cultural differences between the evaluator and violator, the less likely are psychological sanctions which assume a capacity and readiness to subtle cues to get through to the violator, and therefore sanctioning will have to be more physically coercive in order to enforce the norm" (p. 285). Conflict, then, results when there is a breakdown between cultural norms (i.e., the laws as written) and social norms (i.e., the laws as enforced). When certain groups in society fail to embrace the cultural norms and the authority of law enforcement agencies fails to control their behavior, an enhanced police presence may prove necessary to control them, just as the courts may find it necessary to enact more punitive measures. Turk saw blacks, the poor, and the unemployed as representing groups that threaten society's cultural norms and legal order.

## Minority-Threat Theory

Within a decade the work of Blalock and Turk formed the conceptual framework for the **social threat thesis**, or the idea that certain identifiable groups, by their actions or inactions threaten the social, political and, economic order; moreover, those groups were often defined by their race or ethnicity. Sociologist Allen E. Liska (b.1940–d.1998) and associates reframed the social threat thesis, suggesting that it was not simply about political and economic pressures but also reflected threats to morals, values, and personal safety. In a series of works, culminating in *Social Threat and Social Control* (1992), they observed the conditions under which such groups pose a threat to the elites in society, which elicits a punitive response from the criminal justice system. As Barbara D. Warner (1992) notes about the minority-threat theory's main proposition: "Particular situations (e.g., large percentages of nonwhites and income inequality) are perceived as threatening to the normal social order by elites, and that these elites will bring about increased coercive control" (p. 75). While the use of police is not the only mechanism at the disposal of the elites, it certainly is one of the first deployed.

**Minority-threat theory** has been at the center of much recent police-related research, including studies of racial profiling (Petrocelli, Piquero, and Smith 2003), police expenditures (Holmes et al. 2008), police allocation of resources (Ruddell and Thomas 2010), representative policing (Barrick, Hickman, and Strom 2014), and police shootings (Sorenson, Marquart, and Brock 1993). The specific nature of the perceived threat, however, has several manifestations. In an examination of police-citizen complaints across the nation, increases in the percentage of minorities in a community (Jacobs and O'Brien 1998; Sorensen et al. 1993) and whether police officers personally perceive a minority threat (Liska and Yu 1992) show distinctive links to police homicides. In fact, the perception of the race-linked danger—for example, the percentage of a racial minority in the community, rather than cross-racial crime—may be the most crucial variable at work. Moreover, William P. McCarty and colleagues (2012) found in their study of police strength in large U.S. cities in the 1990s that the percentage of blacks in the population was a strong predictor of police strength.

The conflict perspective, especially when both economic and social threats are considered, adds to our understanding of not only crime in America, but also the formal responses of the criminal justice system. As we shall see in chapter 10, conflict theory has broad-ranging implications for criminal justice policies and practices.

## SUMMARY

- The inequities between the "haves" and the have-nots" is best expressed in terms of power.
- Conflict is said to exist between two or more unique groups when they compete or struggle for the same limited resources, including physical space or social position within a geopolitical unit.
- Oppression and coercion are two of the means by which the powerful establish, maintain, and extend their power over others.
- Weber, who was interested in authority relations, felt that in a rational-legal authority, conflict is not only inevitable but also acceptable.
- Simmel saw group interests as playing a role in emergent conflicts as groups seek to further their collective interest and fulfill their needs.

- Marx saw all social life as a struggle—a conflict—between the capitalists, the owners of the means of production, and the proletariat, the workers.

- Crime is, for Marxists, an inevitable by-product of capitalism, as the alienated and demoralized underclass reacts in ways defined by capitalists as deviant.

- Bonger saw capitalism as promoting excessive egoism, which, along with racism, materialism, and false masculinity, underlies much crime.

- Demystification of false consciousness stands at the center of Quinney's ideas on crime and oppression.

- Marxist criminologists described two forms of working class crime: crimes of accommodation and crimes of resistance.

- Marxist criminologists described three forms of elite crime: crimes of economic domination, crimes of repression, and crimes of control.

- Marxist criminologists saw crimes of government as complex; they include illegal and immoral acts directed against those being governed as well as the enemies of the state, internal and external.

- The New Criminology maintained that social justice should frame crime studies.

- Privilege is a key idea for New Criminologists, something largely unknown by the poor, lower socioeconomic classes, racial and ethnic minorities, and women.

- Marxist criminologists are critical of the state for its role in supporting capitalists and their means and goals.

- Marxist criminologists often rely on legal analysis to provide supporting evidence.

- Hagan maintained that power is meaningful only in terms of how it connects actors to one another and ultimately to crime.

- Instrumental power is the ability to use power to achieve specific goals.

- Symbolic power refers to perceptions of the powerful as less vulnerable to control agents.

- Conflict criminologists look at culture and group interests as explaining crime.

- Sellin saw culture conflict as existing in two main forms: primary culture conflict and secondary culture conflict.

- Primary culture conflict had three forms: cross-border culture conflict, colonialism-derived culture conflict, and immigrant-status culture conflict.

- Secondary culture conflict relates to subgroups in a dominant culture and resembles chapter 6's subcultural conflict.

- Vold's group conflict theory assumes a pluralistic societal view and suggests that groups in conflict over group-defined interests tend to solidify in-group loyalties.
- Vold saw crime as the law-breaking behavior of minority power-groups—those with the least power to impact legislation (not necessarily racial and ethnic minority groups)
- Neo-conflict theories have taken elements from both economic conflict and social-cultural conflict perspectives, mixed it with an appreciation for the roles of race, ethnicity, and gender in contemporary society, and created a far more contextualized conflict theory.

## KEY TERMS

capitalism
capitalists
class war
coercion
Colonial Era
colonialism
colonialism-derived culture conflict
conduct norms
conflict
cross-border culture conflict
culture conflict
demystification
excessive egoism
female genital mutilation
group conflict theory
group interests
hegemony
immigrant-status culture conflict

instrumental power relationships
lumpenproletariat
Marxism
minority-threat theory
neo-conflict theories
New Criminology
oppression
power
power-control theory
primary culture conflict
privilege
proletariat
rational-legal authority
secondary culture conflict
social justice
social threat thesis
symbolic power relationships
instrumental power relationships

## CRITICAL REVIEW QUESTIONS

1. Define conflict. How do oppression and coercion help us understand conflict?
2. Compare and contrast the views of Weber and Simmel on conflict.
3. According to Marxism, what is the basis of the conflict-crime connection?
4. Explain the main thesis expressed by each of the following: Bonger, Quinney, and Krisberg. How are they similar? How are they different?
5. What are the main ideas expressed by Chambliss and Hagan. How are they similar? How are they different?
6. How did English laws in the late medieval period support emergent capitalism?

7. What is the basic thesis supporting Sellin's culture conflict theory? Which of the two forms of culture conflict provides, in your opinion, the greatest threat insights into crime and criminality?

8. How are Sellin's statements about primary culture relevant in today's world?

9. How do the assumptions made about human behavior found in Sellin's culture conflict theory and Vold's group conflict theory differ?

10. How is conflict theory useful as a tool to understand conflict between or within nations?

11. What is the greatest strength and the greatest shortcoming of conflict theory?

12. What do the views of Turk and Blalock add to the "social threat thesis"?

13. How did the work of Liska and associates alter the discussion of the threat perceived to originate with racial and ethnic minorities?

14. What elements of both economic conflict and social conflict are central to minority threat theory?

15. What is the greatest strength of neo-conflict theories?

# 10

# From Theory to Practice

*LEARNING OBJECTIVES*

- How the theories covered in this text find expression in various public policies on crime control

- How crime theories influence agencies of social control—the police, courts and corrections

- How crime theories are useful for understanding the nature of police-citizen and police-offender interactions as well as how the police see themselves and how they perform their jobs

# Introduction

This chapter examines how policy analysts and criminal justice practitioners use criminological theories in their work. Some applications of theory are direct and intended; others are more indirect or even unconscious. By looking at the connections between theoretical principles and how they are applied, we enhance our understanding of criminological theory as well as crime-control policies and practices.

# Crime Theories and Crime Control

Criminologists traditionally have had a somewhat ambivalent view of theory's application to practice. Some criminologists believe that "because criminology's research and associated knowledge base is not causally certain, they should not and cannot responsibly inform public policy" (Blomberg, Mestre, and Mann 2013: 571). Other criminologists argue that assisting crime policy makers can further victimize minority populations. In the opinion of these critics, such actions make criminologists part of the problem and not part of the solution.

Crime policy is highly politicized. Public officials may not know—or care—if a particular policy is supported or refuted by crime theory research. Elected officials generally discuss crime only in terms that will appeal to the voting public. The specifics, such as how to determine if there is an increase or decrease in the crime rates or whether a police presence on the street actually reduces crime, are not likely to win votes. Deplorable crimes, including those that end in the death of a child, attract public attention and result in legislation such as the Adam Walsh Child Protection and Safety Act and Megan's Law without any research to support the actions taken. Indeed, much crime policy appears based on buzzwords and metaphors: "zero tolerance," "broken windows," "truth-in-sentencing," and "three-strikes-and-you're out" (Abadinsky 2016).

> Crime control policies and practices can emerge absent empirical proof that they will impact the crime and justice issues to which they allegedly respond.

Both criminologists and public officials support **evidence-based policy (EBP)**; moreover, it has been adopted by agencies across the criminal justice spectrum—from police to parole. EBP refers to the belief that policies should be based on the best scientific evidence available (Cartwright and Stegenga 2011). Various states, including Kentucky, Michigan, Mississippi, and Washington passed legislation mandating that policies be based on evidence. This widespread trend toward mandating EBP exists despite questions about the methodological soundness of much crime research (cf., Boaz et al. 2008; Sullivan, Hunter and Fisher 2013).

The next section looks at the policy implications of the theories discussed in chapters 2 through 9.

## Classical Criminology, Deterrence Theory, and Crime Control Policy

Deterrence theory, as derived from Classical Criminology, forms the basis for the U.S. system of criminal justice, which presumes that unless an offender is a child or suffers from a serious mental defect, he or she has "free will" and, therefore, is accountable for his or her behavior. Furthermore, equal justice requires that offenders be punished based solely on their behavior. The classical concept of proportionality demands that punishment be commensurate with the crime. Finally, classical criminologists see humans as hedonistic beings that must be deterred from behavior that, while pleasurable, is harmful to others.

Deterrence theory is the foundation for the widespread policy of arresting the aggressor in a domestic violence call. This policy is based on a 1980s experiment commonly referred to as the Minneapolis study of domestic violence. Police officers responding to domestic violence calls were required to take one of three predetermined actions—no discretion was allowed—in misdemeanor-level cases when both the suspect and victim were present: (1) arrest, (2) mediation/counsel, or (3) separation (require the suspect to leave the premises and not return for 24-hours). The Minneapolis experiment offered support for deterrence theory: arrest had the most positive outcome—a significant reduction in domestic violence (Sherman and Berk 1984a, 1984b).

Despite the limited research—and caution expressed at the time by the original researchers—a policy of **mandatory arrest** was implemented in many jurisdictions around the nation. Replications of the experiment failed to achieve the same results. Moreover, subsequent research has revealed that mandatory arrest policy did not necessarily reduce domestic abuse and, in many cases, made the situation worse (Sampson, Winship, and Knight 2013). "The evidence shows that, while arrest deters repeat domestic violence in the short run, arrests with brief custody increase the frequency of domestic violence in the long run among offenders in general" (Sherman et al. 1992a, 1992b). What this cautionary tale also reveals is that once policies and associated practices are in place, change is difficult—even when the evidence suggests that it may be the wrong response (Walker 2015; Mays and Ruddell 2015).

> Mandatory arrest is a policy and practice grounded in the Minneapolis domestic violence experiment, whereby officers arrest the aggressor without exception.

*Rational choice theory* tells us that offenders assess the costs and benefits of illegal activities and that they choose to commit a crime only if the expected benefits from that choice exceed the expected costs associated with it (the probability of apprehension and the severity of punishment). Policy based on rational choice focuses on increasing the probability of apprehension—enhanced law enforcement—and severity of punishment, the latter resulting in longer periods of incarceration. However, we know from research that most crimes are not solved—indeed, most are not even reported (Federal Bureau of Investigation 2015). The likelihood of arrest and imprisonment may seem remote to most offenders. Moreover, apply-

Mass incarceration is a term that refers to both the high overall rate of incarceration in the United States and the tendency of the nation's correctional system to house disproportionate numbers of young minority males, especially youth of color.

A crime impact assessment is an architectural planning document intended to identify, predict, evaluate, and mitigate the crime and disorder effects of a development proposal early in the design.

For ethical and political reasons, applying biological models to public policy is untenable.

ing even longer prison sentences more often in a system characterized as **mass incarceration** may prove counterproductive (Comfort 2007).

*Routine activity theory* suggests that there will never be an absence of *motivated offenders* nor sufficient *capable guardians*—people at work generally leave their homes unguarded, although some communities use volunteer citizen-patrols, and others may be protected by the fearsome reputation of some residents. Consequently, an anti-crime policy based on routine activity theory could focus on limiting *suitable targets*. Individuals should be cautioned to avoid the ostentatious displays of jewelry or clothing and expensive automobiles that provide tempting targets for armed robbers and car thieves. Increased guardianship through a neighborhood watch program is another possibility.

*Defensible space's* alleged role in deterring crime also has specific ties to public policy and anti-crime practices. Gated communities where guards or gates allow only residents, guests, and service or delivery vehicles to enter are designed to prevent crime. Speed bumps can impact an offender's automotive entry and escape, as can one-way streets. High-rise public housing is often vulnerable to considerable crime because residents cannot provide adequate guardianship. Newer public housing is tending toward low-rise designs that maximize natural surveillance. Solmaz Amiri (2014) has further recommended that existing federal and state laws requiring developers to provide a formal environmental impact assessment should also include a **crime impact assessment** based on the architecture of defensible space.

## Biology and Crime Control Policy

Crime policy tied to biology is especially challenging. From a legal theory perspective, a person whose crime is the result of a biological defect lacks *mens rea* and should not be punished. Society may choose preventive detention or some other restriction, but the remedy should not be done in the name of *punishment*. In the event that geneticists could identify a crime gene, what should society do about it? If we were unconcerned about moral or legal concerns, public policy would be quite straightforward and simple: isolate or eliminate. Moreover, if criminal behavior results from genetic makeup, policy dictates preventing "crime genes" from being passed on to successive generations. Policy to do this, as noted in chapter 3, was partially implemented in the U.S. and an offshoot of this was horrifically implemented in Nazi Germany.

Patricia A. Brennan and associates (1995) identified several policy implications with regard to *genetics* and crime. They pointed out that we can predict antisocial behavior from the interaction of perinatal factors (i.e., those occurring during pregnancy and delivery) and unstable family environments. Providing prenatal health care to mothers and early hospitalization could reduce perinatal problems. Geneticists tell us that a genetic predisposition does not mean that a specific outcome is inevitable—genes are not destiny (Steen 2001). In fact, there is evidence that the environment may influence genetic makeup; genetic *and* environmental factors interact, and positive environmental influences may offset the genes that promote crime.

Biochemists have also provided evidence that a dysfunctional central nervous system increases susceptibility to psychoactive chemicals. Heroin and cocaine users may be self-medicating. Because the substances are illegal, the user is labeled a criminal. Legalizing the drugs or making substitutes such as methadone available would remove criminal sanctions. It would also impact on drug-trafficking. The policy of increasing law enforcement efforts and penalties has obviously not worked (Pacula, Chriqui, and King 2003; Winterbourne 2012). Perhaps a shift to a drug policy based on treatment would prove beneficial and would certainly be cheaper than our current focus on law enforcement. A recent public opinion poll found that two-thirds of all Americans favor this shift in focus (Pew Research Center 2014).

> While most Americans seem to favor it, shifting the nation's drug policy from a law enforcement response to a treatment response may not be politically feasible.

## Psychology and Crime Control Policy

The goal of crime control policy tied to psychoanalytic theory and behaviorism is the rehabilitation of offenders. *Psychoanalysis* is rarely used to treat adolescents and adults in the criminal justice system, although there is widespread use of therapies based on psychoanalytic theory. A variety of helping professionals (psychiatrists, psychologists, social workers, persons frequently working in courts and prisons, and those employed by public and private agencies) use methods based on psychoanalytic theory.

Criminal justice professionals often apply *behaviorism* in institutional settings such as prisons and training schools. Behavior modification provides positive reinforcement for prosocial behavior. Behavior theory also provides the basis for cognitive behavioral therapy, which is a popular approach in the treatment of offenders (Clark 2010; Tolin 2010).

Interest in *psychopathy* has led to the development of diagnostic tests—but not treatment. There appears to be very little that can be done for those diagnosed as psychopaths (Bonn 2014). Correctional personnel use the PCR-Revised (chapter 4) as a way to manage the potential threat posed by psychopaths. Probation and parole officers can use close supervision techniques to monitor offenders diagnosed as psychopathic.

## Social Structure and Crime Control Policy

Theories of *social structure* have been among the richest sources of public policy initiatives in the history of criminology (Akers and Sellers 2013). The idea of extending opportunities to the disadvantaged fits with a liberal view of the role of government. For example, Richard Cloward and Lloyd Ohlin's (1960) ideas led to significant public policy initiatives. Attorney General Robert Kennedy, after reading *Delinquency and Opportunity*, asked Ohlin to develop a program that addressed the nation's juvenile delinquency problem. The Juvenile Delinquency Prevention and Control Act of 1961 was a direct attempt to extend legitimate opportunities for success to lower-class youth.

After the death of President John F. Kennedy, his successor, Lyndon B. Johnson, extended the act to all of the economically disadvantaged through his **War on Poverty**, which funded initiatives on education, job training, food aid, health care, housing, and community action. However, Cloward and Ohlin's work may have inadvertently created an "us versus them" mentality. Federally funded community legal services sued local and state governments, and rent strikes and demonstrations sponsored by federally funded antipoverty groups generated considerable publicity—garnering the outrage of public officials on the receiving end of this activism. Much of the nation's business community and many in the political sector opposed these programs. Finally, although Washington funded no evaluations of the War on Poverty, President Richard M. Nixon declared the programs a failure and dismantled many of them.

Two fatal flaws that doomed the initiatives related to the War on Poverty offer lessons to anyone attempting to apply a criminological theory to a social problem. The first flaw grew out of the mobilization for political and social empowerment (Moynihan 1969). Program leaders assumed increasingly activist positions on behalf of the poor and disenfranchised. These changes brought them into conflict with local and federal politicians, a conflict they were destined to lose. As Lamar Empey (1982) observed, "Influential members of Congress made it clear that the mandate of the President's Commission was to reduce delinquency, not to reform society or try out sociological theories on American youth." Second, the goals of the opportunity-based programs created obvious problems. If such programs increase the education and job skills of participants, only an expanding economy allows them to secure a level of economic success sufficient to negate the anomic trap. Failure to secure such employment, after investing considerable time and effort, may escalate the anomic condition.

> An academic study led to the nationwide application of a theory-based program to reduce crime and disorder, but politics led to its demise.

## Process Theories and Crime Control Policy

The differential association/social learning tradition troubles some policy makers. The "crime-as-learned-behavior" argument is commonsensible, but some policy makers miss key parts of the theory and may oversimplify *social learning*. For example, when we are young, our parents encourage us to avoid bad companions. Early in school we learn to avoid contact with people identified by teachers and others as troublemakers—and we observe that they are often suspended or expelled from school. Later, as we start our careers, we continue to encounter warnings against bad companions, especially "slackers" and others with poor work habits. This simplistic interpretation overlooks the fact that social learning is not simply a case of "birds of a feather flock together." Controlling the sources of definitions favorable to law-violating behavior is a far more difficult task than avoiding bad companions.

Ronald L. Akers and Christine S. Sellers (2013:100-109) maintain that social learning's influences are evident in a wide range of early delinquency prevention and intervention policies and programs. Some of these policies originated in the 1950s. At Highfields, an alternative residential treatment program for delinquent boys, counselors created a technique called guided group interaction. Peer groups provide prosocial definitions, attitudes, and behavior (Weeks 1958). Since 1977, the Oregon Social Learning Center (OSLC) has operated an ambitious crime prevention program that delivers services to families based on social learning theory (Reid, Patterson, and Snyder 2002). The program, called coercion theory, uses cognitive and behavioral programming to teach parenting skills and problem-solving skills for children faced with stressful situations.

According to *social control theory*, delinquent acts ensue when an individual's bond to society is weakened or broken. Attachments to conventional persons work against crime, whereas the absence of such attachments frees youth from moral constraints. In areas of urban poverty, many children live without parents, creating what Jane Gross (1992) called America's "new orphans." Parents are institutionalized—in prisons, jails, or residential drug programs—or living marginal existences under the influence of drugs or alcohol. Even if present, parents may be unwilling or ill-equipped to care for their offspring. Children farmed out to relatives, friends, foster care, or institutions experience little stability and few, if any, lasting emotional ties.

Social control theory directs policy makers to focus on strengthening social bonds to conventional groups, institutions, and activities. A government program to provide funds to poor families with children was created in 1935. Aid to Families with Dependent Children (AFDC) was replaced with Temporary Assistance for Needy Families (TANF) in 1996. Most states have time limits of five years, and recipients must be working or risk losing benefits. TANF does far less than AFDC did to alleviate poverty (Policy Basics 2015) and, by extension, crime. In 1996, 68 families received TANF for every 100 families in poverty; in 2013, the ratio was 26 families for every 100. Strong social bonds—attachment to others, commitment to conventional goals, involvement in conventional activities—restrict acting in self-interest. "New orphans" have far fewer opportunities to develop social capital and are much more likely to suffer from what Sampson and Laub refer to as cumulative disadvantages.

> Simply keeping bad models away from a child does not guarantee that other social learning forces will not promote a delinquent orientation.

> Coercion theory addresses the aggressive and anti-social behavior resulting from ineffectual parental responses to escalating problem behavior by children.

## Labeling, Restorative Justice and Crime Control Policy

*Labeling theory* is one of the richest theoretical perspectives. Proponents of public policy based on labeling theory seek to reduce the stigma that attaches to those labeled a delinquent or criminal. For example, **decriminalization** refers to a reduction in the number of outlawed behaviors (e.g., possession of small amounts of marijuana). **Diversion** attempts to avoid unnecessarily stigmatizing persons who violate the law by providing alternatives to official criminal justice processing. The police or prosecutor's office can operate diversion programs for adults and juveniles, referring certain offenders to treatment, counseling, or employment training programs instead of official processing. However, many observers of the criminal justice system criticize diversion for contributing to **net widening** (Blomberg 1980)—if there were no diversion programs available, the police would not arrest, and prosecutors would not charge. As an unintended consequence, diversion may add to the number of people under the control of the criminal justice system (Austin and Krisberg 1981).

Labeling theorists are all too aware of incarceration's negative effects. Given that incarceration may facilitate secondary deviation, many system critics rally around **deinstitutionalization**, the removal of inmates from prisons, jails, and juvenile detention centers. Most states no longer incarcerate **status offenders**—children whose behavior is prohibited only because of their age, such as truancy and underage drinking. The Juvenile Justice and Delinquency Prevention Act of 1974 and subsequent federal legislation mandate the removal of juveniles from jails intended to house adults, although many states have been slow to act (Mays and Winfree 2012).

> In recognition of the power of a negative label to limit opportunities, most states no longer incarcerate status offenders.

Labeling theorists also acknowledge the state's power over the individual. It is not surprising, therefore, that during the 1960s and 1970s, labeling supporters championed the extension of **due process guarantees** to juveniles. As a result of *Kent v. United States* (1966) and *In re Gault* (1967), juveniles accused of acts of delinquency are accorded the right to counsel, as well as other due process rights. The U.S. Supreme Court ruled that the adult standard of guilt "beyond a reasonable doubt" must be used in cases of alleged delinquency, rather than the traditional standard of the "preponderance of evidence (*In re Winship* 1971). In *Breed v. Jones* (1975), the U.S. Supreme Court held that trying a juvenile in adult court after being tried in a juvenile court constituted double jeopardy. However, juveniles do not enjoy the full range of adult due process protections, including, for example, the right to a jury trial (*McKiever v. Pennsylvania* 1971). Moreover, pretrial detention was not viewed as a violation of the juvenile's due process rights (*Schall v. Martin* 1984).

> Labeling theory guides the 4-Ds—decriminalization, diversion, deinstitutionalization and due process guarantees—an impact few other theories can match.

Edwin Schur (1973:30) warned that labeling can set in motion "a complex process of response and counter-response with an initial act of rule-violation and developing into elaborated delinquent self-conceptions and a full-fledged delinquent career." Some researchers reported that the majority of those whose first referral to juvenile court was a status offense did go on to more serious act of delinquency. For example, there is evidence that youngsters adjudicated in juvenile court on their first referral were *less* likely to have criminal records as adults than those whose referrals were delayed until further misbehavior occurred (Brown et al. 1991). As suggested in box 10.1, however, reducing the likelihood of a deviant label's attachment to an ex-offender is generally viewed as a good objective.

**Restorative justice (RJ)** is based on the *reintegrative shaming* that rule violators can be brought back into the community, healing the rifts that their misbehavior caused. RJ has historical roots in Western and non-Western cultural traditions (Braithwaite 1999). Ancient Arab, Greek, Roman, and Germanic peoples practiced restorative or healing rituals.

---

**BOX 10.1**

### Removing Barriers to the Reintegration of Ex-Offenders

The impact of labeling is felt by those who have a criminal record in the form of a denial of employment and education opportunity. Three examples of efforts to remove these barriers are insightful. First, there is a movement, sometimes referred to as "ban the box"—that part of an employment application asking about a criminal record—that seeks to improve the employability of those with a criminal record. About a dozen states and over fifty cities and counties have taken steps to remove barriers to government employment, and sometimes private employment, for qualified workers with criminal records, specifically by removing conviction history questions from job applications. They typically do not prevent employers from asking questions about a criminal record, but simply postpone the question to later in the interview. Georgia, the first state in the South to endorse the movement, requires state agencies to offer qualified applicants the chance in a follow-up interview to contest the content and relevance of a criminal record and to provide information that demonstrates rehabilitation.

Second, in an effort to minimize the legal harm caused by a criminal record, some states have removed various statutory restrictions on gaining licenses necessary for employment, and a few have even enacted "fair employment" laws for ex-offenders. New York City's "Fair Chance Law," for example, prohibits the denial of employment or license because of a conviction unless there is a "direct relationship" between the conviction and the specific employment or license or it involves an "unreasonable risk" to persons or property. A direct relationship requires a showing that the nature of the criminal conduct for which the person was convicted has a direct bearing on the fitness or ability to carry out duties or responsibilities related to the employment or license. The statute requires that a public or private employer provide, on request, a written statement setting forth the reasons for a denial of license or employment and provides for enforcement by the New York State Commission on Human Rights.

Finally, the Federal Bonding Program, which is administered through state employment services agencies, has a long-standing program that provides bonding for probationers and parolees without any cost to either the employee or the employer. Established in 1966 by the U.S. Department of Labor, the Federal Bonding Program guarantees the honesty of at-risk job seekers, such as those on probation or parole. Employers receive the bonds free-of-charge as an incentive to hire hard-to-place job applicants. This approach could be extended with government offering cost-free insurance and limiting the liability of employers who employ ex-offenders.

*Sources:* Eisen (2014); Rankin (2015); U.S. Department of Labor (2016).

Buddhists, Hindus, Taoists, and Confucianists all recognize the importance of restoring community harmony and balance after a wrongful or disruptive act. Contemporary aboriginal peoples around the globe, including the United States, employ peacemaking and reintegration models.

American criminal law views the state as victim, with the "actual" crime victim placed in a passive and secondary role (Carlson 1993). Restorative justice (RJ) "views crime as a violation of one person by another, rather than against the state" (Maloney and Umbreit 1995: 43). Emerging during the 1970s as part of the victim's movement, restorative justice promotes maximum involvement of the victim, the offender, and the community (Bazemore and Maloney 1994; Bazemore and Schiff 2001). Instead of simply punishing those who commit crimes (retributive justice), RJ's focus is on allowing the offender the opportunity to make amends to his or her victim (Umbreit 1994).

> Disintegrative shaming makes criminal labels hard to shake; the goal of reintegrative shaming is the return of offenders to the status of productive citizen.

Restorative justice entails a variety of different practices, including apologies, restitution, and acknowledgments of harm and injury, as well as other efforts to provide healing and reintegration of offenders into their communities (with or without punishment). Restorative justice usually involves direct communication, often with a facilitator, between victims and offenders (Menkel-Meadow 2007). Perpetrators must listen to the human side of the injuries they have caused and take responsibility for repairing the resulting damage.

Not everyone views RJ and its methods as a positive policy or practice, nor is the evidence overwhelming that it has the intended impact on victims or perpetrators. For example, victim rights advocacy groups have been critical of restorative justice: The RJ process "can cast victims as little more than props in a psychodrama focused on the offender, to restore him (and thereby render him less likely to offend again)" (Smith 2001: 5). Finally, in their meta-analysis of restorative justice programs, Lawrence Sherman and Heather Strang (2008) revealed that the results of face-to-face conferencing ranged from moderate reductions in recidivism to no differences to increased offending.

## Conflict Theories and Crime Control Policies

Immigration policies have been the source of considerable divisiveness not only in the United States but around the globe, as nations deal with massive migration, sometimes caused by intra-national culture conflicts such as those in Rwanda, Sudan, and, more recently Syria. In the United States, the nation's policy on immigration has merged with the War on Terror, so that securing the nation's border against terrorists and illegal immigration are viewed as compatible policies.

> The merger of policies on immigration and counterterrorism can create cultural and social conflict within a nation and between nations.

Conflict theory can yield unique insights into the nation's drug laws and drug control policy. As we learned in chapter 9, Austin Turk (1969) maintained that authorities criminalize the behavior of culturally and racially dissimilar subordinate groups when they see them as threatening. Allen Liska and Jiang Yu (1992:55) contend that the size of the dissimilar group was important: smaller dissimilar subordinate groups pose less of a threat than do larger ones (i.e., 20 to 30 percent of the population). Larger groups can threaten the social and political order established by the power elites. For example, when the media portrayed the United States in the 1980s as in the midst of a crack cocaine epidemic, states enacted different sentencing guidelines for persons convicted of possessing crack cocaine versus powder cocaine (see box 10.2).

## Crime Theory and Criminal Justice Practice

Crime theories guide criminal justice practice in policing, the courts, and corrections. We focus on some of the applications to law enforcement, including the theories that influence police practice as well as the theories that influence how society views the police. Over the past 50 years or so, criminologists have shown an increased interest in linking their theories to law enforcement.

**Box 10.2    Consider This: Drug Law Wars—Crack Cocaine vs. Powder Cocaine**

Crack cocaine and powder cocaine are chemically identical but delivered differently. Creating crack from cocaine expands the amount of product available for sale. Smoking crack is a more efficient delivery system than snorting cocaine. Crack is less expensive on a per dose basis and is more frequently used by blacks.

The Anti-Drug Abuse Act of 1986 made the sentence for individuals trafficking in 500 grams of cocaine or 5 grams of crack—a ratio of 100 to 1 for drugs that are pharmacologically identical—a minimum of 5 years imprisonment. By the mid-1990s, nearly 90 percent of defendants charged with the possession of crack cocaine were black, 7 percent were Hispanic, and 5 percent were white; for powder cocaine, 40 percent were black, another 40 percent were Hispanic, and 18 percent were white.

The nation's appellate courts ignored challenges to the sentencing laws as unfair and inequitable. In late 2007, the Supreme Court affirmed the right of a judge to sentence Derrick Kimbrough to a shorter sentence than was required by the sentencing guidelines. This decision signaled a major change. The U.S. Sentencing Commission next called for a thorough revamping of cocaine sentencing disparities. In 2010, Congress passed the Fair Sentencing Act, which reduced but did not eliminate the disparities. Possession of 28 grams of crack cocaine is punished by a 5-year mandatory minimum sentence for a first offense versus 500 grams of powder cocaine to trigger the same sentence—a disparity of 18 to 1. In 2011, the law was applied retroactively to reduce the sentences of federal offenders. The law also does not impact the majority of drug offenders convicted under state laws patterned on the original federal drug legislation.

*Sources: Edwards v. United States* (1997); *Kimbrough v. United Sates* (2007); U.S. Sentencing Commission (1995); The Sentencing Project 2004.

## Classical Criminology, Deterrence Theories, and the Police

Many police practices have deterrence theory ties (Gay, Schell, and Schack 1977).

- *Deterring speeders:* Placing police cars, sometimes with lights flashing, in high-visibility locations on highways is intended to slow traffic. The same goal is behind informing radio and television stations about DUI checkpoints or random stops on local streets and highways. Overt or highly visible speed cameras are intended to deter certain dangerous driving patterns, but the research suggests that covert or hidden cameras that provide immediate feedback to derelict drivers may achieve higher compliance levels (Marciano and Norman 2015).

- *Preventive patrol:* From cruising by local parks, recreational centers, and school grounds to stopping and questioning "suspicious persons," the intent of nearly all police patrol practices is deterrence. As revealed in the 1970s Kansas City preventive patrol experiment, such practices have their limitations, at least with respect to reducing crime and citizen perceptions (Pate et al. 1976).

- *Hot-spot patrols:* Targeting a location with an influx of specialized police units—**hot-spot patrols**—evolved from fusing social ecology, routine activities, and rational choice theories. Flooding an area identified as a crime-rate outlier with higher-than-normal levels of police patrols and specialized anti-crime units results in more arrests and forces offenders to make choices (Sherman and Weisburd 1995). Staying put and engaging in more crime will likely result in an arrest and possibly a criminal sanction. The outcome is lower crime (Sherman et al. 1997; Weisburd and Eck 2004)—or criminals may simply move their activities to less heavily-policed areas: *displacement*. And, of course, increasing the police presence in one area requires a reduction of policing in other areas—a zero sum outcome. As suggested in Box 10.3, disagreement exists about what is actually happening.

Deterrence-based practices form the core of many police responses to crime and justice issues.

## Biological Theories and the Police

Whether we can discern a biological basis of crime, current informal police practices may flow from a biogenic perspective. Consider each of the following characterizations of police work and biological input.

- *Physical characteristics and body-typing suspects*: Police officers may learn from experience to look for physical characteristics that mark a person as a threat. For example, the arresting officers described Rodney King at his 1993 civil rights trial as "a monster" largely due to his physique and alleged drug use. He was, in the terminology of the street, "buffed-out." Consider too that such "crimi-

| B | **Conflicting Deterrence Arguments** |
|---|---|
| O | |
| X | |
| 10.3 | |

There is the possibility that increasing enforcement in one area will drive down the crime rates of nearby areas as well—the **diffusion of crime-control benefits hypothesis**. In contrast, the **spatial displacement hypothesis** suggests that hot-spot practices may reduce one area's crime rates because criminals move to nearby areas where crime-control efforts are less aggressive. Empirical studies tend not to support spatial displacement. Focused anticrime efforts rarely yield total crime displacement; if it does occur, it seems to be relatively low in impact and not widespread.

In an effort to resolve the issue, David Weisburd and associates simultaneously examined both displacement and diffusion hypotheses. In Jersey City, New Jersey, they closely monitored two areas that had substantial street-level crime and disorder. They watched for displacement into two neighboring locales. These catchment areas did not receive the enhanced police activities provided to the target areas. The researchers collected systematic observational data, supplemented with interviews and ethnographic field observations, for the both target and catchment areas. While the limited focus of the study restricts its generalizability, the researchers reported that the displacement that occurs does not undermine the use of enhanced police services in specific high-crime areas.

*Sources*: Barr and Pease (1990); Braga et al. (1999); Clarke and Weisburd (1994); Sherman and Rogan (1995); Weisburd et al. (2006).

nal anthropology" markers could include not only well-developed physiques (a mesomorphic somatotype), but also "shifty" eyes (a physiognomic fragment) and twisted, upturned, or flattened noses (atavistic anomalies).

> Biogenic theories rarely apply to police work, although disproved ideas about the physical characteristics of criminals may influence some officers.

- The use of these markers by police is very much a hit-and-miss proposition. However, the police practice of singling out persons for stops because they fit a physical profile may not only violate the suspect's civil rights, but it may also place the officers in legal jeopardy (Del Carmen and Walker 2011).

## Psychological Theories and the Police

Police work has strong ties to various psychological theories. These ties reflect both who the police are, as well as what they do.

- *Psychometric testing and police recruits:* Police departments frequently use personality inventories to screen job applicants and determine candidate suitability for promotion. The 1967 Presidential Commission on Law Enforcement recommended the Minnesota Multiphasic Personality Inventory (MMPI), an idea reinforced by the 1973 report of the National Advisory Commission on Criminal Justice Standards and Goals. As Geoffrey Alpert (1993:103) observed: "A balance must be reached among screening in, selecting out, and avoiding discriminatory practices. It is to be hoped that the psychological test will be used simply to screen out [unsuitable] candidates." A recent survey found that 9 in 10 police departments and nearly all large departments psychologically screened police recruit applicants (Cochrane, Tett and Vandecreek 2003).

- *The police personality and problematic police practices:* The term **police personality** describes undesired characteristics found among sworn officers. The chief one, claims Arthur Niederhoffer (1969), is authoritarianism. **Authoritarianism** refers to a personality type characterized by undemocratic tendencies, dogmatism, cynicism, and a readiness to condemn others solely based on race or ethnicity (Adorno et al. 1985). Personality researchers report that officers are more authoritarian than are members of the public. However, it is unclear whether high authoritarians are drawn to police work or whether policing creates high authoritarianism (Lipset 1969; Van Maanen 1973). It is also unclear whether *all* aspects of authoritarianism are out of place in the police occupation (Anson, Mann and Sherman 1986).

- *Criminal profiling:* Law enforcement agencies (including violent-crime task forces and special investigative units) use personality theory in **criminal profiling**, often employing descriptors found in psychopathy (cf., Egger 1990; Hare 1996b; Holmes 1990; Ressler, Burgess, and Douglas 1988). The goal of profiling is to bring together all relevant information on a single subject and identify a pattern of human behavior. A major criticism of personality theory and the psychopathy hypothesis is that they are overly concerned with using past behavior to predict future behavior, a pattern followed by police investigators pursuing serial offenders (e.g., rapists, burglars, and murderers). Police investigators are less concerned with learning why a crime was committed than with developing a list of possible suspects and/or potential victims. Profiling includes the MO—*modus operandi*—a Latin term meaning method of working used to describe the particular manner in which a crime is committed.

> Psychology tells us a great deal about police as a profession, as well as providing some insights into some parts of police investigatory practices.

## Structural Theories and the Police

Observations about *community malaise* and *disorder* have reshaped the role of police in the community. In other words, if the "quality of life crimes" are not aggressively policed, the net result will be higher rates of more serious crime.

- *Community policing:* Specific programs, sometimes called "broken windows policing," that flowed from concerns about "quality of life crimes" exhibit close kinship to ecological theories. For example, **community policing** is an approach to police work designed to bring officers and their communities into closer contact. The police help broker services that improve the appearance of, and the pride residents have in, a community, including better trash collection, removal of graffiti and abandoned vehicles, and the boarding up or destruction of abandoned structures. An emphasis on policing street disorder—such as aggressive panhandlers, streetwalkers, and disorderly or intimidating youths—encourages residents to spend more time on the streets. These programs meet with generally positive results, particularly an improved public perception of police (Eck and Spelman 1987; Hayeslip 1989; Moore and Trojanowicz 1988).

* *Strain and police corruption:* The concept of strain also provides insights into **police corruption,** the misuse of authority by police officers for personal gain or the benefit of others (Carter 1990). Society's desire for law and order contrasts with its antipathy toward governmental authority. This dynamic tension often places police officers in an anomic trap, caught between competing goals: the arrest, indictment, and conviction of offenders on the one hand, and the rule of law on the other. Consequently, some perjure themselves, engage in entrapment, falsify evidence, give incriminating statements, and even plant evidence at crime scenes. Sometimes they administer "street justice," use of extra-legal force. Officers also may suppress evidence or information that might lead to an arrest. Police deviance can result from strains created by an ambiguous social system that pressures the police to respond efficiently to crime but restrains their ability to do so with due process protections.

* *Police subculture and problematic police practices:* Researchers have also described a **police subculture** that promotes a sexist and macho role perception (Martin 1980). Moreover, managing the stress of police work takes subcultural forms. Outsiders can easily interpret the ridiculing of suspects and the use of racial or sexual joking as callous or worse (Pogrebin and Poole 1988). The police subculture does little to deflect this criticism. One response to these multifaceted problems is to increase police cultural awareness by means of multicultural programming. Academy programs and in-service training address this problem by informing officers about the multiple meanings attached to various acts within communities they police (Roberg and Kuykendall 1993). Another response is to increase minority recruitment, but this practice may overlook the issue of occupational socialization into the police subculture.

> Many of the problematic practices associated with police misuse of authority can be linked to the strains associated with police work itself.

## Social Process Theories and the Police

In addition to *what* they do, *who* the police are and *how* they perceive their world seem to have links to differential association and social learning theories. If police work attracts certain types of people, then society must rely on psychological screening devices to keep out the undesirable ones (assuming the psychological measurements are accurate). If who police officers are is related to police work, then we need to study professional socialization, which involves social learning.

- *Police cynicism and learned behavior:* Police researchers describe officers as cynical, although there is disagreement among researchers as to the sources and implications of police cynicism (Anson, Mann, and Sherman 1986; Niederhoffer 1969; Regoli 1976). A cynical officer is one who views the public and other institutions, including the Supreme Court, with a measure of distrust and even hostility. Researchers suggest that cynicism might be functional for some aspects of police work—officers may learn to protect themselves from aspects of their work that are unpleasant, including interactions with citizens who are hostile to the police in their investigations or if officers perceive that the criminal justice system is not responding appropriately to crime (Caplan 2003; Klinger 1997; Sobol 2010). In short, cynicism functions like chapter 7's techniques of neutralization, providing a learned way for officers to "protect" themselves from what they view as certain unpleasant aspects of their work world.

- *Police corruption and social process theories:* Police corruption is often linked to pressures from deviant peers and the need for group solidarity. Officers who refuse to "play along" may be ostracized or worse (Stoddard 1968; Walker 1992; Westley 1970).

- *Prosocial police practices and social process theories:* For more than 70 years, the Police Athletic League (PAL) has encouraged youths to interact with off-duty officers as a source of positive contacts. PAL emphasizes positive, supportive interactions rather than negative, confrontational ones. Other programs employ uniformed police officers as promoters of positive social bonds. Drug Abuse Resistance Education (DARE) used officers as instructors and role models to teach youths about the dangers of drugs; Gang Resistance Education and Training (G.R.E.A.T.) also promoted participation in conventional activities and the development of prosocial attitudes, orientations, and behavior. Interestingly, evaluations of DARE revealed no results or even negative ones (i.e., increases in the problem behavior), whereas evaluations of G.R.E.A.T. showed far more promising results (cf., Esbensen, Osgood et al. 2013; West and O'Neal 2004).

Process theories yield insights into many aspects of the police occupation, from how officers view the public to the modeling of prosocial behavior.

## Labeling Theory, Reintegrative Justice Theory, and the Police

Law enforcement officers play a central role in the movement from primary to secondary deviance. Police are also essential to the RJ process.

- *Police discretionary powers and criminal labeling:* Discretionary decisions by officers on patrol often determine whether a person will enter the criminal justice system. Officers opting for a warning or reprimand instead of formal processing, particularly with juveniles and adults engaging in minor law-violating behavior, may prevent deviance amplification.

- *Profiling:* Labeling theory may also explain police responses to various identifiable groups, particularly ethnic and racial groups. Stereotyping and the related practice of racial profiling underlie a significant portion of police practices. Officers sometimes must make immediate decisions with very few cues available. For example, they may react to and stop a young black male driving a luxury vehicle, while they might ignore an older white male driving a similar car.

- *Police involvement in family group conferencing:* Braithwaite (1997) observed that the police are crucial gatekeepers in restorative justice practices; he stressed that police are essential to the process and should not be stigmatized. New Zealand police officers play pivotal roles in **family group conferencing,** a program that brings all parties together to begin healing the wounds caused by crime. A youth service officer reads the charges and participates in the decision-making process with the family group (Goenner 2000). We find similar programs in Australia, a handful of U. S. states (e.g., Minnesota, Montana, and Vermont), and several Canadian provinces (Bazemore and Umbreit 2001:5). Preliminary results from programs that involve the police directly in RJ goal attainment are promising (McCold and Wachtel 1998; Sherman et al. 1998). However, officers who are willing to participate in RJ programs may find themselves devalued by their peers (Winfree 2003), while decentralization of policing services may serve as an impediment to its widespread adoption (Winfree 2009).

> Labeling theory explains the police role in disintegrative shaming; reintegrative shaming essentializes the police role in reintegrating offenders.

## Conflict Theories and the Police ·

Conflict theory yields insight into disputes between officers and management. Problematic interactions between police and citizens also have origins in conflict theory.

- *Police strikes as conflict situations:* When police officers disagree with management about issues ranging from salaries to fringe benefits to shift work, the differences are usually resolved through negotiation. On rare occasions, the conflict has resulted in a strike. In most jurisdictions, strikes are illegal. In Cincinnati (1918), Boston (1919), and San Francisco (1975) (Ayers 1977; Bopp, Chignell, and Maddox 1977) strikes turned violent. Police may feel disconnected from the lawmaking process, particularly when their peaceful efforts to resolve conflict fail.

- *Minority-threat theory and police-citizen interactions:* The police may view certain groups as **symbolic assailants**—persons to watch and with whom to exercise high levels of caution during citizen-police contacts. Minority-threat theory provides the theoretical underpinning for highly negative and emotionally charged citizen-police interactions. Influenced by society-wide racism that sees ethnic minorities as threats to the social order, police officers sometimes abuse their authority. Some police experts see body cameras as a means to resolve conflicts. However, the evidence has not yet confirmed that position (Miller, Toliver, and Police Executive Research Forum 2014).

Conflict theory explains problematic police-citizen interactions.

## SUMMARY

- Much crime policy appears based on buzzwords and metaphors.
- Evidence-based policy increasingly plays a significant role in creating new policies and associated practices.
- Deterrence theory forms the basis for the U.S. criminal justice system, evidence of its significance and durability as a perspective on crime.
- Mandatory arrest has become a widespread practice in spite of the absence of corroborating evidence—in fact, there is much evidence that such arrests lead to more violence.
- Policies that hold offenders strictly accountable and rely on imprisonment to deter crime could worsen the nation's system of "mass incarceration."
- Many of the policy implications associated with routine activity theory rely on proactive measures taken by potential victims.
- Crime impact assessments could help urban developers "design out" crime from new developments and urban renewal.
- Crime policies that derive from biological theories have proven controversial and difficult to implement, especially in a democracy.
- Providing prenatal and perinatal care to high-risk mothers may offset the influence of forces shown by biocriminologists to cause crime and delinquency.
- Many drug users self-medicate with illegal drugs to offset the negative consequences of other physical and psychological problems.
- Changing policies regarding the drug problem from enforcement to treatment is a complex undertaking.
- Psychoanalysis has proven a useful tool in the arsenal of correctional officers.
- Behaviorism is a central theme in many systems of reward and punishment used to control criminal conduct generally and the behavior of prisoners in particular.

- Psychopaths may not be "salvageable" by any therapy or treatment; containment is the more feasible outcome.
- The War on Poverty was a prime example of the influence of structural theory on public policy, which ran afoul of political agendas on the left and right.
- The policy of requiring convicted felons and delinquents to avoid contact with "known" offenders is an oversimplification (and underestimation) of social learning theory.
- Holding parents accountable for their children's actions is rooted in social control theory.
- Labeling theory is the basis of the 4-Ds: decriminalization, diversion, deinstitutionalization and due process.
- Labeling proponents suggest that it is difficult to "un-label" offenders, especially when official labeling is at work (i.e., the criminal and juvenile justice systems).
- Restorative justice represents a philosophical reversal of labeling: rather than stigmatizing and marginalizing offenders, RJ seeks to reintegrate them.
- Although pharmacologically identical, crack cocaine and powder cocaine are treated differently by the criminal justice system.
- Police practices such as preventive partial and deterring speeders are based on deterrence, despite a lack of evidence supporting the practices.
- Hot-spot patrolling has been shown to be an effective means of reducing crime, although there is disagreement as to how it works.
- Biology seems to influence police work through the adoption of stereotypes about certain offender body types, physical characteristics, and profiling.
- Psychological theories inform policing agencies about whom to avoid and whom to hire as police officers.
- Specialized investigative groups in many police agencies employ criminal profiling theories and practices to apprehend violent and problematic offenders.
- Structural theories of crime support various community policing practices, especially those designed to improve police-community relations and a community's quality of life.
- Structural theories explain problematic police behavior, including corruption as a response to the strains associated with police work and unlawful actions committed by members of the police subculture.
- Learning theories give insights into police conduct and how beliefs are formed.

- Police are instrumental in strengthening the social bond in a number of critical ways, from PAL to DARE to G.R.E.A.T.
- Labeling theory explains the police role in disintegrative shaming; reintegrative shaming essentializes the police role in reintegrating offenders.
- Conflict theory provides unique insights into internal police disagreements and external police-citizen interactions.

## KEY TERMS

| | |
|---|---|
| authoritarianism | hot-spot patrols |
| community policing | mandatory arrest |
| crime impact assessment | mass incarceration |
| criminal profiling | net widening |
| decriminalization | police personality |
| deinstitutionalization | police subculture |
| diffusion of crime-control | restorative justice (RJ) |
| benefits hypothesis | restorative justice (RJ) |
| diversion | spatial displacement hypothesis |
| due process guarantees | status offender |
| evidence-based policy (EBP) | symbolic assailants |
| family group conferencing | War on Poverty |

## CRITICAL REVIEW QUESTIONS

1. Which deterrence-related criminal justice practices strike you as most likely to be successful? Which ones are likely to fail?

2. Which of this chapter's policy implications do you think poses the greatest threat to democratic ideals? Which one holds the greatest promise for reducing crime?

3. Which psychological theory contains social policy implications that not only would be difficult to implement but also might raise serious constitutional issues?

4. Should the criminal justice system increase or decrease its reliance on psychometric testing when selecting personnel? Why do you feel this way?

5. How should the criminal justice system treat law violators with very low IQs compared to those who fully appreciate the nature of their illegal acts?

6. Which of the personality-based policies and practices do you think poses the greatest threat to democratic ideals?

7. Identify the most important policy implications derived from structural theories. Provide the basis of support for your selections.

8. Identify the most important practical applications for both social disorganization and anomie theories. Provide the basis of support for your selections.

9. What single policy implication that derives from social learning theory do you see as holding the greatest hope for reducing crime or delinquency?

10. What single policy implication that derives from social control theory do you see as holding the greatest hope for reducing crime or delinquency?

11. Which theory has the greater impact on police practices, social learning or social control? Defend your selection with information from the text or other sources.

12. Critics of RJ suggest that while its intent is benevolent, it could result in greater harm than existing criminal justice practices. What is the basis of this concern?

13. "The police play the single most important role in labeling an adult as a criminal or a juvenile as a delinquent." Attack or defend this statement.

14. Which single policy implication associated with conflict theory seems to pose the greatest threat to the fair administration of justice? Explain your selection.

15. The various forms of conflict theory all have implications for the courts, police, and corrections. In which specific instance or practice do you believe that conflict theory best explains what is happening? Explain your selection.

# Glossary of Terms

**A**

Ability (5): Term used by Eysenck to refer to innate intelligence; one of his four higher-order factors of personality; also called g.

Absolute deterrence (2): The idea that rule breakers either see the error of their ways (perhaps after being caught and punished) or the potential losses they face—the net result being that they refrain from all crime in the future; see *general deterrence, individual/specific deterrence,* and *restrictive deterrence.*

Adolescence/Adulthood stage (4): Begins at around age 13 and continues to death; characterized by sexual maturity; the fifth of Freud's stages of psychosexual development; see *anal stage, genital stage, latent stage,* and *oral stage.*

Adolescent-limited (AL) offenders (5): Children begin offending with the start of adolescence and cease offending around age 18; compare with Moffitt's *life-course persistent (LCP) offenders.*

Adoption studies (3): Comparative studies of the crime and delinquency rates of adopted children with those of both their biological *and* their adoptive parents.

Agonists (3): A substance that mimics another substance and elicits a reaction; for example, morphine stimulates the receptor sites in the brain normally excited only by naturally occurring endorphins; see *antagonists.*

Anal stage (4): Begins at ages 1–3; the anus is the primary source of sexual interest and gratification; the second of Freud's stages of psychosexual development; see *adolescence/adulthood stage, genital stage, latent stage,* and *oral stage.*

Anomic trap (6): The state of being caught between culturally defined goals and socially delimited means; see *anomie.*

Anomie (6): Term popularized by Durkheim to refer to the societal condition characterized by a confusion or absence of norms and rules; generally follows great social upheavals, which can include defeat or victory in war and economic downturns or upward spirals; normlessness.

Anomie theory (6): Durkheim's theory was based on societal wide normlessness; Merton's theory was based on a disjuncture between socially prescribed means and culturally defined goals.

Antagonists (3): Chemical substances that inhibit the action of a receptor site; they can counteract the effect of an agonist by their ability to block receptor sites without triggering cell activity; see *agonists.*

Apostasy (1): Rejecting a formerly held religious belief system—for many religions, an act punishable by death.

Associative learning (5): The retention of information or rote memorization of simple facts and skills; level I learning in Jensen's theory; compare with *conceptual learning.*

Atavism (3): The product of immature evolution exhibiting physical stigmata or signs; also *atavist* as a person with these characteristics; see *stigmata.*

Attractiveness (2): The material or symbolic value of persons or property; part of routine activities theory; see *exposure, guardianship,* and *proximity.*

Authoritarianism (10): Personality type characterized by favoring blind submission to authority and exercising control over others, often cynical with a readiness to condemn others based on ethnicity; stubborn and narrow-minded.

Autonomy (6): The desire to be independent from external control; one of Miller's six focal concerns of lower-class culture; see *excitement, fate, smartness, toughness,* and *trouble*.

Authority-conflict pathway (5): Before age 12, children start with stubborn conduct, move to defiance, and settle into authority avoidance; one of three pathways to criminality described by Loeber and Hay; compare with *covert pathway* and *overt pathway*.

Axon (3): Long slender portion of a nerve cell that carries electrical impulses away from the neuron.

# B

Behaviorism (5): A psychological learning theory that emphasizes the objective, measurable investigation of individual actions and reactions.

Biocriminology (3): The scientific study of the biological and genetic causes of crime; a subdiscipline of criminology.

Biological pushes (7): Qualities such as restlessness, discontent, hostility, rebellion, and feelings of inferiority that push youth to engage in delinquency; part of Reckless' containment theory; see *psychological pushes, social pulls,* and *social pushes*.

"Broken windows" theory (1): A metaphor for disorder in a crime-ridden neighborhood; first proposed by Kelling and Wilson, the thinking is that if a single window in a building is broken, soon more broken windows will appear; if the signs of disorder are not addressed, the neighborhood will be characterized by a sense of malaise and disconnectedness.

# C

Capable guardian (2): People (e.g., homeowner, police patrols, or a lone traveler) or precautions (e.g., bars on the windows, steel door, or alarm system) that dissuade a motivated offender from targeting a property; part of routine activities theory; see *motivated offender* and *suitable target*.

Capitalism (9): The political, economic, and social theory that promotes private ownership and control of a nation's commerce and industry; contrast with Marxism.

Capitalists (9): Owners of the means of production in Marxism.

Career criminals (5): Chronic offenders who engage in a high volume of crime over a period of time.

Cathexis (4): Psychic energy that attaches to objects of sexual gratification; part of Freud's psychoanalytic model; see to *fixation* and *regression*.

Causation (1): Refers to anything that produces an outcome or effect; for X to cause Y, X must precede Y in time, there must be a statistical correlation between X and Y, and the relationship between X and Y must not be the result of a third variable, Z (absence of spuriousness).

Celerity (2): The elapsed time between when an offense occurs and when the sanction is applied; the sanction should be prompt; part of deterrence theory; see *certainty* and *severity*.

Central nervous system (3): The brain and spinal column; a complex of nerve tissues that control all bodily activities.

Certainty (2): The probability that an individual will receive a sanction for their offense; part of deterrence theory; see *celerity* and *severity*.

Chicago School, The (6): A group of sociologists and other social scientists at the University of Chicago that explored the distribution of crime and delinquency in the city of Chicago shortly after the turn of the twentieth century.

Choice structuring (2): The process whereby individuals assess their skills and needs in light of a specific crime's characteristics; part of rational choice theory; see *event decision* and *involvement decision*.

Chromosomes (3): High-density genetic storage devices, the carriers of human hereditary characteristics that reside in all of the body's cell nuclei.

Class war (9): The ultimate struggle between capitalists and the proletariat for control of society, according to Marxism.

Classical conditioning (5): Subjects learn to connect a neutral stimulus (e.g. the sound of a bell) that is placed before a naturally occurring response (e.g. food triggering a dog's salivation) even when the trigger is not present—the dog is conditioned to salivate at the sound of the bell; the focus is on involuntary, automatic behaviors; see *operant conditioning*.

Classical criminology (1): One of three main thematic orientations to criminology; the emphasis is on humans as rational beings endowed with free will to choose between crime and law-abiding behavior; justice should be based on equality and proportionality; compare with *conflict criminology* and *positivist criminology*.

Classical School (2): Philosophical, legal and practical origins of deterrence theory; based on the work of Cesare Beccaria and Jeremy Bentham; see *classical criminology*.

Clinical psychologists (4): Practitioners who treat mental disorders and provide psychological services; see *forensic psychologists*.

Coercion (9): Forced compliance, often (but not exclusively) imposed by a legal authority; see *oppression*.

Cognitive learning theory (5): Human behavior is motivated by conscious activity such as thinking, reasoning, or remembering; cognitions cannot be observed but Rotter's theory emphasized that expectations about outcomes will determine whether people engage in certain behaviors.

Collective efficacy (6): The ability of a neighborhood to exercise informal control over the behavior of all individuals living there and to share responsibility for creating an environment in which crime and other undesirable behaviors are less likely to occur.

Colonial era (9): The years from 1500 to 1800 when Britain, France, Portugal, Spain, and the Netherlands took control of distant lands, denying original inhabitants the right to rule themselves.

Colonialism (9): Policy of establishing political dominance over a geographic area; the controlling nation generally settled its own citizens in the colonized area intending to exploit the region in perpetuity.

Colonialism-derived culture conflict (9): One of Sellin's three forms of primary culture conflict derived from the oppressive practices associated with colonialism; for example, the 300-year-plus conflict between various Native American tribes and the United States government; see *cross-border culture conflict* and *immigrant-status culture conflict*.

Communitarianism (8): Interdependencies of people living in a particular area characterized by high levels of mutuality and trust.

Community malaise (1): The condition suffered by residents of a geographic area who feel a generalized sense of despair and disconnectedness from one another, resulting in a lack of emotional investment in their community or each other.

Community policing (10): Approach to the role of police that promotes closer contacts with citizens, establishment of partnerships, and the use of problem-solving techniques to address proactively the conditions that threaten public safety, including crime, social disorder, and fear of crime.

Conceptual learning (5): The ability to manipulate and transform information; level II learning in Jensen's theory; compare with *associative learning*.

Concentrated disadvantage (6): Living conditions in a specific geographic area that reduce the chances of success or positive life outcomes for residents.

Concentric zones (6): Five areas identified in the city of Chicago with different land use and populations as well as other physical, economic, and social characteristics; Zone I was the central business district.

Concepts (1): A mental representation for a thing, object, or idea; an abstract idea generalized from particular circumstances—for example, gang is a concept that stands for a relatively organized group of persons that share a sense of belonging.

Concordance (3): Measurement of the extent of similarity; used in twin studies for the degree to which twins share a particular behavior or condition.

Conduct norms (9): Social rules requiring people to act in a specific manner in a particular situation.

Conflict (9): The condition that exists when individuals or groups compete for the same physical space, resources, power, or social position.

Conflict criminology (1): One of three main thematic orientations to criminology; the emphasis is on power relationships in society—those with the power and wealth wish to keep both; those without strive to change the situation; compare with *classical criminology* and *positivist criminology*.

Conformists (6): Group that accepts both the goals (ends) and the means dictated by society; they respond to Merton's anomic trap by striving to achieve success by following the rules; compare with *ritualists*, *rebels*, *retreatists*, and *innovators*.

Conscious (4): Phenomena about which an individual is currently aware; also called the "here and now" of our existence; one of Freud's three mental processes; compare with *preconscious* and *unconscious*.

Containment theory (7): Theory proposed by Reckless whereby people are pulled away from conventional society or pushed toward misbehavior; see *biological pushes*, *psychological pushes*, *social pulls*, and *social pushes*.

Correlation (1): Evidence of a statistical relationship between two or more entities such that a change in the value of one of the entities produces a change in the remaining entity or entities; not equivalent to causation.

Cost-benefits analysis (2): A systematic process whereby the benefits (gains) associated with a given situation or action are added and any costs (losses) are subtracted, leaving the "net profit" resulting from taking an action.

Covert pathway (5): Minor hidden behavior is the first step to criminal behavior followed by misconduct that escalates to property damage (e.g., vandalism and arson) and moderate forms of delinquency (e.g., burglary, car theft, and fraud); one of three pathways to criminality described by Loeber and Hay; compare with *authority-conflict pathway* and *overt pathway*.

Crime (1): The violation of a criminal law.

Crime impact assessment (10): Report that predicts, identifies, evaluates, and proposes mitigating actions for potential crime and disorder effects of a proposed development.

Criminal (1): A person who has committed a crime; the official designation requires an arrest, trial, conviction, and sentencing.

Criminal career (5): The type, volume, nature, and length of a person's involvement in crime.

Criminal personality theory (5): Eysenck's theory to explain the links between aberrant personality characteristics and crime; a mix of behaviorism, biology, and personality theories, it is the only psychological theory specifically designed to explain criminality.

Criminal profiling (10): Investigative tool to examine evidence from crime scenes, victims, and witnesses to infer characteristics about the offender based on the behavior during the crime and to narrow the field of suspects—includes psychological variables such as personality traits and psychopathologies as well as demographic variables such as age and location; the Federal Bureau of Investigation describes its technique of bringing together all relevant information on a single subject and identifying a pattern of human behavior as criminal investigative analysis.

Criminal-propensity thesis (5): Gottfredson and Hirschi proposed that the tendency to commit crime is not biologically determined; they distinguish between the inclination to commit crime and the actual act—crime declines uniformly as offenders age.

Cross-border culture conflict (9): One of Sellin's three forms of primary culture conflict that occurs when two distinct cultures share a physical border with one another; see *colonialism-derived culture conflict* and *immigrant-status culture conflict*.

Cultural transmission theories (6): Shaw and McKay's term for the general process whereby one generation conveys to the next generation various elements of its culture.

Culture (6): Refers to the totality of a society's beliefs and moral values.

Culture conflict (9): The mental and physical clashes that occur when the values and beliefs of two groups collide.

Cumulative continuity (5): Failure in one aspect of life (i.e. school) increases the probability of failure in another (i.e. work).

Cumulative disadvantage (8): The accumulated total of negative life experiences that limit the chances for an individual to succeed; tied to labeling theory.

**D**

Decriminalization (10): Changing the laws to reduce the number of behaviors punished by the criminal justice system.

Defensible space (6): Physical characteristics of a residential environment that help inhabitants become the prime contributors to their own security.

Deinstitutionalization (10): Practice that removes detention in juvenile facilities, jail, or prison as punishment for juveniles or those accused of minor offenses.

Demystification (9): Removing mystery or obscurity so that the true nature of practices is clear; Quinney advocated demystifying the false consciousness about crime that the government promotes so that oppression of lower classes continues.

Dendrites (3): The branched extensions that compose most of the receptive surface of a neuron; they conduct impulses received from other cells across synapses toward the cell body.

Deoxyribonucleic acid (3): DNA; the molecular basis of heredity—the genetic instructions for development, functioning and reproduction.

Desistance (5): The ending point of a criminal career; contrast with *onset*.

Determinism (1): In social science, the idea that forces beyond the person's control cause all or some human behavior; see *positivist criminology*.

Deterrence (1): The prospect of punishment or its application as a means of preventing the occurrence of future crimes.

Developmental criminology (5): Loeber and LeBlanc's perspective that identifies causal factors that predate delinquency and studies life cycle transitions and other factors that affect offending at different times in an individual's life.

Developmental psychology (5): A branch of psychology that explores how and why humans grow, develop, and adapt over the course of their lifetime.

Deviance amplification (8): An idea that refers to the process whereby the actions of an official agency, often the police, increase the negative aspects of the behavior controlled by that agency, further devaluing those engaged in it; part of labeling theory.

Differential anticipation/expectation theory (7): Engaging in a crime depends on the consequences expected, prior learning experience, the quality of the bonds established with others, and perceived opportunities for success or failure; Glaser's theory combined aspects of differential association, control theories, rational choice theory, operant conditioning, and strain theory.

Differential associations (7): We learn attitudes and behavior from significant others (parents, relatives, friends); our associations vary in terms of frequency, duration, priority, and intensity.

Differential association theory (7): Sutherland's theory predicted that people become criminals when attitudes favorable to the violation of law outweigh attitudes favorable to following the law; criminal behavior results from the strength of an individual's criminal associations and is a cumulative learning process.

Differential association-reinforcement theory (7): Burgess and Akers' theory expands on differential association theory by adding the element of operant conditioning as the force that supports learning.

Differential deterrability (2): The idea that formal (and possibly informal) sanctions are more likely to work for some people and not for others.

Differential opportunity theory (6): Chances to achieve society's success goals are not equally distributed; when legitimate pathways are closed, people seek alternative routes; Cloward and Ohlin merged strain and cultural transmission theories to explain how delinquent subcultures begin, develop, persist or change over time.

Differential reinforcement theory (7): The theory adds psychological learning processes (i.e., behaviorism and operant conditioning) to differential association theory; the strength of criminal behavior depends on the amount of reinforcement.

Diffusion of crime-control benefits hypothesis (10): The deterrence-related idea that increasing enforcement in one area will drive down the crime rates of nearby areas as well; contrast with *spatial displacement hypothesis*.

Discriminative stimuli (7): Signals that certain behavior is appropriate or inappropriate—likely to be rewarded or not.

Disintegrative shaming (8): Stigmatizes the offender and devalues their status in the group through exclusionary rituals that deny reentry into the community; contrast with *reintegrative shaming*.

Displacement (4): The expression of unacceptable id impulses through an acceptable outlet; one of Freud's four defense mechanisms; see *reaction formation*, *repression*, and *sublimation*.

Diversion (10): Formal and informal programs to help juvenile or adult law violators avoid deeper penetration into the criminal justice system.

Dizygotic twins (3): DZ; fraternal twins; evolved from two separate eggs, fertilized by different spermatocytes.

Dopamine (3): One of about 100 neurotransmitters found in the central nervous system; received special attention because of its role in the regulation of mood and affect and because of its role in motivation and reward processes.

Double failures (6): Cloward and Ohlin's term for offenders unable to access either legitimate or illegitimate opportunity structures to achieve success goals.

Dramatization of evil (8): Tannenbaum's idea that explains how society transfers and affixes the evil of a deed to individuals, creating the status of person as evil.

Dream interpretation (4): Exploration of the meaning in patient's dreams; one of three techniques used by psychoanalysts to elicit repressed information; see *free association* and *transference*.

Drift theory (7): Matza's idea that youth are not totally committed to delinquent groups or values; rather, they move freely between normative and non-normative elements in society; subterranean values are important to understanding drift.

Due process guarantees (10): The right to life, liberty and property free from government interference granted by the Fifth and Fourteenth Amendments to the U.S. Constitution.

Duration (7): Associations differ in terms of how long the contacts last; part of Sutherland's differential association theory; see *frequency, intensity* and *priority*.

## E

Ecological fallacy (6): Making inappropriate *individual*-level inferences from *group*-level data; often associated with social disorganization theory.

Ecology (6): The branch of biology that studies the relationships between organisms and their environment.

Ego (4): Associated with the anal stage, it acts as a mediator through which infants modify their id drives by contact with the physical world around them; the second of Freud's three psychic phenomena to evolve during psychosexual development see *id* and *superego*.

Electra complex (4): A psychological phenomenon that can emerge in girls during the genital stage of psychosexual development; inappropriate sexual thoughts about the father.

Epigenetic studies (3): Biogenic research that examines the influence of environmental forces that essentially turn off genetic switches, causing cells to misread DNA.

Equality (1): Idea that all people should be treated the same; in criminal justice, this refers to the application of law.

Equilibrium (4): According to Freud, this is the delicate balance between the highly charged unwanted id impulses and the expenditure of psychic energy to oppose them.

Eugenics (3): Altering hereditary qualities of people by selectively breeding in certain desirable characteristics and breeding out unwanted characteristics.

Event decision (2): Occurs quickly without much thought on the offender's part prior to commission of the criminal act based on already assessed information; part of rational choice theory; see *choice structuring* and *involvement decision*.

Event-propensity theory (7): Another term for *self-control theory*.

Evidence-based policy (EBP) (10): Policies based on the best scientific evidence available; developed from evidence-based medicine that used clinical trials and randomized controlled experiments to determine best practices; also called evidence-based policy and practice (EBPP).

Excessive egoism (9): Greed and self-interest promoted by capitalism.

Excitement (6): Tendency to seek thrills, risk, and danger; one of Miller's six focal concerns of lower-class culture; see *autonomy, fate, smartness, toughness*, and *trouble*.

Expectancy theory (5): People weigh the possible consequences of their actions, including criminal behavior, in terms of recollections about what has happened in similar circumstances.

Expected utility principle (2): Decisions about engaging in a behavior in which the outcome is uncertain are made based on the individual's best available knowledge about the probability of potential rewards versus the probability of possible costs.

Experimental psychology (5): Subdiscipline of psychology that employs experimental methods to study behavior and associated processes.

Experimenter type (5): Offender who "dabbles" in delinquency during younger years but quits entirely in middle to late adolescence; contrast with *persister type*.

Exposure (2): The visibility and physical accessibility of the target; part of routine activities theory; see *attractiveness, guardianship*, and *proximity*.

Extraversion (5): A personality trait characterized by lively energy levels that are directed outside of the individual, manifesting as impulsive sociability; one of Eysenck's three personality temperaments; see *neuroticism* and *psychoticism*.

## F

Family group conferencing (10): A restorative justice program based on reintegrative shaming that brings all involved parties—perpetrators, victims, criminal justice personnel, and members of the community—together to begin healing the wounds caused by criminal events.

Fate (6): The idea of being lucky or unlucky; one of Miller's six focal concerns of lower-class culture; see *autonomy, excitement, smartness, toughness*, and *trouble*.

Feeblemindedness (5): A person who suffers from a mental defect other than insanity who cannot manage his or her own life; a nineteenth and early twentieth century diagnosis for a mentally deficient person largely abandoned by the 1920s.

Felonies (1): Violations of the law punishable by more than one year in a correctional facility operated by a state or the federal government; some felonies are punishable by death.

Female genital mutilation (9): The practices of primarily African nations that include the circumcision of female children (i.e., remove all or part of the clitoris) at an early age.

Fixation (4): Occurs when the strength of an attachment to one stage of sexual gratification remains particularly strong even as the individual ages to the next stage of psychosexual development; part of Freud's psychoanalytic model; see *cathexis* and *regression*.

Focused deterrence (2): Targeting specific criminal behavior committed by a small number of chronic offenders; a problem-oriented policing strategy in which police interact directly with the targeted offenders and use all means available to communicate incentives for compliance, alternatives to their current crime path, and examples of consequences if they persist in criminal activity; see *pulling levers*.

Forensic psychologists (4): Practitioners of clinical psychology who investigate crimes (e.g., criminal profilers) or testify as expert witnesses in court (e.g., sanity and competency hearings).

Free association (4): A practice in which the patient verbally expresses ideas as they come to mind; one of three techniques used by psychoanalysts to elicit repressed information; see *dream interpretation* and *transference*.

Free will (1): The ability to make choices voluntarily; in criminology, the ability to distinguish between right or wrong—to decide to obey or to break the law.

Frequency (7): How often one associates with a particular contact; part of Sutherland's differential association theory; see *duration, intensity* and *priority*.

# G

g (5): Innate intelligence; see *ability*.

General deterrence (2): The focus of this type of deterrence is society and the idea that people aware of punishment applied to a particular behavior will view the penalty as too costly and will decide not to engage in the targeted behavior; see *specific/individual deterrence, restrictive deterrence*, and *absolute deterrence*.

General strain theory (6): GST; Agnew suggested multiple sources of strain interact with individual traits to produce criminal behavior (e.g. inequity as well as the inability to reach goals causes strain); whereas other strain theories look at the inability to attain something desired, Agnew looked at delinquent acts as attempts to avoid negative situations.

Genes (3): The basic physical and functional unit of heredity; humans are thought to have about 20–25,000 genes.

Genital stage (4): Begins at ages 3-5; pleasure seeking shifts from anus to genitals; the third of Freud's stages of psychosexual development; see *adolescence/adulthood stage, anal stage, latent stage*, and *oral stage*.

Gestural forgiveness (8): A key part of reintegrative shaming, this ceremonial practice consists of a member of the harmed community forgiving the shamed person and the community welcoming him or her back into the group.

Group conflict theory (9): When groups in society hold conflicting values; conflict can result, particularly if groups in positions of authority weave their values into the law to protect their interests and criminalize the interests of groups with less power.

Group interests (9): The needs, goals, status, power, influence, and other concerns of a collective; conflict develops when other groups infringe on those interests.

Guardianship (2): The ability (and presence) of persons or objects to prevent crime from occurring; part of routine activities theory; see *attractiveness, exposure,* and *proximity.*

## H

Harrison Narcotics Tax Act (1): Congress passed the Act in 1914, which made it a crime to possess and traffic in opiates.

Hate crime (8): A criminal act precipitated by the victim's race, gender, sexual orientation, or other protected status.

Hedonism (1): The pursuit of pleasure, especially as one seeks to maximize pleasure over pain; part of *classical criminology.*

Hegemony (9): Dominance over another country or group of people.

Heritability (3): The concept that traits and characteristics can be transmitted biologically from one generation to the next.

Homeostasis (3): The tendency of the body to seek a state of balance or equilibrium.

Hot-spot patrols (10): Police practice of targeting specific geographic areas identified by crime analysts as troublesome locations.

Human genome (3): The complete set of genetic information in the chromosomes of an organism, including its genes and DNA sequences.

Hypothesis (1): A proposed relationship between two or more variables based on informed ideas about how those variables are interrelated; must be testable through observation or experimentation.

## I

Id (4): A mass of powerful drives that consist of instincts and impulses seeking immediate discharge or gratification and lacking any restraint; the first of Freud's three psychic phenomena to evolve during psychosexual development; a see *ego* and *superego.*

Illegitimate opportunities (6): Access to unlawful means to obtain socially desired goals.

Image (6): The capacity of an area's physical design to impart a sense of security for residents and a warning against intruders; part of Newman's defensible space thesis; see *milieu, territoriality,* and *natural surveillance.*

Imitation (7): Learning through observing what happens to others; *modeling* is the same concept.

Immigrant-status culture conflict (9): One of Sellin's three forms of primary culture conflict that occurs when immigrants leave their home culture to live in another; see *colonialism-derived culture conflict* and *cross-border culture conflict.*

Individual deterrence (2): The focus of this type of deterrence is the individual; if punished for a particular behavior, he or she will modify or change his or her behavior; same as *specific deterrence.*

Inner containment (7): Inner strengths that help youths resist pulls into delinquent behavior; examples include self-control, good self-concept, the ability to internalize societal norms, and the ability to tolerate frustrations; part of Reckless' theory of containment see *outer containment.*

Innovators (6): Group that responds to Merton's anomic trap by using illegal means to gain societally defined success goals; compare with *conformists, ritualists, rebels,* and *retreatists.*

Instrumental conditioning (5): Another term for *operant conditioning.*

Instrumental power relationships (9): The possession of direct means—capital and political influence—to achieve specific goals.

Intensity (7): Associations differ in terms of the emotional quality of relationships, affecting the importance of the association to the individual; part of Sutherland's differential association theory; see *duration, frequency,* and *priority.*

Interstitial area (6): Area between an industrial zone and a residential zone characterized by a high volume of crime; see *the Chicago School* and *social disorganization*.

Involvement decision (2): A multistage process that ends with the decision to get involved in crime; part of rational choice theory; see *involvement decision* and *event decision*.

IQ score (5): A numerical representation of an individual's intelligence as measured by a psychometric test.

**K**

Karyotype studies (3): A gene-linked research approach that examines chromosomes in cells, which can identify genetic problems as the cause of a disorder or disease; see *XYY male*.

**L**

Late-onset offenders (5): Criminals who begin their careers well after adolescence—rarely studied because they are a minority within the offender population.

Latent stage (4): Begins at age 5 through adolescence; the child loses interest in sexual organs as expanded relationships with same-sex and age playmates become paramount in their lives; the fourth of Freud's stages of psychosexual development; see *adolescence/adulthood stage*, *anal stage*, *genital stage*, and *oral stage*.

Legitimate opportunities (6): Access to lawful means to obtain culturally desired goals.

Life-course persistent (LCP) offenders (5): Offenders embark on delinquency and crime paths by age 4 and younger and participate in increasingly serious crime as they age; compare with Moffitt's *adolescent-limited (AL) offenders*.

Lower-class culture thesis (6): Crime occurs in the lower class because of different focal concerns that put it in conflict with the dominant culture.

Lumpenproletariat (9): The lowest stratum of the underclass (outcasts, vagrants, and criminals lacking class identification and solidarity); according to Marx, rabble sometimes bribed by capitalists to work against the interests of the working class.

**M**

*Mala in se* (1): Latin for "evil in itself," refers to crimes that are intrinsically evil, such as murder.

*Mala prohibita* (1): Latin for "wrong because it is prohibited," which refers to activities that have been outlawed because they violate certain societal standards, such as the sale of a controlled substance; see *mala in se*.

Mandatory arrests (10): Policy requiring police to arrest the aggressor without exception; based on the Minneapolis domestic violence experiment.

Marxism (9): The socioeconomic and political philosophy of Karl Marx that divided society into capitalists and workers (proletariat), predicting that the conflict would eventually be resolved by a class war, transforming society into a socialist paradise; contrast with capitalism.

Mass incarceration (10): The high rate of incarceration in the United States marked by the disproportionate numbers of imprisoned minority males.

Master status (8): A person's perceived social standing; the primary identifying characteristic of an individual—the lens through which others view an individual as well as how the individual views him- or herself.

*Mens rea* (1): An individual's mental state at the time of the committing a crime; to be legally liable, the act must have been willful and the outcome intended.

Milieu (6): Addresses features of a physical space that might influence security, such as the proximity of a park or shopping mall; part of Newman's defensible space thesis; see *image*, *natural surveillance*, and *territoriality*.

Minority-threat theory (9): The view that ethnic minority groups threaten white dominance, subjecting them to increased coercive control, including arrest, detainment, adjudication and imprisonment.

Misdemeanors (1): Crimes or law violations punishable by one year or less in a correctional facility operated by a city, county, or the federal government; may also be punishable by a fine.

Modeling (7): See *imitation*.

Modeling theory (5): Humans are capable of learning through observing the actions of another person or through one's imagination; also called *observational learning theory*.

Monozygotic twins (3): MZ; identical twins who share the same genetic material; evolved from a single fertilized egg.

Moral insanity (4): Nineteenth century term used to describe people today referred to as psychopaths.

Motivated offender (2): People (teenagers, the poor, drug users) with few resources who turn to crime to acquire what they want; part of routine activities theory that maintains there is an unlimited supply of motivated offenders.

Motivating definitions (7): Two types of signals underlie *discriminative stimuli:* (1) those that put deviance/criminality in a positive light; and (2) those that allow the offender to neutralize negative aspects of the crime.

## N

National Prohibition Act (1): Known informally as the Volstead Act, this legislation of 1919 enforced the provisions of the Eighteenth Amendment prohibiting the manufacture, sale, or transportation of intoxicating liquors.

Natural law (2): A philosophical view that some elements of justice are universal and derived from nature rather than from the rules of society; contrast with *positive law.*

Natural surveillance (6): The ability of residents to keep a close watch over an area; part of Newman's defensible space thesis; see *image, milieu,* and *territoriality.*

Nature (1): In positivistic criminology, the idea that we can seek answers to crime causation questions from genetic, biological, or other innate properties associated with the individual.

Negative punishment (5): The *removal* of a desirable stimulus (e.g. taking away a favorite toy) following offending behavior to decrease the undesired behavior; part of Skinnerian operant conditioning; see *negative reinforcement, positive punishment,* and *positive reinforcement.*

Negative reinforcement (5): The *removal* of a potentially undesirable result (e.g. studying to avoid a bad grade); part of Skinnerian operant conditioning; see *negative punishment, positive punishment,* and *positive reinforcement.*

Negotiations (8): All involved parties—victims, the state, and the alleged perpetrator—engage in discussions about what will happen to the individual initially designated as having a spoiled identity; one of Schur's four elements in the labeling process; see *retrospective interpretation, role engulfment,* and *stereotyping.*

Neoclassicism (2): Added mitigation or aggravation based on past criminal record, mental state, age, and gender to the Classical School's emphasis on fee will.

Neo-conflict theories (9): Emerging conflict theories that focus on the societal disadvantages faced by various ethnic groups in the United States.

Net widening (10): Legal and correctional practices that expand the net of social control, resulting in more people being controlled by the criminal justice system.

Neurons (3): Specialized cells that send nerve impulses or electrochemical information.

Neuroses (4): Mild personality disorders that may include depression, anxiety, or obsessive behavior.

Neurotic extravert (5): Persons who require high stimulation levels from their environments; one of Eysenck's two personality types most prone to crime; see *psychotic extravert.*

Neuroticism (5): A personality trait associated with anxiety, depression and other negative psychological states; one of Eysenck's three personality temperaments; see *extraversion* and *psychoticism.*

Neurotransmitters (3): Chemicals that transmit signals across synapses.

Neuve Classical School (2): New generation of deterrence theories that emerged in the late twentieth and early twenty-first centuries, primarily rational choice and routine activities theories.

New Criminology (9): A 1970s movement within criminology that criticized traditional criminology as serving the power elite's interests; framed crime studies in a concern for social justice.

Nucleotides (3): The building blocks of nucleic acid, including DNA.

Nurture (1): In positivistic criminology, the idea that we can seek answers to crime causation questions from within the social environment.

## O

Observational learning theory (5): Bandura identified 4 steps in non-direct learning: attention, retention, reproduction, and motivation. Same as *modeling theory*.

Oedipus complex (4): A psychological phenomenon that can emerge in boys during the genital stage of psychosexual development; inappropriate sexual thoughts about the mother.

Onset (5): The beginning point of a criminal career; contrast with *desistance*.

Operant behavior (7): Voluntary and brain-mediated activities; guided by the principles of Skinnerian operant conditioning; see *respondent behavior*.

Operant conditioning (5): Skinner's use of reinforcement or punishment to increase or decrease behavior; an association is formed between the behavior and the consequences for that behavior; focuses on strengthening or weakening voluntary behaviors; also called instrumental conditioning.

Oppositional ideologues (3): A person who unequivocally supports one side in a binary argument (either A or B is right) and selects or fabricates the evidence to support his or her position.

Oppression (9): Refers to the imposition of excessive, severe, or unreasonable burdens on others; see coercion.

Oral stage (4): Begins at birth to age 18 months; the mouth, lips, and tongue are the predominant organs of pleasure for the infant; the first of Freud's stages of psychosexual development; see *adolescence/adulthood stage, anal stage, genital stage*, and *latent stage*.

Ordinances (1): Legislation enacted by local authorities, such as a village, town, city or municipality; intended to control minor forms of misbehavior through the application of fines.

Outer containment (7): Social forces are essential to help youths build bonds to resist pulls into juvenile delinquency; they include family, schools, religious and other institutions, role models, and supportive relationships; part of Reckless' theory of containment; see *inner containment*.

Overt pathway (5): Bullying is the first step to criminal behavior, followed by fighting, then major aggressive acts, including assault and rape; one of three pathways to criminality described by Loeber and Hay; compare with *authority-conflict pathway* and *covert pathway*.

## P

Perceptual deterrence (2): Refers to the idea that the *perceived* certainty, severity, and celerity of punishment are inversely related to the decisions to commit crime made by would-be offenders; perception is the key element.

Persister type (5): Offender who engages in delinquent behavior at a young age and continues engaging in delinquent and criminal conduct into adulthood; contrast with *experimenter type*.

Personal control (7): The ability of the individual to refrain from meeting needs in ways that conflict with the norms and rules of the community.

Phrenology (3): A nineteenth century pseudo-science claiming that the shape of the head revealed the "inner person," including the propensity to commit crime.

Police corruption (10): The misuse of authority by police officers for personal gain or the benefit of others.

Police personality (10): The idea that police officers have distinct and unique psychological and social characteristics characterized by undemocratic tendencies, cynicism, and a readiness to condemn others solely based on race or ethnicity; see *authoritarianism* and *police subculture*.

Police subculture (10): The beliefs, attitudes, and behaviors exhibited by law enforcement officer; tends to promote an "us-versus-them" view of the world; see *authoritarianism* and *police personality*.

Positive law (2): Law created through the political process, the rules and regulations of a particular society—distinguished from *natural law*.

Positive punishment (5): Administering an unpleasant stimulus (e.g. grounding a teenager after taking the car without permission) after an offending behavior to reduce the undesired behavior; part of Skinnerian operant conditioning; see *negative reinforcement, negative punishment*, and *positive reinforcement*.

Positive reinforcement (5): The *presence* of a desirable stimulus (e.g., a new toy for good behavior) increases the probability of the desired behavior; part of Skinnerian operant conditioning; see *negative punishment, negative reinforcement*, and *positive punishment*.

Positivism (1): A philosophical position that all events are knowable using one or more physical senses and rejection of metaphysical answers; in research, using scientific methods to understand social behavior.

Positivist criminology (1): One of three main thematic orientations to criminology; the emphasis is on scientific answers to the reasons for both crime and criminals; compare with *classical criminology* and *conflict criminology*.

Power (9): The ability of a group to attain its goals, implement its policies, and influence the behavior of others.

Power-control theory (9): Gender difference in criminal activity results from the family structure; patriarchal and egalitarian family structures exercise different social controls over girls and boys, resulting in different attitudes toward risk taking.

Preconscious (4): Thoughts and memories just below the surface that easily can be called into conscious awareness, standing as a buffer between conscious and unconscious; one of Freud's three mental processes; compare with *conscious* and *unconscious*.

Predatory crime (2): Violent crimes against persons and crimes of theft in which the victim is present.

Prestige symbols (8): Positive labels conveying acceptance, distinction and valued status.

Primary culture conflict (9): Conflict that results when a culture imposes its legal norms on people socialized in a different culture; Sellin identified three forms—*cross-border culture conflict, colonialism-derived culture conflict*, and *immigrant-status culture conflict*.

Primary deviation (8): An initial foray into criminal activity that represents little threat that the actor or society will see the behavior as part of a deviant career.

Principle of differential association (7): The idea that an individual turns to crime when he or she is exposed to an excess of definitions favorable to law violations compared with unfavorable definitions.

Principle of differential reinforcement (7): Given two or more forms of behavior, the one retained and repeated is the one most highly rewarded.

Priority (7): Associations differ in terms of their ordering in the life cycle—those with the highest priority occur earlier in one's life; part of Sutherland's differential association theory; see *duration, frequency*, and *intensity*.

Privilege (9): That which is valued; class, power, and status are essential and interrelated aspects of privilege.

Proletariat (9): The working class in Marxism.

Proportionality (1): The legal concept whereby the punishment fits the crime; opposite of individualized justice or punishments fitted to individual offenders.

Proximity (2): The physical distance between potential targets and populations of potential offenders; part of routine activities theory; see *attractiveness, exposure,* and *guardianship.*

Psyche (4): Greek word that means the soul.

Psychiatry (4): A branch of medicine concerned primarily with the study and treatment of mental disorders.

Psychoanalysis (4): Generally associated with Freud, this branch of psychiatry aims to induce the patient to give up the repressions belonging to his or her early life, replacing them with reactions that would correspond better to a psychically mature condition.

Psychological pushes (7): Psychological elements that make delinquency more likely, such as inner tensions, unhappiness, hostility, and aggressiveness; part of Reckless' theory of containment; see *biological pushes, social pulls,* and *social pushes.*

Psychology (4): Both an area of scientific study and an academic discipline, it examines individual human and animal behavior; chiefly concerned with the mind and mental processes.

Psychopath (4): A personality disorder characterized by long-term antisocial behavior, diminished empathy and remorse, and disinhibited, aggressive, violent, or bold behavior.

Psychoses (4): A commonly used psychological term that describes severe personality disorders, such that the victim suffers a break with reality; may include hallucinations and delusional beliefs; see *neuroses.*

Psychosexual development (4): According to Freud, humans pass through five developmental stages: *adolescence/adulthood, anal, genital, latent* and *oral.*

Psychosexual maturity (4): Freud's term for the final stop on the psychosexual development journey; adulthood.

Psychotic extravert (5): Persons who are cruel, hostile, insensitive to others, and unemotional—but not necessarily "out of touch with reality"; one of Eysenck's two personality types most prone to crime; see *neurotic extravert.*

Psychoticism (5): A personality trait in which the person is aggressive, impulsive, impersonal, cold and lacking in empathy for others; one of Eysenck's three personality temperaments; see *extraversion* and *neuroticism.*

"Pulling levers" (2): The focused deterrence intervention in which the police communicate directly and repeatedly with offenders that they are under scrutiny and all available sanctions will be applied for not complying with the law; the strategy can include interagency enforcement—police, probation, parole, state and federal prosecutors, and federal enforcement agencies.

## R

Rational-legal authority (9): Weber's description of authority based on administrative and legal order, where laws and rules are fairly and equally applied to everyone.

Reaction formation (4): Mechanism that allows an individual to replace socially unacceptable behavior with behavior that is socially acceptable; one of Freud's four defense mechanisms; see *displacement, repression,* and *sublimation.*

Reaction formation thesis (6): Cohen's idea that delinquent subcultures take the larger culture's norms (middle-class values) and turn them upside down—rejecting the standards they cannot attain.

Rebels (6): Group that responds to Merton's anomic trap by rejecting societal goals and attempting to overthrow the existing social order and its cultural values; compare with *innovators, conformists, retreatists,* and *ritualists.*

Regression (4): Reversion to a previous mode of gratification, as in moving backward from the adolescence/adulthood stage to the genital stage; part of Freud's psychoanalytic model; see *cathexis* and *fixation.*

Reintegrative shaming (8): Punishment should focus on the offender's behavior with the goal of returning the individual to the community through ritualistic reinforcement of the person's status within the group; contrast with *disintegrative shaming.*

Repression (4): Mechanism to prevent unwanted id impulses, memories, desires, or wish-fulfilling fantasies from entering the conscious-thought level; one of Freud's four defense mechanisms; see *displacement, reaction formation,* and *sublimation.*

Respondent behavior (7): Automatic and reflexive behavior (i.e., blinking); guided by the principles of Skinnerian instrumental conditioning; see *operant behavior.*

Restorative justice (RJ) (10): An alternative justice practice to heal the harm caused by an offender to the victim and to the community and to reintegrate rule violators into the community; see *reintegrative shaming* and *disintegrative shaming.*

Restrictive deterrence (2): Offenders may refrain from repeating a specific behavior for which they were punished, but they modify their criminal conduct rather than abandoning it.

Retreatists (6): Group that responds to Merton's anomic trap by abandoning all attempts to reach conventional social goals in favor of a deviant adaptation (e.g., abusing alcohol and drugs); compare with *innovators, conformists, rebels,* and *ritualists.*

Retrospective interpretation (8): Looking to the past for previously unseen causes of present undesired behavior; one of Schur's four elements in the labeling process; see *negotiations, role engulfment,* and *stereotyping.*

Reuptake (3): Refers to the reabsorption of a neurotransmitter by the presynaptic nerve ending that previously secreted it; recycling of neurochemicals.

Ritualists (6): Group that responds to Merton's anomic trap by rigidly adhering to and accepting their station in life; compare with *innovators, rebels, retreatists,* and *conformists.*

Role engulfment (8): The social-psychological process by which the individual assumes his or her master status—the sum total of Shur's *negotiations, retrospective interpretation,* and *stereotyping.*

## S

Secondary culture conflict (9): Conflict within a dominant culture when a group emerges that has significantly different values and conduct norms.

Secondary deviation (8): Activity that occurs when labeled persons reorganize their behavior according to society's reactions and respond to society in terms of that negative label.

Secondary sanctioning (8): Losses or negative experiences (e.g. poor employment prospects, reliance on welfare) endured by persons labeled as criminals in addition to loss of respect and freedom.

Self-control theory (7): Proposed by Gottfredson and Hirschi, this theory suggests that only socialization (primarily effective parenting) overcomes the natural tendencies toward self-centered activities; if self-control is not learned by age 10, individuals will follow their selfish inclinations and engage in impulsive, reckless behaviors; also called *event-propensity theory.*

Self-medication (3): Self-administered treatment of a chemical deficiency or dysfunction without a doctor's prescription, sometimes using illegal substances.

Self-fulfilling prophecy (8): The sociological principle that what people believe to be real becomes real in its consequences.

Serotonin (3): A neurotransmitter involved in sleep, mood, depression, and anxiety; moderates primitive drives such as aggression, sex, and food seeking, while improving the ability to interact socially.

Severity (2): The fear of the sanction for an offense must outweigh the pleasure associated with it; part of deterrence theory; see *certainty* and *celerity*.

Shame (8): A painful emotion caused by feelings of guilt or failure, particularly when embarrassing behavior is made public and threatens a person's value or standing in the community.

Shaming (8): Public expressions of disapproval with the intention of informing others about the offensive behavior and invoking remorse in the offender.

Sharia law (1): Islamic law that regulates both public and private aspects of individuals' lives; based on an Arabic word meaning "way" or "path."

Smartness (6): The ability to "con" and act shrewdly; one of Miller's six focal concerns of lower-class culture; see *autonomy, excitement,* fate, *trouble,* and *toughness*.

Social altruism (8): A community's willingness to share scarce resources for the aid and comfort of their members; these resources are distinct from those provided by the state.

Social bond (7): Relationships that connect an individual to society and its moral constraints; these attachments and commitments constrain egocentric and norm-violating tendencies.

Social contract (2): The Age of Enlightenment ideal in which people are both self-interested and rational; they will submit to political authority in order to live in a civil society giving up selfish interests to the state as long as everyone else does the same—a balance between individual rights and societal rules.

Social disorganization (6): Any disturbance, disruption, conflict, or lack of consensus within a social group or given society that makes harmonious functioning of social controls and social institutions impossible without significant adjustments.

Social disorganization theory (6): Theory developed by the Chicago School that links crime directly to neighborhood socioecological characteristics.

Social exclusion (8): Application of a negative label that limits and restricts a person's social networks.

Social equilibrium (6): A working balance between all the interconnected parts within a social system and the external environment in which it exits.

Social fear (8): The anticipation of the shame and loss of social standing associated with various labels (e.g., unemployed, criminal).

Social justice (9): A condition of equality, self-determination, and liberation that results in the elimination of all conditions of human suffering.

Social learning theory (7): Akers' expansion of Sutherland's differential association theory through the addition of operant conditioning principles to the process of learning.

Social process (7): Any identifiable, repetitive pattern of interaction between humans in a group or social context.

Social pulls (7): Forces in one's social environment such as youth gangs or other criminal subcultures that make the delinquent path attractive to some youth; part of Reckless' theory of containment see *biological pushes, psychological pushes,* and *social pushes*.

Social pushes (7): Forces in one's social environment, such as poverty, minority-group status, and family conflicts that force youth in the direction of delinquency; part of Reckless' theory of containment; see *biological pushes, psychological pushes,* and *social pulls*.

Social threat thesis (9): Some identifiable groups, by their actions or inactions, threaten the political and economic order as well as values, eliciting a punitive response from the criminal justice system.

Sociopath (4): Person who exhibits antisocial attitudes and behavior caused by social and environmental conditions.

Soma (3): Cell body.

Spatial displacement hypothesis (10): The idea that hot-spot practices reduce an area's crime rates because criminals move to nearby areas where crime-control efforts are less aggressive; contrast with *diffusion of crime-control benefits hypothesis.*

Specific deterrence (2): Same as *individual deterrence.*

Spoiled identity (8): The permanent attachment of a negative label (e.g. criminal, pervert, child molester) to an individual that disqualifies him or her from social acceptance; the net result of stigmatization on master status.

Spuriousness (1): If a mathematical relationship between two variables can be eliminated by the introduction of a third variable, the original relationship is false.

Stake in conformity (7): The extent to which a child feels connected to and engaged in normative behavior.

Status characteristics hypothesis (8): Personal characteristics are the determining factors in the application of labels by social control agencies; researchers using the hypothesis to explore how different criminal justice agencies apply formal labels.

Status degradation ceremonies (8): Public denunciations of people identified as undesirable, untrustworthy, and devalued—include arrest, charging, preliminary court appearance, trial, and sentencing.

Status offender (10): Behavior that is designated as deviant only because of the age of the offender.

Stereotyping (8): The process of assigning a simplistic and unchanging mental image or pattern to an individual or group based on visual or auditory cues; one of Schur's four elements in the labeling process; see *negotiations, retrospective interpretation,* and *role engulfment.*

Stigma symbols (8): Negative labels conveying an undesirable quality, rejection, and devalued status.

Stigmata (3): Nonphysical and physical characteristics (e.g. facial asymmetry, an enormous jaw, prominent cheekbones, large ears, fleshy lips, abnormal teeth, receding chin, excessive arm length) that indicated to early biocriminologists an evolutionary throwback.

Stigmatization (8): The process of labeling and devaluing an individual and his or her status in the community.

Strain theory (6): Merton's idea that normlessness arises out of a contradiction (*strain*) between culturally endorsed success goals and the means to attain them legitimately.

Subculture (6): An identifiable subgroup within a larger culture, whose culture, beliefs, or interests may differ from those of the larger culture.

Sublimation (4): Unconscious transformation of socially unacceptable impulses into socially acceptable actions or behavior; one of Freud's four defense mechanisms; see *displacement, reaction formation,* and *repression.*

Subterranean values (7): Norms and expectations that set youth culture apart from the dominant culture of a society; promotion of risky, exciting behavior outside behavioral standards.

Suitable target (2): Potential person, place or thing to victimize; part of routine activities theory; see *capable guardian* and *motivated offender.*

Superego (4): Sometimes referred to as a conscience-like mechanism, it exercises a criticizing power over the ego; the third of Freud's three psychic phenomena to evolve during psychosexual development; see *ego* and *id.*

Supermales (3): A label attached to XYY males; a specific type of "born criminal" that proved to be largely a media myth.

Symbol (8): A thing that stands for something else, usually a material object that represents an abstract idea.

Symbolic assailants (10): Individuals designated by the police as meriting surveillance because of membership in a dangerous group or suspicious behavior.

Symbolic interactionism (8): A sociological perspective that if something is perceived to be a certain way, no matter the objective reality, the perceived reality shapes the outcome.

Symbolic power relationships (9): Societal perspective on power elites—generally seen as less vulnerable to control agents because they have more power (i.e. corporate executives vs. those who commit street crimes).

Synapses (3): The point at which an impulse passes from one neuron to another.

Synaptic vesicles (3): Button-like sacs that extend from the ends of axons that store sensitive electrochemicals.

**T**

Tautology (1): An argument constructed so that the first claim is supported by the same claim in the second statement.

Technique of neutralization (7): Techniques that allow youth to rationalize crime or a rule violation.

Territoriality (6): Home as valued possession to be protected; part of Newman's defensible space thesis; see *image, milieu,* and *natural surveillance.*

Theory (1): An explanation of a real-world occurrence based on systematic observations about the phenomenon or class of phenomena under study.

Time discounting (2): People tend to devalue a future reward in favor of one that is more immediate.

Torts (1): Civil wrongs or injuries not subject to criminal litigation.

Toughness (6): Physical prowess and daring; one of Miller's six focal concerns of lower-class culture; see *autonomy, excitement, fate, smartness,* and *trouble.*

Trajectories (5): Long-term developmental pathways over the life course.

Transference (4): Patient develops a negative or positive emotional attitude toward his or her therapist; one of three techniques used by psychoanalysts to elicit repressed information; see *dream interpretation* and *free association.*

Transitory events (5): Short-term, specific life events that are part of life-course trajectories and mark movement from one status to another.

Transporters (3): Proteins located on the surface of the sending neurons that latch onto the neurotransmitters and transport them back inside the cell body for use at a later time.

Trouble (6): Engaging in law-violating behavior; one of Miller's six focal concerns of lower-class culture; see *autonomy, excitement, fate, smartness,* and *toughness.*

Turning points (5): Changes in life-course trajectories.

Twin studies (3): A research method that allows researchers to examine the overall role of genes in the development of a trait or disorder, including criminal propensity.

**U**

Unconscious (4): Repressed memories and attendant emotions very difficult to pull into the conscious level; one of Freud's three mental processes; compare with *conscious* and *preconscious.*

**V**

Variable (1): Something that is inconsistent or subject to change (exists in different amounts or types); in research, it is a measurable form of a specific *concept* and takes one of 3 forms: independent, variable, controlled.

Victimologist (2): Social scientists who study what happens to individuals who fall prey to criminal events.

**W**

War on Poverty (10): Unofficial name for the program initiated in 1964 by President Lyndon B. Johnson that consisted of multiple pieces of federal legislation to address poverty in the United States.

# References

Abadinsky, H. (2013). *Organized Crime*, 10th ed. Belmont, CA: Cengage.

Abadinsky, H. (2014a). *Drug Abuse: A Comprehensive Introduction*, 8th ed. Belmont, CA: Cengage.

Abadinsky, H. (2014b). *Law, Courts, and Justice in America*. Long Grove, IL: Waveland Press.

Abadinsky, H. (2016). "Some Musings about Buzzwords and Metaphors in Criminal Justice," *ACJS Today* 61 (March):23–27.

Adorno, T., E. Frenkel-Brunswick, D. L. Levinson, and R. N. Sanford. (1985). *The Authoritarian Personality*. New York: Harper and Row.

Agnew, R. (1985). "A revised strain theory of delinquency." *Social Forces* 64:151–67.

Agnew, R. (1992). "Foundation for a general strain theory of crime and delinquency." *Criminology* 30: 47–87.

Aichhorn, A. (1973[1935]). *Wayward Youth*. New York: Viking Press.

Akers, R. L. (1968). "Problems in the sociology of deviance: Social definitions and behavior." *Social Forces* 46: 455–65.

Akers, R. L. (1973). *Deviant Behavior: A Social Learning Approach*. Belmont, CA: Wadsworth.

Akers, R. L. (1985). *Deviant Behavior: A Social Learning Approach*, 3rd ed. Belmont, CA: Wadsworth.

Akers, R. L. (1998). *Social Learning and Social Structure: A General Theory of Crime and Deviance*. Boston: Northeastern University Press.

Akers, R. L., and C. S. Sellers. (2013). *Criminological Theories: Introduction, Evaluation, and Application*, 6th ed. New York: Oxford University Press.

Akins, S., C. L. Smith, and C. Mosher. (2010). "Pathways to adult alcohol use across race/ethnic groups: An application of general strain and social learning theories." *Journal of Drug Issues* 40:321–52.

Alpert, G. P. (1993). "Hiring and promoting police officers in small departments: Limiting the role of psychological testing." Pp. 96–105 in *Critical Issues in Policing*, Eds. R. G. Dunham and G. P. Alpert. Long Grove, IL: Waveland Press.

American Psychological Association. (2013). *Diagnostic and Statistical Manual of Mental Disorders*, 5th ed. Arlington, VA: APA.

Amiri, S. (2014). *Testing a Geospatial Predictive Policing Strategy: Application of Arcgis 3D Analyst Tools for Forecasting Commission of Residential Burglaries* (Unpublished doctoral dissertation). Washington State University.

Anderson, K. B. (2002). "Richard Quinney's journey: The Marxist dimension." *Crime and Delinquency* 48:232–42.

Anderson, N. E. and K. A. Kiehl. (2014). "The psychopath magnetized: Insights from brain imaging." *Trends in Cognitive Science* 16 (January):52–60.

Andrews, D. A. (1980). "Some experimental investigations of the principles of differential association through deliberate manipulation of the structure of service systems." *American Sociological Review* 44:448–62.

Anson, R. J., D. Mann, and D. Sherman. (1986). "Niederhoffer's cynicism scale: Reliability and beyond." *Journal of Criminal Justice* 14:295–305.

Antonaccio, O., and C. R. Tittle. (2007). "A cross-national test of Bonger's theory of criminology and economic conditions." *Criminology* 45:925–58.

Anwar, S., and T. A. Loughran. (2011). "Testing a Bayesian learning theory of deterrence among serious juvenile offenders." *Criminology* 49:667–98.

Appleby, N. (2010). "Labeling the innocent: How government counter-terrorism advice creates labels that contribute to the problem." *Critical Studies in Terrorism* 3:421–36.

Armstrong, E. G. (2000). "Constructions of cultural conflict and crime." *Sociological Imagination* 37:114–26.

Arrigo, B. A., and S. Shipley. (2001). "The confusion over psychopathy (I): Historical considerations." *International Journal of Offender Therapy and Comparative Criminology* 45:325–44.

Austin, J., and B. Krisberg. (1981). "Wider, strong, and different nets: The dialectics of criminal justice reform." *Journal of Research in Crime and Delinquency* 18:165–96.

Ayers, R. M. (1977). "Case studies of police strikes in two cities—Albuquerque and Oklahoma City." *Journal of Police Science and Administration* 5:19–31.

Babiak, P., C. S. Neumann, and R. D. Hare. (2010). "Corporate psychopathy: Talking the walk." *Behavioral Sciences and the Law* 28:174–93.

Bachman, R., R. Paternoster, and S. Ward. (1992). "The rationality of sexual offending: Testing a deterrence/rational choice conception of sexual assault." *Law and Society Review* 26:343–72.

*Bailey et al. v. Drexel Furniture Company*, 259 U.S. 20, 42S.Ct. 449, L.Ed. 817 (1922a).

*Bailey et al. v. George et al.*, 259 U.S. 16, 42 S.Ct. 419, 66 L.Ed. 816 (1922b).

Balkan, S., R. J. Berger, and J. Schmidt. (1980). *Crime and Deviance in America: A Critical Approach.* Belmont, CA: Wadsworth.

Bandura, A. (1974). "Behavioral theory and the models of man." *American Psychologist* 28:859–69.

Bandura, A., and A. Huston. (1961). "Identification as a process of incidental learning." *Journal of Abnormal and Social Psychology* 63:311–18.

Barnes, J. C., K. M. Beaver, and B. B. Boutwell. (2011). "Examining the genetic underpinnings of Moffitt's developmental taxonomy: A behavioral genetic analysis." *Criminology* 49:923–54.

Baron, S. W. (2011). "When formal sanctions encourage violent offending: How violent peers and violent codes undermine deterrence." *Justice Quarterly* 30:926–55.

Barr, R., and K. Pease. (1990). "Crime placement, displacement and deflection." Pp. 277–318 in *Crime and Justice: A Review of Research* (vol. 12), Eds. M. Tonry and N. Morris. Chicago: University of Chicago Press.

Barrick, K. (2007). *Being Labeled a Felon and Its Consequences for Recidivism: An Examination of Contingency Effects* (Unpublished dissertation). Florida State University, Tallahassee, FL.

Barrick, K. (2014). "A review of prior tests of labeling theory." Chapter 5 in *Labeling Theory: Empirical Tests*, Eds. D. Farrington and J. Murray. Advancements in Criminological Theory, Volume 18. New Brunswick, NJ: Transaction.

Barrick, K., M. J. Hickman, and K. J. Strom. (2014). "Representative policing and violence towards the police." *Policing* 8:193–204.

Bartol, C. R. (1991). *Criminal Behavior: A Psychological Approach*, 3rd ed. Englewood Cliffs, NJ: Prentice-Hall.

Bartol, C. R. (1999). *Criminal Behavior: A Psychosocial Approach*, 5th ed. Upper Saddle River, NJ: Prentice-Hall.

Barton, M. S., B. L. Jensen, and J. M. Kaufman. (2010). "Social disorganization theory and the college campus." *Journal of Criminal Justice* 38:245–54.

Bazemore, G., and D. Maloney. (1994). "Rehabilitating community service toward restorative service sanctions in a balanced justice system." *Federal Probation* 58:24.

Bazemore, G., and M. Schiff. (2001). *Restorative Community Justice: Repairing Harm and Transforming Communities.* Cincinnati, OH: Anderson.

Bazemore, G., and M. Umbreit. (2001). "A comparison of four restorative conferencing models." *Juvenile Justice Bulletin*, February. Washington, DC: Office of Juvenile Justice and Delinquency Prevention.

Beaver, K. M., J. C. Barnes, J. S. May, and J. A. Schwartz. (2011). "Psychopathic personality traits, genetic risk, and gene environment correlations." *Criminal Justice and Behavior* 38:896–912.

Beaver, K. M., M. W. Rowland, J. A. Schwartz, and J. L. Nedelec. (2011). "The genetic origins of psychopathic personality traits in adult males and females: The results of an adoption-based study." *Journal of Criminal Justice* 39:426–32.

Beaver, K. M., J. P. Wright, and M. DeLisi. (2007). "Self-control as an executive function: Reformulating Gottfredson and Hirschi's parental socialization thesis." *Criminal Justice and Behavior* 34:1345–61.

Beccaria, C. (1963[1764]). *On Crimes and Punishments*. Trans. H. Paolucci. Indianapolis, IN: Bobbs-Merrill.

Becker, G. S. (1968). "Crime and punishment: An economic approach." *Journal of Political Economy* 76:169–217.

Becker, H. S. (1963). *Outsiders: Studies in the Sociology of Deviance*. New York: Free Press.

Bellamy, J. (2004). *The Law of Treason in England in the Later Middle Ages* (Reprinted ed.), Cambridge: Cambridge University Press.

Bellair, P. E. (1997). "Social interaction and community crime: Examining the importance of neighbor networks." *Criminology* 35:677–703.

Bentham, J. (1948[1789]). *An Introduction to the Principles of Morals and Legislation*. New York: Kegan Paul.

Berkout, O. V., A. M. Gross, and K. K. Kellum. (2013). "Behaving badly: A perspective on mechanisms of dysfunction in psychopathy." *Aggression and Violent Behavior* 18:620–29.

Bernberg, J. G., and M. D. Krohn. (2003). "Labeling, life chances, and adult crime: The direct and indirect effects of official interventions in adolescence on crime in early childhood." *Criminology* 41:1287–317.

Bernberg, J. G., M. D. Krohn, and C. J. Rivera. (2006). "Official labeling, criminal embeddedness, and subsequent delinquency: A longitudinal test of labeling theory." *Journal of Research in Crime and Delinquency* 43:67–88.

Berryessa, C. M., N. A. Martinez-Martin, and M. A. Allyse. (2013). "Ethical, legal and social issues surrounding research on genetic contributions to anti-social behavior." *Aggression and Violent Behavior* 18:605–10.

Bird, A. (2007). "Perceptions of epigenetics." *Nature: International Weekly Journal of Science* 447:396–98.

Black, D. (1976). *The Behavior of Law*. Orlando, FL: Academic Press.

Blackstone, W. (1962[1760]). *Commentaries on the Laws of England*. Boston: Beacon Press.

Blackwell, B. S. (2000). "Perceived sanction threats, gender, and crime: A test and elaboration of power-control theory." *Criminology* 38:439–88.

Blalock, H. M. (1967). *Towards a Theory of Minority Group Relations*. New York: John Wiley.

Blank, R. H. (2013). *Intervention in the Brain: Politics, Policy, and Ethnics*. Cambridge, MA: MIT Press.

Block, B. P., and J. Hostettler. (1997). *Hanging in the Balance: A History of the Abolition of Capital Punishment in Britain*. Winchester: Waterside Press.

Blomberg, T. G. (1980). "Widening the net: An anomaly in the evaluation of diversion programs." Pp. 572–592 in *Handbook of Criminal Justice Evaluation*, Eds. M. Klein and K. Teilmann. Beverly Hills, CA: Sage.

Blomberg, T. G., J. Mestre, and K. Mann. (2013). "Seeking causality in a world of contingency." *Criminology and Public Policy* 12 (November):571–84.

Blumstein, A., J. Cohen, and D. Nagin, Eds. (1978). *Deterrence and Incapacitation: Estimating the Effects of Criminal Sanctions on Crime Rates*. Washington, DC: National Academy of Sciences.

Blumstein, A., J. Cohen, J. Roth, and C. Visher, Eds. (1986). *Criminal Careers and "Career Criminals."* 2 vols. Washington, DC: National Academy Press.

Boaz, A., L. Grayson, R. Levitt, and W. Solesbury. (2008). "Does evidence-based policy work? Learning from the UK experience." *Evidence & Policy* 4:233–53.

Bonger, W. (1969[1916]). *Criminality and Economic Conditions*. Bloomington: Indiana University Press.

Bonn, S. A. (2014). "How to tell a sociopath from a psychopath." *Psychology Today* Online. Retrieved from https://www.psychologytoday.com/blog/wicked-deeds/201401/how-tell-sociopath-psychopath

Bopp, W. J., P. Chignell, and C. Maddox. (1977). "The San Francisco police strike of 1975: A Case study." *Journal of Police Science and Administration* 5:32–42.

Boudon, R. (2003). "Beyond rational choice theory." *Annual Review of Sociology* 29:1–21.

*Bowers v. Hardwick*. 478 U.S. 186 (1986).

Boyle, J. (1992). "Natural law and the ethics of traditions." Pp. 3–30 in *Natural Law Theory*, Ed. R. P. George. Oxford, UK: Oxford University Press.

Bradshaw, E.A. (2011). "A rose by any other name: State criminality and the limits of social learning theory." *The Hilltop Review* 5:1–12.

Braga, A. A., and R. V. Clarke. (2014). "Explaining High-Risk Concentrations of Crime in the City: Social Disorganization, Crime Opportunities, and Important Next Steps." *Journal of Research in Crime and Delinquency* 51 (4):480–98.

Braga, A. A., and D. L. Weisburd. (2012). "The effects of focused deterrence strategies on crime: A systematic review and meta-analysis of the empirical evidence." *Journal of Research on Crime and Delinquency* 49:323–58.

Braga, A. A., D. Weisburd, E. Waring. L. Green-Mazzerolle, W. Spelman, and F. Gajewski. (1999). "Problem-oriented policing in violent crime places: A randomized controlled experiment." *Criminology* 37: 541–80.

Braithwaite, J. (1989). "The state of criminology: Theoretical decay or renaissance?" *Australian and New Zealand Journal of Criminology* 22:129–35.

Braithwaite, J. (1997). "Charles Tittle's control balance and criminological theory." *Theoretical Criminology* 1:77–97.

Braithwaite, J. (1999). "Restorative justice: Assessing optimistic and pessimistic accounts." Pp. 1–127 in *Crime and Justice: A Review of Research*, Ed. M. Tonry. Chicago: University of Chicago Press.

Braithwaite, J. (2000). "Shame and criminal justice." *Canadian Journal of Criminology* 42:281–99.

*Breed v. Jones*, 421 U.S. 519 (1975).

Brennan, P. A., S. Mednick, and J. Volavka. (1995). "Biomedical factors in crime." Pp. 65–90 in *Crime*, Eds. J. Q. Wilson and J. Petersilia. San Francisco: Institute for Contemporary Studies.

Brown, W. K., T. Miller, R. L. Jenkins, and W. A. Rhodes. (1991). "The human costs of 'giving the kid another chance.'" *International Journal of Offender Therapy and Comparative Criminology* 35:296–302.

Brunner, H. G., M. Nelson, X. D. Breakefield, H. H. Ropes, and A. van Oost. (1994). "Abnormal behavior associated with a point mutation in the structural gene for monoamine oxidase A." *Science* 262:578–80.

*Buck v. Bell*, 274 U.S.C. 200 (1927).

Burgess, R., and R. L. Akers. (1966). "A differential-association-reinforcement theory of criminal behavior." *Social Problems* 14:128–47.

Bursik, R. J. (1988). "Social disorganization and theories of crime and delinquency: Problems and prospects." *Criminology* 26:519–51.

Burt, C. H., and R. L. Simons. (2014). "Pulling back the curtain on heritability studies: Biosocial criminology in the postgenomic era." *Criminology* 52:223–62.

Burt, C. H., and R. L. Simons. (2015). "Heritability studies in the postgenomic era: The fatal flaw is conceptual." *Criminology* 53:103–12.

Burt, C. L. (1935). *The Subnormal Mind*. London: Oxford University Press. Republished London: Oxford University Press.

Cao, L. (2007). "Returning to normality anomie and crime in China." *International Journal of Offender Therapy and Comparative Criminology* 51:40–51.

Caplan, J. (2003). "Police cynicism: Police survival tool." *The Police Journal* 76:304–13.

Carlson, J. M. (1993) *Restorative Justice: Beyond Crime and Punishment* (Unpublished master's thesis). Mankato State University, Minnesota.

Carter, D. (1990). "Drug-related corruption of police officers: A contemporary typology." *Journal of Criminal Justice* 18:85–98.

Cartwright, N., and J. Stegenga. (2011). "A theory of evidence for evidence-based policy." *Proceedings of the British Academy* 171:289–319.

Carveth, D. L. (2010). "Superego, conscience, and the nature and types of guilt." *Modern Psychoanalysis* 35:106–30.

Caspi, A., T. E. Moffitt, P. A. Silva, M. Stouthamer-Loeber, R. F. Krueger, and P. A. Schmutte. (1994). "Are some people crime-prone? Replications of personality-crime relationship across countries, genders, races, and methods." *Criminology* 32:163–96.

Chambliss, W. J. (1964). "A sociological analysis of the law and vagrancy." *Social Problem* 12:67–77.

Chambliss, W. J. (1976). "The state and criminal law." Pp. 66–106 in *Whose Law, What Order? A Conflict Approach to Criminology*, Eds. W. J. Chambliss and M. Mankoff. New York: Wiley.

Chambliss, W. J. (1988). *Exploring Criminology*. New York: Macmillan.

Chambliss, W. J. (1989a). "State-organized crime." *Criminology* 27:188–90.

Chambliss, W. J. (1989b). "On trashing Marxist criminology." *Criminology* 27:231–38.

Chambliss, W. J., and R. Seidman. (1982). *Law, Order and Power*. Reading, MA: Addison-Wesley.

Chamlin, M., and J. K. Cochran. (1997). "Social altruism and crime." *Criminology* 35:203–27.

Chen, X. (2010). "Desire for autonomy and adolescent delinquency: A latent growth curve analysis." *Criminal Justice and Behavior* 37:989–1004.

Chichinadze, K., M. Chichinadze, and A. Lazarashvili. (2011). "Hormonal and neurochemical mechanisms of aggression and a new classification of aggressive behavior." *Aggression and Violent Behavior* 16:461–71.

Chiricos, T., K. Barrick, W. Bales, and S. Bontrager. (2007). "The labeling of convicted felons and its consequences for recidivism." *Criminology* 45:547–81.

Christiansen, K. O. (1977). "A review of studies of criminality among twins." Pp. 45–58 in *Biosocial Bases of Criminal Behavior*, Eds. S. Mednick and K. O. Christiansen. New York: Gardner.

Clark, G. R., M. A. Telfer, D. Baker, and M. Rosen. (1970). "Sex chromosomes, crime and psychosis." *American Journal of Psychiatry* 126 (11):1659–63.

Clark, P. P. (2010). "Preventing future crime with cognitive behavioral therapy." *NIJ Journal* 265:22–25.

Clarke, R. V., and D. Weisburd. (1994). "Diffusion of crime control benefits: Observation on the reverse of displacement." Pp. 165–183 in *Crime Prevention Studies* (vol. 3), Ed. R. V. Clarke. Monsey, NJ: Criminal Justice Press.

Cleckley, H. M. (1941). *The Mask of Sanity*. St. Louis: Mosby.

Clinard, M. B., and R. Quinney. (1967). *Criminal Behavior Systems: A Typology*. New York: Holt, Rinehart and Winston.

Cloninger, S. (1993). *Theories of Personality: Understanding Persons*. Englewood Cliffs, NJ: Prentice-Hall.

Clotfelter, C. T., and P. J. Cook. (1991). *Selling Hope: State Lotteries in America*. Cambridge, MA: Harvard University Press.

Cloward, R., and L. Ohlin. (1960). *Delinquency and Opportunity: A Theory of Delinquent Gangs*. Glencoe, IL: Free Press.

Cochrane, R. E., R. P. Tett, and L. Vandecreek. (2003). "Psychological testing and the selection of police officers: A national survey." *Criminal Justice and Behavior* 30:511–37.

Cohen, A. K. (1955). *Delinquent Boys: The Culture of the Gang*. New York: Free Press.

Cohen, L. E., and M. Felson. (1979). "Social change and crime rate trends: A routine activity approach." *American Sociological Review* 44:588–608.

Cohen, L. E., J. R. Kluehel, and K. C. Land. (1981). "Social inequality and predatory criminal victimizations: An exposition and test of a formal theory." *American Sociological Review* 46:505–24.

Coid, J., M. Yang, S. Ullrich, A. Roberts, P. Moran, P. Bebbington, T. Brugha, R. Jenkins, M. Farrell, G. Lewis, N. Singleton, and R. D. Hare. (2009). "Psychopathy among prisoners in England and Wales." *International Journal of Law and Psychiatry* 32:134–41.

Comfort, M. (2007). "Punishment beyond the legal offender." *Annual Review of Law and Social Science* 3:271–96.

Cooley, C. H. (1922). *Human Nature and the Social Order. New* York: Scribner.

Cornish, D. B., and R. V. Clarke. (1986). *The Reasoning Criminal: Rational Choice Perspectives on Offending*. New York: Springer-Verlag.

Crank, J., C. M. Koski, M. Johnson, E. Ramirez, A. Shelden, and S. Peterson. (2010). "Hot corridors, deterrence, and guardianship: An assessment of the Omaha metro safety initiative." *Journal of Criminal Justice* 38:430–38.

Curran, D., and C. M. Renzetti. (1994). *Theories of Crime*. Boston: Allyn &Bacon.

Darwin, C. (1859). *On the Origin of the Species*. London: John Murray.

Darwin, C. (1981[1871]). *Descent of Man, and Selection in Relation to Sex*. Princeton, NJ: Princeton University Press.

Da Silva, D. R., D. Rijo, and R. T. Salekin. (2012). "Child and adolescent psychopathy: A state-of-the-art reflection on the construct and etiological theories." *Journal of Criminal Justice* 40:269–77.

Davenport, C. B. (1915). *The Feebly Inhibited*. Publication No. 236. Washington, DC: Carnegie Institute of Washington.

Davies, S., and J. Tanner. (2003). "The long arm of the law: Effects of labeling on employment." *The Sociological Quarterly* 44:385–404.

Degler, C. N. (1991). *In Search of Human Nature: The Decline and Revival of Darwinism in American Thought*. New York: Oxford University Press.

Del Carmen, R. V., and J. T. Walker. (2011). *Briefs in 100 Leading Cases in Law Enforcement*, 8th ed. Cincinnati, OH: Anderson.

DeLisi, M. (2009). "Psychopathy is the unified theory of crime." *Youth Violence and Juvenile Justice* 7:256–73.

Dobbs, D. (2013). "The social life of genes." *Pacific Standard* (September/October): 40–49.

Domhoff, G. W. (2014). *Who Rules America? The Triumph of the Corporate Rich*, 7th ed. New York: McGraw-Hill Education.

Durkheim, E. (1961[1925]). *Moral Education*. Glencoe, IL: FreePress.

Eck, J. E., and W. Spelman. (1987). "Who ya gonna call? The police as problem-busters." *Crime and Delinquency* 33:31–52.

*Edwards v. United States*, U.S. S.Ct. 96-1492, 61 CrL3015(1997).

Egger, S. A. (1990). *Serial Murder: An Elusive Phenomenon*. New York: Praeger.

Ehrlich. I. (1975). "The deterrence effect of capital punishment: A question to life and death." *The American Economic Review* 65:397–417.

Eisen, R. (2014). "States slowly adopting laws to ease ex-felons' path to employment." Lexis-Nexis Legal Newsroom. Labor and Employment Law. Retrieved from https://www.lexisnexis.com/legalnewsroom/labor-employment/b/labor-employment-top-blogs/archive/2014/08/05/states-slowly-adopting-laws-to-ease-ex-felons-39-path-to-employment.aspx#sthash.7KgajCuP.dpuf

Elliott, M. A. (1967). "Social disorganization." In *Dictionary of Sociology and Related Sciences*, Ed. H. Pratt. Totowa, NJ: Littlefield, Adams.

Ellis, L., and A. Walsh. (2000). *Criminology: A Global Perspective*. Boston: Allyn & Bacon.

Eme, R. (2009). "Male life-course persistent antisocial behavior: A review of neurodevelopmental factors." *Aggression and Violent Behavior* 14:348–58.

Empey, L. (1982). *American Delinquency*. Homewood, IL: Dorsey.

Empey, L., and M. L. Erickson. (1972). *The Provo Experiment: Evaluating Community Control of Delinquency*. Lexington, MA: Heath.

Engels, F. (1958[1845]). *The Condition of the Working Class in England*. Oxford, UK: Blackwell.

Englebert, P. (2000). "Pre-colonial institutions: Post-colonial states, and economic development in tropical Africa." *Political Research Quarterly* 53:7–36.

Erickson, K. T. (1966). *Wayward Puritans*. New York: Wiley.

Erickson, M. H. (1929). "A study of the relationship between intelligence and crime." *Journal of Criminal Law and Criminology* 19:592–635.

Ermann, M. D., and R. Lundman. (1992). *Corporate and Governmental Deviance: Problems of Organizational Behavior in Contemporary Society*. New York: Oxford University Press.

Esbensen, F. A., D. W. Osgood, D. Peterson, T. J. Taylor, and D. C. Carson. (2013). "Short- and long-term outcome results from a multisite evaluation of the G.R.E.A.T. program." *Criminology & Public Policy* 12:375–411.

Eysenck, H. J. (1969). "The technology of consent." *New Scientist*, 26:688–90.

Eysenck, H. J. (1973). *The Inequality of Man*. San Diego, CA: Edits.

Eysenck, H. J. (1977). *Crime and Personality*, 2nd ed. London: Routledge and Kegan Paul.

Eysenck, H. J., and I. H. Gudjonsson. (1989). *The Causes and Cures of Criminality*. New York: Plenum.

Fallon, J. H. (2006). "Neuroanatomical background to understanding the brain of the young psychopath." *Ohio State Journal of Criminal Law* 3:341–67.

Federal Bureau of Investigation. (2015). *Crime in the United States, 2014*. Washington, DC: Federal Bureau of Investigation.

Felson, M. (1993). "Review of Choosing Crime by K. Tunnell." *American Journal of Sociology* 98:1497–99.

Felson, M., and M Eckert. (2016). *Crime and Everyday Life*, 5th ed. Thousand Oaks, CA: Sage.

Ferguson, C. J. and K. M. Beaver. (2009). "Natural born killers: The genetic origins of extreme violence." *Aggression and Violent Behavior* 14:286–294.

Forst, B. E. (1983). "Capital punishment and deterrence: Conflicting evidence?" *Journal of Criminal Law and Criminology* 74:927–42.

Fox, K. A., J. Lane, and R. L. Akers. (2010). "Do perceptions of neighborhood predict crime or victimization? An examination of gang members versus non-gang member jail inmates." *Journal of Criminal Justice* 38:720–29.

Fox, V. (1946). "Intelligence, race, and age as selective factors in crime." *Journal of Criminal Law and Criminology* 37:141–52.

Fraga, M. F., E. Ballestar, M. F. Paz, S. Ropero, F. Setien, M. L. Ballestar, D. Heine-Suñer, J. C. Cigudosa, M. Urioste, J. Benitez, M. Boix-Chornet, A. Sanchez-Aguilera, C. Ling, E. Carlsson, P. Poulsen, A. Vaag, Z. Stephan, T. D. Spector, Y.-Z. Wu, C. Plass, and M. Esteller. (2005). "Epigenetic differences arise during the lifetime of monozygotic twins." *Proceeding of the National Academy of Sciences of the United States of America* 102:10604–609.

Freedman, J. L. (1984). "Effects of television violence on aggressiveness." *Psychological Bulletin* 96:227–46.

Freedman, J. L. (1986). "Television violence and aggression: A rejoinder." *Psychological Bulletin* 100:372–78.

Freud, S. (1933). *New Introductory Lectures on Psychoanalysis*. New York: Norton.

Freud, S. (1938) *Psychopathology of Everyday Life*. New York: Penguin Books.

Fuchs, J. (1965). *Natural Law: A Theoretical Investigation*. New York: Sheed and Ward.

Galton, F. (1906). "Eugenics: Its definition, scope, and aims." *American Journal of Sociology* 19:1–25.

Garfinkel, H. (1956). "Conditions of successful degradation ceremonies." *American Journal of Sociology* 61:420–24.

Gay, W. G., T. H. Schell, and S. Schack. (1977). *Routine Patrol: Improving Police Productivity*. Washington, DC: U.S. Government Printing Office.

Geerken, M. R., and W. R. Gove. (1975). "Deterrence: Some theoretical considerations." *Law and Society Review* 9:497–513.

Gibbs, J. (1968). "Crime, punishment and deterrence." *Southwest Social Science Quarterly* 48:515–30.

Gibbs, J. (1975). *Crime, Punishment, and Deterrence*. New York: Elsevier.

Gill, A. (1978). "The misuse of genetics in the race-IQ controversy." *San Jose Studies* 4:23–43.

Glaser, D. (1978). *Crime in Our Changing Society*. New York: Holt, Rinehart and Winston.

Glueck, S., and E. Glueck. (1950). *Unraveling Juvenile Delinquency*. New York: The Commonwealth Fund.

Glueck, S. and E. Glueck. (1956). *Physique and Delinquency*. Cambridge, MA: Harvard University Press.

Goddard, H. H. (1914). *Feeblemindedness: Its Causes and Consequences*. New York: Macmillan.

Goddard, H. H. (1921). "Feeblemindedness and delinquency." *Journal of Psycho-Asthenics* 25:168–76.

Goenner, T. (2000). "Conflict, crime, communication, cooperation—Restorative justice as a new way of dealing with the consequences of criminal acts." Unpublished paper. Tübingen, Germany: University of Tübingen.

Goffman, E. (1963). *Stigma*. Englewood Cliffs, NJ: Prentice-Hall.

Gold, S. (1980). "The CAP control theory of drug abuse." Pp. 8–11 in *Theories of Drug Abuse: Selected Contemporary Perspectives*, Eds. D. J. Lettieri, M. Sayers, and H. W. Pearson. Rockville, MD:

Goode, E. (1984). *Drugs in American Society*, 2nd ed. New York: Knopf.

Gordon, R. (1976). "Prevalence: The rare datum in delinquency measurement and its implications for the theory of delinquency." Pp. 201–284 in *The Juvenile Justice System*, Ed. M. W. Klein. Beverly Hills, CA: Sage.

Gordon, R. (1987). "SES versus IQ in the race—IQ–delinquency model." *International Journal of Sociology and Social Policy* 7:42–62.

Goring, C. (1913). *The English Convict: A Statistical Study*. London: Darling and Sons.

Gottfredson, M. R., and T. Hirschi. (1986). "The true value of lambda would appear to be zero: An essay on career criminals, criminal careers, selective incapacitation, cohort studies, and related topics." *Criminology* 24:213–34.

Gottfredson, M. R., and T. Hirschi. (1989). "A propensity-event theory of crime." Pp. 57–67 in *Advances in Criminological Theory* (vol. 1), Eds. W. S. Laufer and F. Adler. New Brunswick, NJ: Transaction.

Gottfredson, M. R., and T. Hirschi. (1990). *A General Theory of Crime.* Stanford, CA: Stanford University Press.

Gross, J. (1992). "Collapse of inner city families creates America's new orphans: Death, drugs, and jail leave voids in childhood." *New York Times* (March 28), p. A1.

Hagan, J. (1989). *Structural Criminology.* New Brunswick, NJ: Rutgers University Press.

Hagan, J. (1990). "The structuration of gender and deviance: A power control theory of vulnerability to crime and the search for deviant role exits." *Canadian Review of Sociology and Anthropology* 27:137–56.

Hagan, J., and F. Kay. (1990). "Gender and delinquency in white-collar families: A power-control perspective." *Crime and Delinquency* 36:391–407.

*Hammer v. Dagenhart et al.*, 247 U.S. 251, 38 S.Ct. 529,L.Ed. 1101 (1918).

Hare, R. D. (1996a). "Psychopathology: A clinical construct whose time has come." *Criminal Justice and Behavior* 23:25–54.

Hare, R. D. (1996b). "Psychopathy and antisocial personality disorder: A case of diagnostic confusion." *Psychiatric Times* 13:39–40.

Hare, R. D. (1998). "The PCL-R: Some issues concerning its misuse." *Legal and Criminological Psychology* 3: 99–119.

Hare, R. D. (2007). *Hare Psychopathy Checklist-revised (PCL-R): Technical Manual,* 2nd ed. Toronto, Ontario, Canada: Multi-Health Systems.

Harrison Narcotics Tax Act, Ch. 1, 38 Stat. 785 (1914).

Hart, S. D., R. D. Hare, and A. E. Forth. (1994). "Psychopathy as a risk marker for violence: Development and validation of a screening version of Revised Psychopathy Checklist." Pp. 81–98 in *Violence and Mental Disorder: Developments of Risk Assessment,* Eds. J. Monahan and H. J. Steadman. Chicago, IL: University of Chicago Press.

Hay, C. (1998). "Parental sanctions and delinquent behavior: Toward clarification of Braithwaite's theory of reintegrative shaming." *Theoretical Criminology* 2:419–43.

Hay, C. (2001). "An exploratory test of Braithwaite's reintegrative shaming theory." *Journal of Research in Crime and Delinquency* 38:132–53.

Hayeslip, D. W. (1989). *Local-Level Drug Enforcement: New Strategies.* National Institute of Justice Research in Action. Washington, DC: U.S. Government Printing Office.

Healy, W., A. F. Bronner, and A. M. Bowers. (1930). *The Structure and Meaning of Psychoanalysis.* New York: Knopf.

Herrnstein, R. J., and C. Murray. (1994). *The Bell Curve: Intelligence and Class Structure in American Life.* New York: Free Press.

Hirschi, T. (1969). *Causes of Delinquency.* Berkeley: University of California Press.

Hirschi, T., and M. J. Hindelang. (1977). "Intelligence and delinquency: A revisionist review." *American Sociological Review* 42:571–86.

Hjalmarsson, R. (2008). "Criminal justice involvement and high school completion." *Journal of Urban Economics* 63: 613–30.

Hoeve, M., G. J. Stams, C. E. van der Put, J. S. Dubas, P. H. van der Laan, and J. R. Gerris. (2012). "A meta-analysis of attachment to parents and delinquency." *Journal of Abnormal Child Psychology* 40:771–85.

Hoffman, B. F. (1977). "Two new cases of XYY chromosome complement." *Canadian Psychiatric Association Journal* 22:447–55.

Hollin, C. R. (1989). *Psychology and Crime: An Introduction to Criminological Psychology.* London: Routledge.

Holmes, R. M. (1990). *Profiling Violent Crimes*. Newbury Park, CA: Sage.

Holmes, M. D., D. W. Smith, A. B. Freng, and E. A. Muñoz. (2008). "Minority threat, crime control, and police resource allocation in the southwestern United States." *Crime and Delinquency* 54:128–52.

Hooton, E. (1939). *The American Criminal: An Anthropological Study*. Cambridge, MA: Harvard University Press.

Horney, J., and I. H. Marshall. (1992). "Risk perceptions among serious offenders: The role of crime and punishment." *Criminology* 30:575–92.

Houston, J. (1995). *Correctional Management: Functions, Skills and Systems*. Chicago: Nelson-Hall.

Howard, G. J., G. Newman, and W. A. Pridemore. (2000). "Theory, method, and data in comparative criminology." Pp. 139–211 in *Criminal Justice*, Vol. 4, Ed. D. Duffee. Washington, DC: U.S. Department of Justice.

Hutchings, B., and S. A. Mednick. (1977). "Criminality in adoptees and their biological parents: A pilot study." Pp. 127–141 in *Biosocial Bases of Criminal Behavior*, Eds. S.A. Mednick and K.O. Christiansen. New York: Gardner.

*In re Gault*, 387 U.S. 1; 18 L.Ed. 2d 527, 87 S.Ct. 1428(1967).

*In re Winship*, 397 U.S. 358 (1970); 397 U.S. 358 (1971).

Ivory, D., and B. Vlasic. (2015). "$900 million penalty for GM's deadly defect leaves many cold." *New York Times* (September 18), pp. B1–2.

Jackson, D. B., and C. Hay. (2013). "The conditional impact of official labeling on subsequent delinquency: Considering the attenuating role of family attachment." *Journal of Research in Crime and Delinquency* 50:300–22.

Jacobs, D., and R. O'Brien. (1998). "The determinants of deadly force: A structural analysis of police violence." *American Journal of Sociology* 103:837–62.

Jacobs, J. (1961). *The Death and Life of Great American Cities*. New York: Vintage Books.

Jacobs, B. (2010). "Deterrence and deterrability" *Criminology* 48:417–41.

Jacobs, B. and M. Cherbonneau. (2014). "Auto theft and restrictive deterrence." *Justice Quarterly* 31:344–67.

Jacobs, P. A., M. Brunton, M. Melville, R. P. Brittain, and W. F. McClemont. (1965). "Aggressive behavior, mental sub-normality and the XYY male." *Nature* 208:1351–52.

Jeffery, C. R. (1965). "Criminal behavior and learning theory." *Journal of Criminal Law, Criminology, and Police Science* 56:294–300.

Jeffery C. R. (1971). *Crime Prevention through Environmental Design*. Beverly Hills, CA: Sage.

Jensen, A. R. (1969). "How much can we boost I.Q. and scholastic achievement?" *Harvard Educational Review* 39:1–123.

Jensen, G. F. (1972). "Parents, peers, and delinquent action: A test of the differential association perspective." *American Journal of Sociology* 78:63–72.

Kelling, G. L., T. Pate, D. Dieckman, and C. E. Brown. (1974). *The Kansas City Preventive Patrol Experiment: A Summary Report*. Washington, DC: Police Foundation.

*Kent v. United States*, 383 U.S.C. 541 (1966).

Kiehl, K. A. (2014). *The Psychopath Whisperer: The Science of Those without a Conscience*. New York: Crown.

Kiehl, K. A., and J. Buckholtz. (2010). "Inside the mind of a psychopath." *Scientific American Mind* (September/October):22–29.

Kiehl, K. A. and M. B. Hoffman. (2011). "The criminal psychopath: History, neuroscience, treatment, and economics." *Jurimetrics* 51:355–97.

*Kimbrough v. United States*, 128 S. Ct. 558 (2007).

Klein, L. R., B. Forst, and V. Filatov. (1978). "The deterrent effect of capital punishment: An assessment of the estimates." Pp. 336–360 in *Deterrence and Incapacitation: Estimating the Effects of Criminal Sanctions on Crime Rates*, Eds. A. Blumstein, J. Cohen, and D. Nagin. Washington, DC: National Academy of Sciences.

Klinger, D. A. (1997), "Negotiating order in patrol work: An ecological theory of police response to deviance." *Criminology* 35:277–306.

Klochko, M. A. (2006). "Time preference and learning versus selection." *Rationality and Society* 18:305–31.

Klochko, M. A. (2008). "Individual time preferences in prison population: The effects of rehabilitation programs on women vs. men in Ukraine." Pp. 185–206 in *Beyond Little Vera: Women's Bodies, Women's Welfare in Russia and Central/Eastern Europe, Ohio Slavic Papers* (vol. 7), Eds. A. Brintlinger and N. Kolchevska. Columbus, OH: The Ohio State University.

Kornhauser, R. (1978). *Social Sources of Delinquency. Chicago*: University of Chicago Press.

Kreek, J. M., D. A. Nielsen, E. R. Butelman, and K. S. LaForge. (2005). "Genetic influences on impulsivity, risk taking, stress responsivity and vulnerability to drug abuse and addiction." *Nature Neuroscience* 8:1450–57.

Krisberg, B. (1975). *Crime and Privilege: Toward a New Criminology.* Englewood Cliffs, NJ: Prentice-Hall.

Krisberg, B., and J. F. Austin. (1993). *Reinventing Juvenile Justice.* Newbury Park, CA: Sage.

Lange, J. (1930). *Crime and Destiny.* Trans. Charlotte Haldane. New York: Charles Boni.

Lange, M., J. Mahoney, and M. vom Hau. (2006). "Colonialism and development: A comparative analysis of Spanish and British colonies." *The American Journal of Sociology* 111(5):1412–62.

Laub, J. H., R. J. Sampson, and L. C. Allen. (2001). "Explaining crime over the life course: Toward a theory of age-graded informal social control." Pp. 97–112 in *Explaining Criminals and Crime*, Eds. R. Paternoster and R. Bachman. Los Angeles: Roxbury.

*Lawrence v. Texas*, 539 U.S. 558, 2003.

Lederberg, J. (1969). "The meaning of Dr. Jensen's study of IQ disparities." *Washington Post*, 29 March.

Lee, N. (1995). "Culture conflict and crime in Alaskan native villages." *Journal of Criminal Justice* 23:177–89.

Lemert, E. (1951). *Social Pathology.* New York: McGraw-Hill.

Levy, L. (1988). *Original Intent of the Framers' Constitution.* Chicago: Ivan R. Dee.

Liberman, A., D. S. Kirk, and K. Kim. (2014). "Labeling effects of first juvenile arrests: Secondary deviance and secondary sanctioning." *Criminology* 52:345–70.

Lipset, S. M. (1969). "Why cops hate liberals—and vice versa." *Atlantic Monthly* 223:76–83.

Liska, A. E. (Ed.) (1992). *Social Threat and Social Control.* Albany: The State University of New York Press.

Liska, A. E., and M. B. Chamlin. (1984). "Social structure and crime control among macrosocial units." *American Journal of Sociology* 90:383–95.

Liska, A. E., and J. Yu. (1992). "Specifying and testing the threat hypothesis: Police use of deadly force." Pp. 53–69 in *Social Threat and Social Control*, Ed. A. E. Liska. Albany: The State University of New York Press.

Little, C. M. (2003). "Female genital circumcision: Medical and cultural considerations." *Journal of Cultural Diversity* 10:30–34.

Locurto, C. (1991). *Sense and Nonsense about IQ: The Case of Uniqueness.* New York: Praeger.

Loeber, R., and D. F. Hay. (1994). "Developmental approaches to aggression and conduct problems." Pp. 488–516 in *Development through Life: A Handbook for Clinicians*, Eds. M. L. Rutter and D. F. Hay. Oxford, UK: Blackwell.

Loeber, R., K. Kennan, and Q. Zhang. (1997). "Boys' experimentation and persistence in developmental pathways toward serious delinquency." *Journal of Child and Family Studies* 6: 321–57.

Loeber, R., and M. LeBlanc. (1990). "Toward a developmental criminology." Pp. 375–473 in *Crime and Justice*, Eds. N. Morris and M. Tonry. Chicago: University of Chicago Press.

Loeber, R., and M. Stouthamer-Loeber. (1998). "Development of juvenile aggression and violence: Some common misconceptions and controversies." *American Psychologist* 53:242–59.

Lombardo, P. "Eugenic sterilization laws." Image Archive on the American Eugenics Movement, Dolan DNA Learning Center, Cold Spring Harbor Laboratory. Retrieved from http://www.eugenicsarchive.org/html/eugenics/essay8text.html

Lombroso, C. (1876). *L'uomo Delinquente* [The Criminal Man]. Milan: Hoepli.

Lombroso-Ferrero, G. (1979[1911]). *Criminal Man, According to the Classification of Cesare Lombroso*. New York: Putnam.

Loughran, T. A., A. R. Piquero, J. Fagan, and E. P. Mulvey. (2012). "Differential deterrence: Studying heterogeneity and changes in perceptual deterrence among serious youthful offenders." *Crime and Delinquency* 58:3–27.

Loughran, T. A., G. Pogarsky, A. R. Piquero, and R. Paternoster. (2012). "Re-examining the functional form of certainty effects in deterrence theory." *Justice Quarterly* 29:712–41.

Lu, H. (1998). *Community Policing—Rhetoric or Reality? The Contemporary Chinese Community-Based Policing System in Shanghai* (Unpublished doctoral dissertation). Arizona State University.

Lyons, R. (1968). "Genetic abnormality is linked to crime: Genetics links to violent crimes." *New York Times* (April 21), p. 1.

MacDougall, W. (1908). *An Introduction to Social Psychology*. London: Methuen.

Maimon, D., M. Alper, B. Sobesto, and M. Cukier. (2014). "Restrictive deterrence effects of a warning banner in an attacked computer system." *Criminology* 52:33–59.

Maloney, D. M., and M. S. Umbreit. (1995). "Managing change: Toward a balance and restorative justice model." *Perspectives* 19:43–46.

Mankoff, M. (1971). "Societal reaction and career deviance: A critical analysis." *The Sociological Quarterly* 12:204–18.

Marciano, H., and J. Norman. (2015). "Overt vs. covert speed cameras in combination with delayed vs. immediate feedback to the offender." *Accident Analysis & Prevention* 79:231–40.

Martin, S. O. (1980). *Breaking and Entering: Policewomen on Patrol*. Berkeley: University of California Press.

Marx, K. (1867). *Das Kapital*. Hamburg, Germany: Verlag von Otto Meisner.

Marx, K. (1956). *Selected Writings in Sociology and Social Philosophy*. Trans. T. B. Bottomore. New York: McGraw-Hill.

Marx, K. (1984[1853]). "On capital punishment." *Monthly Review—An Independent Socialist Magazine* 36:44–45.

Marx, K. (1964[1862]). "Class conflict and law." Pp. 200–230 in *Karl Marx: Selected Writings for Sociology and Social Philosophy*, Eds. T. B. Bottomore and M. Rubel. London: McGraw-Hill.

Massey, D. S. (2015). "Brave new world of biosocial science." *Criminology* 53:127–31.

Matsueda, R. L. (1992). "Reflected appraisals, parental labeling, and delinquency: Specifying a symbolic interactionist theory." *American Journal of Sociology* 97:1577–611.

Matza, D. (1964). *Delinquency and Drift*. New York: Wiley.

Matza, D., and G. Sykes. (1961). "Juvenile delinquency and subterranean values." *American Sociological Review* 26:712–19.

Mays, G. L., and R. Ruddell. (2015). *Making Sense of Criminal Justice: Policies and Practices*, 2nd ed. New York: Oxford University Press.

Mays, G. L., and L. T. Winfree, Jr. (2012). *Juvenile Justice*. Frederick, MD: Wolters-Kluwer.

Mays, G. L., and L. T. Winfree, Jr. (2014). *Essentials of Corrections*. New York: John Wiley & Sons.

McAndrew, F. T. (2009). "The interacting roles of testosterone and challenges to status in human male aggression." *Aggression and Violent Behavior* 14:330–35.

McCarthy, B. R., and B. L. Smith. (1986). "The conceptualization of discrimination in the juvenile justice process: The impact of administrative factors and screening decisions on juvenile court dispositions." *Criminology* 24:41–64.

McCarty, W. P., L. Ren, and J. S. Zhao. (2012). "Determinants of police strength in large U.S. cities during the 1990s: A fixed-effects panel analysis." *Crime & Delinquency* 58:397–424.

McCold, P., and B. Wachtel. (1998). *Restorative Policing Experiment: The Bethlehem, Pennsylvania, Police Family Group Conferencing Project*. Pipersville, PA: Community Service Foundation.

McColgin, D. L. (2011). "The theotorture of Guantánamo." Pp. 202–203 in *Whose God Rules? Is the United States a Secular Nation or a Theolegal Democracy?*, Eds. N.C. Walker and E. J. Greenlee. New York: Palgrave MacMillan.

McCord, W., and J. Sanchez. (1983). "The treatment of deviant children: A twenty-five-year follow-up study." *Crime and Delinquency* 29:238–53.

McCuish, E. C., R. Corrado, P. Lussier, and S. D. Hart. (2014). "Psychopathic traits and offending trajectories from early adolescence to adulthood." *Journal of Criminal Justice* 42:66–76.

*McKiever v. Pennsylvania*, 403 U.S. 528, 91 S.Ct. 1976, 29L.Ed. 2d 6 (1971).

Mead, G. H. (1934). *Mind, Self and Society*. Chicago: University of Chicago Press

Meier, R. F., and W. T. Johnson. (1977). "Deterrence as social control: The legal and extralegal production of conformity." *American Sociological Review* 42:292–304.

Meloy, J. R. (1997). "The psychology of wickedness: Psychopathy and sadism." *Psychiatric Annals* 27:630–33.

Meloy, J. R., and A. Shiva. (2007). "A psychoanalytic view of the psychopath." Pp. 335–346, *The International Handbook of Psychopathic Disorders and the Law*, Ed. A. Felthouse and H. Sass. New York: Wiley.

Menkel-Meadow, C. (2007). "Restorative justice: What is it and does it work?" *Annual Review of Law and Social Science* 3:161–87.

Merton, R. K. (1938). "Social structure and anomie." *American Sociological Review* 3:672–82.

Merton, R. K. (1957). *Social Theory and Social Structure*. New York: Free Press.

Merton, R. K. (1988). "The Matthew effect in science, II: Cumulative advantage and the symbolism of intellectual property." *Isis* 79:606–23.

Michalowski, R. L. (1985). *Order, Law and Crime: An Introduction to Criminology*. New York: Random House.

Miller, L., J. Toliver, and Police Executive Research Forum. (2014). *Implementing a Body-Worn Camera Program: Recommendations and Lessons Learned*. Washington, DC: Office of Community Oriented Policing Services.

Miller, W. B. (1958). "Lower class culture as a generating milieu of gang delinquency." *Journal of Social Issues* 14:5–19.

Millon, T., M. E. Simonsen, M. Birket-Smith, and R. D. Davis, Eds. (1998). *Psychopathy: Antisocial Criminal, Violent Behavior*. New York: Guilford Press.

Moffitt, T. (1993a). "Adolescence-limited and life-course-persistent anti-social behavior: A developmental taxonomy." *Psychological Review* 100:674–701.

Moffitt, T. (1993b). "The neuropsychology of conduct disorder." *Development and Psychopathology* 5:135–51.

Moffitt, T., D. Lyman, and P. Silva. (1994). "Neuropsychological tests predicting persistent male delinquency." *Criminology* 32:277–300.

Mokros, A., P. Hollerbach, K. Vohs, J. Nitschke, R. Eher, and E. Habermeyer. (2013). "Normative data for the psychopathy check-list revised in German-speaking countries." *Criminal Justice and Behavior* 40:397–412.

Moore, M., and M. B. Morris. (2011). "Political science theories of crime and delinquency." *Journal of Human Behavior in the Social Environment* 21:284–96.

Moore, M. H., and R. Trojanowicz. (1988). *Policing and the Fear of Crime*. Washington, DC: U.S. Government Printing Office.

Morash, M., and M. Chesney-Lind. (1991). "A reformulation and partial test of the power control theory of delinquency." *Justice Quarterly* 8:347–78.

Morenoff, J. D., R. J. Sampson, and S. Raudenbush. (2001). "Neighborhood inequality, collective efficacy, and spatial dynamics of urban violence." *Criminology* 39:517–60.

Morris, R. G., and A. R. Piquero. (2013). "For whom do sanctions deter and label?" *Justice Quarterly* 30:837–68.

Moynihan, D. P. (1969). *Maximum Feasible Misunderstanding: Community Action in the War on Poverty*. New York: Free Press.

Murchison, C. (1926). *Criminal Intelligence*. Worcester, MA: Clark University.

Mustaine, E. E. (1997). "Victimization risks and routine activities: A theoretical examination using a gender-specific and domain-specific model." *American Journal of Criminal Justice* 22:41–70.

Mustaine, E. E., and R. Tewksbury. (1998). "Predicting risks of larceny theft victimization: A routine activities analysis using refined lifestyle measures." *Criminology* 36:829–57.

Myrdal, G. (1944). *An American Dilemma: The Negro Problem and Modern Democracy*. New York: Harper & Brothers.

Nagin, D. S. (1978). "General deterrence: A review of the empirical evidence." Pp. 95–139 in *Deterrence and Incapacitation: Estimating the Effects of Criminal Sanctions on Crime Rates*, Eds. A. Blumstein, J. Cohen, and D. S. Nagin. Washington, DC: National Academy Press.

Nagin, D. S. (1998). "Deterrence and incapacitation." Pp. 345–368 in *Handbook of Crime and Punishment*, Ed. M. Tonry. New York: Oxford University Press.

Nagin, D. S., and G. Pogarsky. (2004). "Time and punishments: Delayed consequences and criminal behavior." *Journal of Quantitative Criminology* 30:295–317.

Nagin, D. S., R. M. Solow, and C. Lum. (2015). "Deterrence, criminal opportunities, and police." *Criminology* 53:74–100.

National Advisory Commission on Criminal Justice Standards and Goals. (1973). *Criminal Justice System*. Washington, DC: U.S. Government Printing Office.

National Juvenile Justice Network (NJJN). (2008). Using Adolescent Brain Research to Inform Policy: A Guide for Juvenile Justice Advocates. Washington, DC: NJJN

National Prohibition Act, P.L. 66–66, 41 Stat. 305 (1920).

Neisser, U., G. Boodoo, T. J. Bourchard, Jr., A. W. Boykin, N. Brody, S. J. Ceci, D. F. Halpern, J. C. Loehlin, R. Perloff, R. J. Sternberg, and S. Urbina. (1996). "Intelligence: Knowns and unknowns." *American Psychologist* 51 (2):77–101.

Neumann, C. S., and R. D. Hare. (2008). "Psychopathic traits in a large community sample: Links to violence, alcohol use, and intelligence." *Journal of Consulting and Clinical Psychology* 76:893–99.

Neumann, C. S., D. S. Schmitt, R. Carter, I. Embley, and R. D. Hare. (2012). "Psychopathic traits in females and males across the globe." *Behavioral Sciences & the Law* 30:557–74.

Newman, O. (1972). *Defensible Space: Crime Prevention through Urban Design*. New York: Macmillan.

Newman, O. (1975). *Defensible Space*. New York: Collins.

Niederhoffer, A. (1969). *Behind the Shield: The Police in Urban Society.* Garden City, NY: Anchor.

Nyangweso, M. (2014). *Female Genital Cutting in Industrialized Countries.* Santa Barbara, CA: Praeger.

Nye, F. I. (1958). *Family Relationships and Delinquent Behavior.* New York: Wiley.

Omer, H., and P. London. (1988). "Metamorphosis in psychotherapy: End of the systems era." *Psychotherapy* 25:171–80.

Pacula, R. L., J. F. Chriqui, and J. King. (2003). "Marijuana decriminalization: What does it mean in the United States?" NBER Working Paper No. 9690. Retrieved from http://www.nber.org/papers/w9690

Pager, D. (2003). "The mark of a criminal record." *American Journal of Sociology* 108:937–75.

Papachristos, A. W., D. M. Hureau, and A. A. Braga. (2013). "The corner and the crew: The influence of geography and social networks on gang violence." *American Sociological Review* 78:417–47.

Park, R. E., E. W. Burgess, and R. D. McKenzie. (1984). *The City.* Chicago: University of Chicago Press.

Passas, N. (1990). "Anomie and corporate deviance." *Contemporary Crises* 14:157–78.

Pate, T., J. W. McCullough, R. A. Bowers, and A. Ferrara. (1976). *Kansas City Peer Review Panel: An Evaluation Report.* Washington, DC: Police Foundation.

Paternoster, R. (1987). "The deterrent effect of perceived severity of punishment: A review of the evidence and issues." *Justice Quarterly* 4:173–217.

Paternoster, R. (1989a). "Absolute and restrictive deterrence in a panel of youth: Explaining the onset, persistence/desistance, and frequent offending." *Social Problems* 36:289–309.

Paternoster, R. (1989b). "Decision to participate in and desist from four types of common delinquency: Deterrence and the rational choice perspective." *Law and Society Review* 23:7–40.

Paternoster, R. (2010). "How much do we really know about criminal deterrence?" *Journal of Criminal Law and Criminology* 100:765–824.

Paternoster, R., and R. Bachman. (2001). *Explaining Criminals and Crime: Essays in Contemporary Criminological Theory.* Los Angeles: Roxbury.

Paternoster, R., and R. Bachman. (2012). "Perceptual deterrence theory." Pp. 649–671 in *The Oxford Handbook of Criminological Theory,* Eds. F. Cullen and P. Wilcox. New York: Oxford University Press

Paternoster, R., and L. Iovanni. (1989). "The labeling perspective and delinquency: An elaboration of the theory and an assessment of the evidence." *Justice Quarterly* 6.

Patterson, G. T. (2003). "Examining the effects of copying and social support on work and life stress among police officers." *Journal of Criminal Justice* 31:215–26.

Pemment, J. (2013). "Psychopathy versus sociopathy: Why the distinction has become crucial." *Aggression and Violent Behavior* 18:458–61.

Pepinsky, H., and P. Jesilow. (1984). *Myths That Cause Crime.* Cabin John, MD: Seven Locks.

Perez, D. M., W. G. Jennings, and A. R. Gover. (2008). "Specifying general strain theory: An ethnically relevant approach." *Deviant Behavior* 29:544–78.

Perez, P. R. (2012). "The etiology of psychopathy: A neuropsychological perspective." *Aggression and Violent Behavior* 17:519–22.

Petrocelli, M., A. R. Piquero, and M. R. Smith. (2003). "Conflict theory and racial profiling: An empirical analysis of police traffic stop data." *Journal of Criminal Justice* 31:1–11.

Pew Research Center. (2014). *America's New Drug Policy Landscape: Two-Thirds Favor Treatment, Not Jail, for Use of Heroin, Cocaine.* Washington, DC: Pew Research Center. Retrieved from http://www.people-press.org/2014/04/02/americas-new-drug-policy-landscape/

Pileggi, N. (1990). *Wise Guy: Life in a Mafia Family.* New York: Pocket Books.

Pistone, J. D. (2004). *The Way of the Wiseguy. Philadelphia*, PA: Running Press.

Pogarsky, G. (2002). "Identifying 'deterrable' offenders: Implications for research on deterrence." *Justice Quarterly* 19:431–52.

Pogrebin, M., and E. D. Poole. (1988). "Humor in the briefing room: A study of the strategic uses of humor among police." *Journal of Contemporary Ethnography* 17:183–210.

Polaschek, D. L. and T. E. Daly. (2013). "Treatment and psychotherapy in forensic settings." *Aggression and Violent Behavior* 18: 592–603.

Policy Basics. (2015). An introduction to TANF. Washington, DC: Center on Budget and Policy Priorities. Retrieved from http://www.cbpp.org/research/policy-basics-an-introduction-to-tanf

Polk, K. (1991). "Book review—A General Theory of Crime." *Crime and Delinquency* 37:575–79.

Porter, S. (1996). "Without conscience or without active conscience? The etiology of psychopathy revisited." *Aggression and Violent Behavior* 1:179–89.

Poythress, N. G. and J. R. Hall. (2011). "Psychopathy and impulsivity reconsidered." *Aggression and Violent Behavior* 16:120–34.

Pratt, T. C., and F. T. Cullen. (2000). "The empirical status of Gottfredson and Hirschi's general theory of crime: A meta-analysis." *Criminology* 38:931–64.

Pratt, T. C., and F. T. Cullen. (2005). "Assessing macro-level predictors and theories of crime: A meta-analysis." *Crime and Justice* 32:373–449.

Pratt, T. C., F. T. Cullen, K. R. Blevins, L. E. Daigle, and T. D. Madensen. (2006). "The empirical status of deterrence theory: A meta-analysis." Chapter 13 in *Taking Stock: The Status of Criminological Theory*, Eds. F. T. Cullen, J. P. Wright, and K. R. Blevins. Edison, NJ: Transaction.

Pratt, T. C., F. T. Cullen, C. S. Sellers, L. T. Winfree, Jr., T. D. Madensen, L. E. Daigle, N. E. Fairn, and J. C. Gau. (2010). "The empirical status of social learning theory: A meta-analysis." *Justice Quarterly* 27:644–69.

Presidential Commission on Law Enforcement and Administration of Justice. (1967). *The Challenge of Crime in a Free Society*. Washington, DC: U.S. Government Printing Office.

Prichard, J. C. (1973[1835]). *Researches into the Physical History of Man*. Reprinted. Chicago: University of Chicago Press.

Quadragno, J. S., and R. J. Antonio. (1975). "Labeling theory as an over-socialized conception of man: The case of mental illness." *Sociology and Social Research* 60:33–45.

Quinney, R. (1973). *Critique of Legal Order: Crime Control in Capitalist Society*. Boston: Little, Brown.

Raine, A. (1993). *The Psychopathology of Crime: Criminal Behavior as a Clinical Disorder*. San Diego, CA: Academic Press.

Raine, A. (2013). *The Anatomy of Violence: The Biological Roots of Crime*. New York: Vintage Books.

Raine, A., M. O'Brien, N. Smiley, A. S. Scerbo, and C. J. Chan. (1990). "Reduced lateralization in verbal dichotic listening in adolescent psychopaths." *Journal of Abnormal Psychiatry* 99:272–77.

Raine, A., T. Lencz, S. Bihrle, L. LaCasse, and P. Colletti. (2000). "Reduced prefrontal gray matter volume and reduced autonomic activity in antisocial personality disorder." *Archives of General Psychiatry* 57:119–27.

Rankin, K. (2015). "New York City's Fair Chance Law Could Help Ex-Offenders Nationwide." Colorlines. Retrieved from https://www.colorlines.com/articles/new-york-city%E2%80%99s-fair-chance-law-could-help-ex-offenders-nationwide

Read, D., and N. L. Read. (2004). "Time discounting over the lifespan." *Organizational Behavior and Human Decision Processes* 94:22–32.

Reckless, W. C. (1961). "A new theory of delinquency and crime." *Federal Probation* 25:4–46.

Reed, G. E., and P. C. Yeager. (1996). "Organizational offending and neoclassical criminology: Challenging the reach of a general theory of crime." *Criminology* 34:357–82.

Regoli, R. M. (1976). "An empirical assessment of Niederhoffer's scale." *Journal of Criminal Justice* 4:231–41.

Reid, J. B., G. R. Patterson, and J. Snyder, Eds. (2002). *Antisocial Behavior in Children and Adolescents: A Developmental Analysis and Model for Intervention.* Washington, DC: American Psychological Association.

Reiff, P., Ed. (1963). *Freud, Therapy and Techniques.* New York: Crowell-Collier.

Reiss, A. J. (1951). "Delinquency and the failure of personal and social controls." *American Sociological Review* 16:196–207.

Regoeczi, W. C., and J. P. Jarvis. (2013). "Beyond the social production of homicide rates: Extending social disorganization theory to explain homicide case outcomes." *Justice Quarterly* 30:983–1014.

Ressler, R. K., A. W. Burgess, and J. E. Douglas. (1988). *Sexual Homicide: Patterns and Motives.* Washington, DC: Federal Bureau of Investigation.

Restivo, E., and M. M. Lanier. (2015). "Measuring the contextual effects and mitigating factors in labeling theory." *Justice Quarterly* 32:116–41.

Reuter, P. (1987). *Racketeering in Legitimate Industries: A Study in the Economics of Intimidation.* Santa Monica, CA: RAND Corporation.

Roberg, R. R., and J. Kuykendall. (1993). *Police and Society.* Belmont, CA: Wadsworth.

Roberts, E. G. (2013). "Are sociopaths and psychopaths one in the same?" *Psychology Standard* (October 2). Retrieved from http://psychologystandard.com/sociopaths-psychopaths-one/

Robison, S. M. (1936). *Can Delinquency Be Measured?* New York: Columbia University Press.

Rommen, H. A. (1998). *The Natural Law: A Study in Legal and Social History and Philosophy.* Trans. T. R. Hanley. Indianapolis, IN: Liberty Fund.

Roshier, B. (1989). *Controlling Crime: The Classical Perspective in Criminology.* Chicago: Lyceum.

Rotter, J. (1954). *Social Learning and Clinical Psychology.* New York: Prentice-Hall.

Rousseau, J. J. (1954[1762]). *The Social Contract. Chicago*: Regenery.

Rowe, D. C. (2002). *Biology and Crime.* Los Angeles: Roxbury.

Ruddell, R., and M. O. Thomas. (2010). "Minority threat and police strength: An examination of the Golden State." *Police Practice and Research* 11:256–73.

Russell, S. (2002). "The continuing relevance of Marxism to theoretical criminology." *Critical Criminology* 11:113–35.

Sampson, R. J. (2002). "Transcending tradition: New directions in community research, Chicago style." *Criminology* 40:213–30.

Sampson, R. J. (2012). *Great American City: Chicago and the Enduring Neighborhood Effect.* Chicago: The University of Chicago Press.

Sampson, R. J. (2013). "The place of context: A theory and strategy for criminology's hard problems" *Criminology* 55:609–27.

Sampson, R. J., and D. J. Bartusch. (1999). "Attitudes toward crime, police, and the law: Individual and neighborhood differences." *National Institute of Justice Research Preview.* Washington, DC: U.S. Department of Justice.

Sampson, R. J., and W. B. Groves. (1989). "Community structure and crime: Testing social disorganization theory." *American Journal of Sociology* 94:774–802.

Sampson, R. J., and J. Laub. (1993). *Crime in the Making: Pathways and Turning Points through Life.* Cambridge, MA: Harvard University Press.

Sampson, R. J., J. D. Morenoff, and T. Gannon-Rowley. (2002). "Assessing 'neighborhood effects': Social processes and new directions in research." *Annual Review of Sociology* 28:443–78.

Sampson, R. J., and S. W. Raudenbush. (1999). "Systematic social observation of public spaces: A new look at disorder in urban neighborhoods." *American Journal of Sociology* 105:603–51.

Sampson, R. J., and S. W. Raudenbush. (2001). "Disorder in urban neighborhoods—Does it lead to crime?" *Research in Brief.* Washington, DC: National Institute of Justice, February.

Sampson, R. J., S. W. Raudenbush, and F. Earls. (1997). "Neighborhood and violent crime: A multilevel study of collective efficacy." *Science* 277: 918–24.

Sampson, R. J., C. Winship, and C. Knight. (2013). "Translating causal claims: Principles and strategies for policy-relevant criminology." *Criminology and Public Policy* 12(4):585–616.

Sarbin, T. R., and J. E. Miller. (1970). "Demonism revisited: The XYY chromosome anomaly." *Issues of Criminology* 5:195–207.

*Schall v. Martin*, 467 U.S. 253 (1984).

Scheff, T. J. (1988). "Shame and conformity: The deference–emotion system." *American Sociological Review* 53:395–406.

Scheiber, N., and P. Cohen. (2015). "By molding tax system, wealthiest save billions." *New York Times* (December 30), p. A1.

Schimmenti, A., C. Caprì, D. La Barbera, and V. Caretti. (2014). "Mafia and psychotherapy." *Criminal Behaviour and Mental Health* 24:321–31.

Schur, E. (1971). *Labeling Deviant Behavior: Its Sociological Implications.* New York: Harper and Row.

Schur, E. (1973). *Radical Non-Intervention: Rethinking the Delinquency Problem.* Englewood Cliffs, NJ: Prentice-Hall.

Schwartz, R. D., and J. Skolnick. (1962). "Two studies of legal stigma." *Social Problems* 10:133–42.

Schwartz, S. J., C. S. Dunkel, and A. S. Waterman. (2009). "Terrorism: An identity theory perspective." *Studies in Conflict & Terrorism* 32:537–59.

Sellers, C. S., and L. T. Winfree, Jr. (1990). "Differential associations and definitions: A panel study of youthful drinking behavior." *International Journal of the Addictions* 25:755–71.

Sellers, C. S., L. T. Winfree, Jr., and R. L. Akers (Eds.). (2012). *Social Learning Theories of Crime.* Burlington, VT: Ashgate.

Sellin, T. (1938). *Culture Conflict and Crime.* New York: Social Science Research Council.

Sentencing Project, The. (2004). "Crack cocaine sentencing police: Unjustified and unreasonable." Washington, DC: The Sentencing Project.

Seo, D., C. J. Patrick, and P. J. Kennealy. (2008). "Role of serotonin and dopamine system interactions in the neurobiology of impulsive aggression and its comorbidity with other clinical disorders." *Aggression and Violent Behavior* 13:383–95.

Shaw, C. R. (1930). *The Jack-Roller: A Delinquent Boy's Own Story.* Philadelphia: Saifer.

Shaw, C. R. (1938). *Brothers in Crime.* Philadelphia: Saifer.

Shaw, C. R., and H. D. McKay. (1942). *Juvenile Delinquency and Urban Areas: A Study of Rates of Delinquency in Relation to Different Characteristics of Local Communities in American Cities.* Chicago: University of Chicago Press.

Shaw, C. R., and H. D. McKay. (1972). *Juvenile Delinquency and Urban Areas: A Study of Rates of Delinquency in Relation to Different Characteristics of Local Communities in American Cities*, rev. ed. Chicago: University of Chicago Press.

Sherman, L. W., and R. Berk. (1984a). "The Minneapolis Domestic Violence Experiment." *Police Foundation Reports* 1:10–18.

Sherman, L. W., and R. Berk. (1984b). "The specific deterrent effects of arrest for domestic assault." *American Sociological Review* 49:261–72.

Sherman, L. W., P. R. Gartin, and M. E. Bueger. (1989). "Hot spots of predatory crime." *Criminology* 27:27–55.

Sherman, L. W., D. Gottfredson, D. MacKenzie, J. Eck, P. Reuter, and S. Bushway. (1997). *Preventing Crime: What works, What Doesn't and What's Promising*. Research report. Washington, DC: U.S. Office of Justice Programs.

Sherman, L. W., and D. P. Rogan. (1995). "Effects of gun seizures on gun violence: 'Hot spots' patrol in Kansas City." *Justice Quarterly* 12:673–94.

Sherman, L. W., J. D. Schmidt, D. P. Rogan, and D. A. Smith (1992a). "The variable effects of arrest on criminal careers: The Milwaukee domestic violence experiment." *Journal of Criminal Law and Criminology* 83:137–69.

Sherman, L. W., and D. Smith, with J. D. Schmidt and D. P. Rogan. (1992b). "Crime, punishment, and stake in conformity: Legal and informal control of domestic violence." *American Sociological Review* 57:680–90.

Sherman, L. W., and H. Strang (2008). *Restorative Justice: The Evidence*. London, UK: The Smith Institute.

Sherman, L. W., H. Strang, J. Barnes, J. Braithwaite, N. Ipken, and M. Teh. (1998). "Experiments in restorative justice: A progress report to the National Police Research Unit in the Canberra Reintegrative Shaming Experiments (RISE)." Canberra: Australian Federal Police and Australian National University.

Sherman, L. W., and D. Weisburd. (1995). "General deterrent effects of police patrol in crime 'hot spots': A randomized controlled trial." *Justice Quarterly* 12:625–48.

Shockley, W. (1967). "A 'try the simplest cases' approach to the heredity–poverty–crime problem." *Proceedings of the National Academy of Sciences* 57:1767–74.

Siegel, L. (1992) *Criminology*, 4th ed. St. Paul, MN: West.

Silberman, M. (1976). "Toward a theory of criminal deterrence." *American Sociological Review* 41:442–61.

Simmel, G. (1955). *Conflict*. Trans. K. H. Wolff. Glencoe, IL: Free Press.

Simon, J. L. (1969). *Basic Research Methods in Social Science: The Art of Empirical Investigation*. New York: Random House.

Simons, R. L., Y. F. Chen, E. A. Stewart, and G. H. Brody. (2003). "Incidents of discrimination and risk for delinquency: A longitudinal test of strain theory with an African American sample." *Justice Quarterly* 20:827–54.

Simons, R. L., M. K. Lei, S. R. H. Beach, G. H. Brody, R. A. Philibert, and F. X. Gibbons. (2011). "Social environment, genes, and aggression: Evidence supporting the differential susceptibility perspective." *American Sociological Review* 76:883–912.

Singer, S. I., and M. Levine. (1988). "Power-control theory, gender, and delinquency: A partial replication with additional evidence on the effects of peers." *Criminology* 26:627–48.

Skeem, J. L., D. L. Polaschek, C. Patrick, and S. O. Lilienfeld. (2011). "Psychopathic personality: Bridging the gap between scientific evidence and public policy." *Psychological Science in the public Interest* 12:95–162.

Skinner, B. F. (1974). *About Behaviorism*. New York: Knopf.

Slife, B. D., S. C. Yanchar, and B. T. Williams. (1999). "Conceptions of determinism in radical behaviorism: A taxonomy." *Behavior and Philosophy* 27:75–96.

Smart, F. (1970). *Neurosis and Crime*. New York: Barnes and Noble.

Smith, D. A. (1986). "The neighborhood context of police behavior." *Crime and Justice* 8:313–41.

Smith, M. E. (2001). *What Future for "Public Safety" and "Restorative Justice" in Community Corrections?* Washington, DC: National Institute of Justice.

Sobol, J. J. (2010). "The social ecology of police attitudes." *Policing: An International Journal of Police Strategies and Management* 33(2):253–69.

Sorensen, J., J. Marquart, and D. Brock. (1993). "Factors related to killings of felons by police officers: A test of the community violence and conflict hypotheses." *Justice Quarterly* 10:417–40.

Spano, R., J. D. Freilich, and J. Bolland. (2008). "Gang membership, gun carrying, and employment: Applying routine activities theory to explain violent victimization among inner city, minority youth living in extreme poverty." *Justice Quarterly* 25:381–410.

Spencer, H. (1961[1864]). *The Study of Sociology*. Ann Arbor: University of Michigan Press.

Spitzer, S. (1975). "Toward a Marxian theory of deviance." *Social Problems* 22: 638–51.

Spradley, J. P. (1970). *You Owe Yourself a Drunk*. Long Grove, IL: Waveland Press.

Stafford, M. C., and M. Warr. (1993). "A reconceptualization of general and specific deterrence." *Journal of Crime and Delinquency* 30: 123–35.

Steen, R. G. (2001). *DNA and Destiny: Nature and Nurture in Human Behavior*. Cambridge, MA: De Capo Press.

Stoddard, E. R. (1968). "The informal 'code' of police deviancy: A group approach to 'blue-coat crime.'" *Journal of Criminal Law, Criminology, and Police Science* 59:201–13.

Strang, H. (2002). *Repair or Revenge: Victims and Restorative Justice*. Oxford, UK: Oxford University Press.

*Strong v. Repide*, 213 U.S. 419 (1909).

Sullivan, R. F. (1973). "The political economics of crime: An introduction to the literature." *Crime and Delinquency* 19:138–49.

Sullivan, T. P., B. A. Hunter, and B. S. Fisher. (2013). Evidence-Based Policy and Practice: The Role of the State in the Advancing Criminal Justice Research, Findings from the Researcher-Practitioner Partnerships Study (RPPS). Washington, DC: U.S. Department of Justice.

Sumner, W. G. (1906). *Folkways: A Study of the Sociological Importance of Usages, Manners, Customs, Mores, and Morals*. Boston: Ginn.

Sutherland, E. H. (1947). *Principles of Criminology*. Philadelphia: Lippincott.

Sutherland, E. H., and D. R. Cressey. (1974). *Criminology*, 9th ed. Philadelphia: Lippincott.

Suttles, G. (1968). *The Social Order of the Slum: Ethnicity and Territory*. Chicago: University of Chicago Press.

Svensson, R. (2015). "An examination of the interaction between morality and deterrence in offending: A research note." *Crime and Delinquency* 61:3–18.

Sweeten, G. (2006). "Who will graduate? Disruption of high school education by arrest and court involvement." *Justice Quarterly* 23:462–80.

Sykes, G., and F. T. Cullen. (1992). *Criminology*, 2nd ed. New York: Harcourt Brace Jovanovich.

Sykes, G., and D. Matza. (1957). "Techniques of neutralization: A theory of delinquency." *American Journal of Sociology* 22:664–70.

Tannenbaum, F. (1938). *Crime and the Community*. New York: Ginn.

Taylor, R. B., S. D. Gottfredson, and S. Brower. (1984). "Block crime and fear: Defensive space, local ties, and territorial functioning." *Journal of Research in Crime and Delinquency* 21: 303–31.

Taylor, I., P. Walton, and J. Young. (1973). *The New Criminology: For a Social Theory of Deviance*. New York: Harper and Row.

Telfer, M. A. (1968). "Are some criminals born that way?" *Think* 34:24–28.

Thomas, W. I., and F. Znaniecki. (1918). *The Polish Peasant in Europe and America*, vol. 1. Chicago: University of Chicago Press.

Thomas, W. I., and D. S. Thomas. (1928). *The Child in America*. New York: Knopf.

Tibbetts, S. G., and A. R. Piquero. (1999). "The influence of gender, low birth weight, and disadvantaged environment in predicting early onset of offending: A test of Moffitt's interactional hypothesis." *Criminology* 37:843–78.

Tillyer, M. S., R. S. Engel, and B. Lovins. (2012). "Beyond Boston: Applying theory to understand and address sustainability issues in focused deterrence initiatives for violence reduction." *Crime and Delinquency* 58:973–97.

Tittle, C. R. (1969). "Crime rates and legal sanctions." *Social Problems* 23: 3–18.

Tittle, C. R., M. J. Burke, and E. F. Jackson. (1986). "Modeling Sutherland's theory of differential association: Toward an empirical clarification." *Social Forces* 65:405–32.

Tittle, C. R., and A. R. Rowe. (1974). "Certainty of arrest and crime rates: A further test of the deterrence hypothesis." *Social Forces* 52:455–62.

Toby, J. (1957). "The differential impact of family disorganization." *American Sociological Review* 22:505–12.

Toby, J. (1959). "Review of Family Relationships and Delinquent Behavior by F. I. Nye." *American Sociological Review* 24:282–83.

Tolin, D. F. (2010). "Is cognitive-behavioral therapy more effective than other therapies? A meta-analytic review." *Clinical Psychology Review* 30:710–20.

Topalli, V., P. R. Giancola, R. E. Tarter, M. Swahn, M. M. Martel, A. J. Godlaski, and K. T. McCoun. (2014). "Persistence of neighborhood disadvantage: An experimental investigation of alcohol and later physical aggression." *Criminal Justice & Behavior* 41:400–16.

Tricarico, D. (1984). *The Italians of Greenwich Village.* Staten Island, NY: Center for Migration Studies of New York.

Tunnell, K. D. (1992). *Choosing Crime: The Criminal Calculus of Property Offenders.* Chicago: Nelson-Hall.

Turk, A. (1969). *Criminality and Legal Order.* Chicago: Rand-McNally.

Tyler, T. P., L. Sherman, and H. Strang. (2007). "Reintegrative shaming, procedural justice, and recidivism: The engagement of offender's psychological mechanisms in the Canberra RISE drinking and driving experiment." *Law and Society Review* 41:553–84.

Twardosz, S. and J. R. Lutzker. (2010). "Child maltreatment and the developing brain: A review of neuroscience perspectives." *Aggression and Violent Behavior* 15:59–68.

Uchida, C. D., M. L. Swatt, S. E. Solomon, and S. Varano. (2014) *Neighborhoods and Crime: Collective Efficacy and Social Cohesion in Miami-Dade County.* Washington, DC: National Institute of Justice.

Ullrich, S., M. Paelecke, L. Kahle, and A. Marneros. (2003). Kategoriale und dimensionale Erfassung von 'psychopathy' bei deutschen Straftätern: Prävalenz, Geschlechts- und Alterseffekte [Categorical and dimensional assessment of "psychopathy" in German offenders: Prevalence, gender differences and age factors]. *Nervenarzt* 74:1002–8.

Umbreit, M. S. (1994). *Victim Meets Offender: The Impact of Restorative Justice and Mediation.* Monsey, NY: Willow Tree Press.

Umukoro, S., A.C. Aladeokin, and A.T. Eduviere. (2013). "Aggressive behavior: A comprehensive review of its neurochemical mechanisms and management." *Aggression and Violent Behavior* 18:195–203.

United Nations Office on Drugs and Crime. (2014). *Global Study on Homicide, 2013.* Vienna, Austria: UNODC.

Urban Institute. (2015). Nine Charts about Wealth Inequality in America. Washington, DC: Urban Institute. Retrieved from apps.urban.org/features/wealth-inequality-charts/

U.S. Department of Labor. (2016). The Federal Bonding Program. Program Background. Washington, DC: U.S. Department of Labor. Retrieved from http://www.bonds4jobs.com/program-background.html

U.S. Sentencing Commission. (1995). *Cocaine and Federal Sentencing Policy.* Washington, DC: U.S. Government Printing Office.

*U.S. v. Doremus.* 249 U.S. 86 (1919).

Van Maanen, J. (1973). "Observations on the making of policemen." *Human Organization* 32:407–18.

Vito, G. F., and T. J. Keil. (1988). "Capital sentencing in Kentucky: An analysis of the factors influencing decision making in the post-Gregg period." *Journal of Criminal Law and Criminology* 79:483–503.

Vold, G. B. (1958). *Theoretical Criminology.* New York: Oxford University Press.

Volkow, N. D., G. J. Wang, J. S. Fowler, J. Logan, S. J. Gatley, A. Gifford, R. Hitzemann, Y. S. Ding, and N. Pappas. (1999). "Prediction of reinforcing responses to psychostimulants in humans by brain dopamine D2 receptor levels." *American Journal of Psychiatry* 156:1440–43.

Wagatsuma, H., and A. Rosett. (1986). "The implications of apology: Law and culture in Japan and the United States." *Law and Society Review* 20:461–98.

Walker, S. (1992). *The Police in America: An Introduction. New* York: McGraw-Hill.

Walker, S. (2015). *Sense and Nonsense about Crime, Drugs, and Communities*, 8th ed. Stamford, CT: Cengage Learning.

Warner, B. D. (1992). "The reporting of crime: A missing link in conflict theory." Pp. 71–88 in *Social Threat and Social Control*, Ed. A. E. Liska. Albany: The State University of New York Press.

Watson, J. D. (1990). "The human genome project: Past, present and future." *Science.* April: 44–49.

Watson, J. B. (1913). "Psychology as the behaviorist views it." *Psychological Review* 20:158–77.

Watson, J. B. (1914). *Behavior: An Introduction to Comparative Psychology.* New York: Holt.

Watson, J. B. (1930). *Behaviorism*, rev. ed. New York: Norton.

*Webb v. United States.* 249 U.S. 96, 99 (1919).

Weber, M. (1947[1918]). *The Theory of Social and Economic Organizations.* Trans. A. M. Henderson and Talcott Parsons. New York: Free Press.

Weber, M. (1978[1925]). "Economy and Law." Pp. 641–900 in *Economy and Society*, Eds. G. Roth and C. Wittich. Berkeley: University of California Press.

Weeks, H. A. (1958). *Youthful Offenders at Highfields.* Ann Arbor,: University of Michigan Press.

Weisburd, D., and J. E. Eck. (2004). "What can police do to reduce crime, disorder and fear?" *Annals of the American Academy of Political and Social Sciences* 593:42–65.

Weisburd, D., E. R. Groff, and S. M. Yang. (2014). "The importance of both opportunity and social disorganization theory in a future research agenda to advance criminological theory and crime prevention at places." *Journal of Research in Crime and Delinquency* 51:499–508.

Weisburd, D., L. A. Wyckoff, J. Ready, J. E. Eck, J. C. Hinkle, and J. Gajewski. (2006). "Does crime just move around the corner? A controlled study of spatial displacement and diffusion of crime control benefits." *Criminology* 44:549–92.

West, S. L., and K. K. O'Neal. (2004). "Project D.A.R.E. Outcome effectiveness revisited." *American Journal of Public Health* 94:1027–29.

Westley, W. (1970). *Violence and the Police: A Sociological Study of Law, Custom and Morality.* Cambridge, MA: MIT Press.

Wheeler, D. L. (1995) "A growing number of scientists reject the concept of race." *Chronicle of Higher Education*, 17 February:A8, A9, A15.

Wikström, P. O., and R. J. Sampson. (2003). "Social mechanisms of community influences on crime and pathways in criminality." Pp. 118–148 in *Causes of Conduct Disorder and Serious Juvenile Delinquency*, Eds. B. Lahey, T. Moffitt, and A. Caspi. New York: Guilford Press.

Wilcox, P., T. D. Madensen, and M. S. Tillyer. (2007). "Guardianship in context: Implications for burglary victimization risk and prevention." *Criminology* 45:771–804.

Wiley, S. A., L. A. Slocum, and F. A. Esbensen. (2013). "The unintended consequences of being stopped or arrested: An exploration of the labeling mechanisms through which police contact leads to subsequent delinquency." *Criminology* 51:927–66.

Wilkins, L. (1965). *Social Deviance: Social Policy, Action and Research*. Englewood Cliffs, NJ: Prentice-Hall.

Williams, K., and R. Hawkins. (1986). "Perceptual research on general deterrence: A critical overview." *Law and Society Review* 20:545–72.

Wilson, J. Q., and G. Kelling. (1982). "Broken windows: The police and neighborhood safety." *Atlantic Monthly*, March:29–38.

Wilson, K. R., D. J. Hansen, and M. Li. (2011). "The traumatic stress response in child maltreatment and resultant neuropsychological effects." *Aggression and Violent Behavior* 16:87–97.

Winfree, Jr., L. T. (2003). "Peacemaking and community harmony: Lessons (and admonitions) from the Navajo peacemaking courts." Pp. 285–306 in *Restorative Justice: Theoretical Foundations*, Eds. E. G. M. Weitekamp and H. J. Kerner. Devon, UK and Portland, OR: Willan Publishing.

Winfree, Jr., L. T. (2009). "Restorative policing and law enforcement in the USA: Problems and prospects." Pp. 245–54 in *Victimology, Victim Assistance and Criminal Justice*, Eds. O. Hagemann, P. Schaefer, and S. Schmidt. Mönchengladbach, Germany: Mönchengladbach University Press.

Winfree, Jr., L. T., C. S. Sellers, and D. Clason. (1993). "Social learning and adolescent deviance abstention: Toward understanding reasons for initiating, quitting and avoiding drugs." *Journal of Quantitative Criminology* 9:101–25.

Winship, C., and S. Korenman. (2011). "Does staying in school make you smarter? The effect of education on IQ in The Bell Curve." Pp. 215-234 in *Intelligence, Genes and Success: Scientists Respond to The Bell Curve*, Eds. B. Devlin, S. G. Feinberg, D. P. Resnick, and K. Roeder. New York: Springer.

Winterbourne, M. (2012). "United States drug policy: The scientific, economic, and social issues surrounding marijuana." Stanford University, *Social Sciences* 95–100.

Wirth, L. (1931). "Culture conflict and misconduct." *Social Forces* 9:484–92.

*Wisconsin v. Yoder*, 406 U.S. 205 (1972).

Wolfgang, M. E., R. M. Figlio, and T. Sellin. (1972). *Delinquency in a Birth Cohort*. Chicago: University of Chicago Press.

Wolny, P. (2005). *Colonialism: A Primary Source Analysis*. New York: Rosen Publishing Group.

Wong, D. (1996). *Paths to Delinquency: Implications for Juvenile Justice in Hong Kong and China* (Unpublished doctoral dissertation). University of Bristol.

World Health Organization. (2016). "Female genital mutilation." Retrieved from http://www.who.int/topics/female_genital_mutilation/en/

Wormald, P. (2001). *The Making of English Law: King Alfred to the Twelfth Century, Legislation and Its Limits*. Oxford, UK: Wiley-Blackwell.

Wright, J., K. Beaver, M. DeLisi, M. Vaughn, D. Boisvert, and J. Vaske. (2008a). "Lombroso's legacy: The miseducation of criminologists." *Journal of Criminal Justice Education* 19:325–38.

Wright, J., K. Beaver, M. DeLisi, and M. Vaughn. (2008b). "Evidence of negligible parenting influences on self-control, delinquent peers, and delinquency in a sample of twins." *Justice Quarterly* 25:544–69.

Wrong, D. H. (1961). "The oversocialized conception of man in modern sociology." *American Sociological Review* 26:183–93.

Yakeley, J., and J. R. Meloy. (2012). "Understanding violence: Does psychoanalytic thinking matter?" *Aggression and Violent Behavior* 17:229–39.

Young, J. (1971). "The role of the police as amplifiers of deviancy, negotiators of reality, and translators of fantasy: Some consequences of our present system of drug control as seen in Notting Hill." Pp. 27–61 in Images *of Deviance*, Ed. S. Cohen. Middlesex, England: Penguin.

Zhao, R., and L. Cao. (2010). "Social change and anomie: A cross-national study." *Social Forces* 88:1209–30.

Zimring, F. E., and G. J. Hawkins. (1973). *Deterrence: The Legal Threat in Crime Control.* Chicago: University of Chicago Press.

# Name Index

# Subject Index